GOLDEN MEN

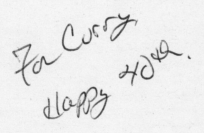

GOLDEN MEN

THE POWER OF GAY MIDLIFE

HAROLD KOODEN, PH.D.
WITH CHARLES FLOWERS

AVON BOOKS ◆ NEW YORK

AVON BOOKS, INC.
An Imprint of HarperCollins *Publishers*
10 East 53rd Street
New York, New York 10022-5299

Copyright © 2000 by Harold Kooden, Ph.D.
Front cover photography by Bob Firth/International Stock
Inside back cover author photo by Donna Aceto
Published by arrangement with the authors
ISBN: 0-380-80443-3
www.harpercollins.com

Library of Congress Cataloging in Publication Data:
Kooden, Harold.
  Golden men : the power of gay midlife / Harold Kooden with Charles Flowers.—1st ed.
  p.cm.
Includes bibliographical references
  1. Middle aged gay men—United States—Psychology. 2. Middle aged gay men—United States—Attitudes. 3. Middle aged gay men—United States—Social conditions. 4. Self-esteem in men—United States. 5. Body image in men—United States. 6. Self perception in men—United States. I. Flowers, Charles. II. Title.
HQ76.14.K66   99-055639
305.244—dc21

First Avon Trade Paperback Printing: February 2000

Printed in the U.S.A.

OPM   10 9 8 7 6 5 4 3 2

This book is dedicated to all those deceased gay men who but for AIDS would have been such good role models of vibrant and exciting, middle-aged gay men.

And to Bernice Neugarten, Ph.D., who first taught me that aging is a lifetime process of development.

CONTENTS

Part Three—SOUL

ACKNOWLEDGMENTS

This book could not have been written without those many gay men who have shared their life stories with me. Some were friends, some were clients, and some were both. I gratefully thank them for having given of themselves and letting me share with you their stories in the fullest sense of brotherhood.

This book is about the landscape in my life's journey, from where I came and how I have grown to be the person I am. Having had a schizophrenic mother who tried her best, a musician father who was never there, an unhappy older brother who became a marine, a loving sister who was the only solid piece of earth in my life, having been arrested for being gay when I was fourteen, and been programmed not to be successful or have a good life, I have taken a path that has truly been an adventure—leaving this dysfunctional family and struggling to become a happy adult. All kinds of people that I have encountered became extremely important for my growth and development so that I have a rich range of acknowledgments.

I therefore want to begin by acknowledging those loving persons who had a direct bearing upon my emotional and intellectual life. Sadly, some of these important people are no longer alive—they had been so lovingly supportive of my personal growth, my professional development, and my activism. I miss our not being witnesses to one another's lives and not being able to discuss this book with them—

Bill Khin, Marty Levine, and Joe Reed. Barry Douglas, Patrick Kelley, and Paul Paroski would also have had much to add. My dialogue with them continues in absentia.

Given my discovery that blood-family relationships can be supportive, I would like to acknowledge those loving and enduring relationships that daily affirm me. These people nurture my spirit and give me the strength to continue trying to make this a better world for all. Having always had unconditional love from my sister, Dianna Lee Davidson, was clearly one of those live-saving supports as well as having love and respect from my four nephews, Wayne and Greg Kooden and Matt and Josh Davidson, who have made me an integral part of their families. Experiencing my brother, Jess Kooden, move from being an active homophobe to becoming a proud brother continues to give me faith in the process of enlightenment and reconciliation. I give thanks to Margaret Kooden, my sister-in-law, for always making me welcomed and loved in her home. A lifetime thank you to the Corey family where I continue to experience being a loved member of an extended blood family.

That I still am part of my late lover's blood family (the Blacks, Bynos, and Premingers) as I was when he was alive only furthers my belief in the importance of how we gay men invent and maintain our own families in our own creative ways. Also from my late lover, I inherited his loving circle of friends from the Chorus Angelorum: Ben McFall, Florence Levitt, Nancy Parish and Elizabeth Sniffen. Other important families to me have been the Dachs and the Breuers. And speaking of different kinds of families, I must include the Eureka family, the gay men with whom I shared summers on Fire Island.

As will be very clear from this book, I believe strongly in the importance of friendships that are an integral part of the chosen family—a family to which I am committed that consists of loving friends, some of whom may be related by blood. All these are people, both living and dead, with whom I have or have had a significant connection. The dimensions of our connection cover the wonderful range of human interaction—loving, spiritual, sexual, collegial, mentoring, and/or playmate. Some of them are like brothers and sisters, others like cousins and all are part of my world: Mark Adise, Linda Arkin and Lynne Alterman, Nick Ashton, Steve Ault, Sam Blazer, Joanne Collier, Dario Corea and Gerd Schacker, Frank Donnelly, Jack Doren, Susan Frankel, Carline Frazier, Barbara Fried, John Fritz and George Michell, Carlos Garay and Frank Youmans, Arlene Goldberg and Ann Taylor, Susan Gore and Ann Wigodsky, Liliane Hecart, Mark Hughes, Nancy and Dan Jordan, Dennis Mack, Bruce and Jennifer Miller, Dale Olson, David Perry, Carol and Bill Polak, Celeste Polak, Ruth Richard, Al Sbordone, Michael Shernoff, Madeline Silver, Marion Steel, Fred and Judy Strassberger, Susan Strauss, Joyce Warshow and Dorothy Sander, Don Wharton, Mark Wind, George Worthington and Manuel Yesckas. And a special acknowledgment to my late lover, Jim Black, who taught me about the grand party of life. And thank you to Friedrich Schmitz, my partner-in-life, for his patience in putting up with all the interruptions in our time together so that I could work on the book and for proving to me that mutual passion and love can happen at any age, a further validation of all that I am saying in this book.

Many of the people that I would have included in the above list have also had a very direct connection with this book. So I am choosing to put them into the literary acknowledgments though they rightfully are part of my chosen family. First of all, the literary debts would almost be endless—many will become clear as you read this book but I want to mention one who opened a world to me and began my life of activism—John Stuart Mill. When I read *On Liberty*, the ideas of activism and feminism sprang forth and I began to understand the individual's relationship to the greater good.

I would like to acknowledge those people from my past who helped influence my thinking—many of the early feminists and gay activists who challenged and opened new doors for me. There are the pioneers and friends, who personally influenced me, such as Walter Lear, Allen Young, Evelyn Hooker, Don Clark, Ed Morales, Steve Morin, and my political mentor and constant friend, Doris Miller. Always with me is my loving friend, Ginny Apuzzo, whose steadfastness to her ideals and commitment to our community was a constant reminder of the importance of our debt to the community—partial payment of my debt is this book.

I would also like to thank those people who directly and indirectly gave me the emotional support for seeing this book to its finish. Their presence in my life has validated what I am trying to share with my readers. My thanks to Roger Enlow for urging me to start writing about my ideas in the early days of GRID (Gay Related Immune Deficiency). Longtime friend Charles Silverstein later urged me to write an article on self-disclosure, therapy, and gay men. Then at the suggestion of Barbara Sang, I wrote a first draft of a paper about gay men's midlife but nothing came of it. Douglas Kimmel, a former classmate and friend, saw this draft and felt that these ideas should be developed and published. Without his prompting, I would not have produced and published my original paper on gay men and aging.

If it were not for Michael Denneny, no more would have been done. A senior editor at St. Martin's, he read the paper and told me "There is a book here, write it!" Frankly, if it had come from anyone else, I probably would have ignored it. So began the long process of expanding a professional paper to make it meaningful for other gay men. One clear inspiration for me was my college classmate and friend, Arnold Rachman, a clinician who had persevered in doing the books of his dreams. A deep gratitude to Lee Breuer, whom I have known since the fifth grade, for listening to me and helping me to clarify my ideas and giving me the loving encouragement that I did have something worthwhile to say. Another friend, Camille Lavington, having written her own book and dealt with the publishing process, prepared me for this process.

When I was ready to approach an agent, I talked with Jed Mattes, also a longtime, political colleague of mine. He saw the potential of the book and made the perfect suggestion of Charles Flowers as co-author—all the accolades that I want to say concerning Charles will be in the afterword of this book. Thanks to Jed's insight and support, we met an editor who immediately understood the relevance of the book and bought the proposal—Charlotte Abbott. Charlotte's early support and enthusiasm were an inspiration, and her comments helped me to shape and develop my ideas even further. We were lucky, when Charlotte left Avon, to land in the hands of our present editor, Hamilton Cain. Hamilton's humor and intelligence made our editorial conversations exciting, and in our discussions, many of the distinctions between gay and nongay fell away and we became men just talking about midlife.

Finally, there are those friends who have read drafts and made suggestions: Sam Schoenbaum who gave the idea of the afterword and other reformatting suggestions and Reverend M. Zell Schwartzman who had read drafts of both the professional paper and book and was especially helpful on the spirituality issues. It was important that one of the initial readers be my gay nephew, Josh, who is the prototypical audience for this book. Besides his many useful comments, he helped remind me that New York is not the center of the gay male world!

And the final acknowledgment is to you, the reader, for being part of our community and taking up the challenge to continue the process of re-creation in your new identity as a Golden Man.

Last I want to say that I truly feel blessed in having a rich and global life (greatly enhanced by my lover Friedrich and my work with the International Lesbian and Gay Association) in which blood family, chosen family, gay, nongay, white, Black, Hispanic, rich, poor, young, old are all intertwined. It is a great life and it keeps getting better and better and I deeply thank all of you who have contributed to this.

GOLDEN
MEN

From Golden Boy to Golden Man:
A Journey of Transformation

I have always enjoyed talking to gay men. As a therapist, I have spent over thirty years listening to gay men talk about their lives, their fears and dreams, hopes and doubts. As a gay man, I have spent even more time listening to gay men tell their stories—not just of coming out and living as gay men, but also of approaching and surviving middle age. In many of the stories, some difficult questions kept surfacing: What makes a gay man age well? Why do some gay men surrender to the negative stereotypes, while others thrive? This book is my attempt to answer such questions.

The stories I have to share come from many perspectives, yet the personal angle is paramount among my other identities as therapist and activist. Basically, I'm a gay man who has been through midlife and is here to tell you that life gets better, not worse, as you age. My friends and clients have taught me so much because we were all tackling the same issues surrounding the shifting priorities of work, family, relationships, politics, and pleasure. Working together with other gay men on these issues has convinced me that gay men can create a dynamic life of integrity and wholeness *through-out their entire life span*, not just when they first come out.

I came out over two decades before Stonewall. I started cruising as a preteen, was arrested because of police entrapment and sentenced at fourteen for being gay, then left California at eighteen to move in with a lover in 1954. In my twenties, I was a worker, student, and political activist in the civil rights, anti-war, and radical health movements. After graduating from the University of Chicago with a doctorate in human development and clinical psychology, I moved to New York in 1967 to work in community mental health programs. My first jobs were at hospitals in the South Bronx and Fort Greene, Brooklyn, in primarily Hispanic and African-American neighborhoods. I first began seeing lesbians and gay men as clients during the early seventies while involved in the radical mental health movement, but I didn't come out professionally until my midthirties, and I didn't begin a private practice until 1977.

So why a book about gay men and aging? Aren't there already books out there about aging? Can't we learn from them? Well, yes and no. There are some very good books about aging on the market, but none of them fully address the phenomenon of aging from a gay perspective. In 1998, The MacArthur Foundation published *Successful Aging*, the results of its ten-year study on aging. The words *gay* or *lesbian* or *homosexual* are not to be found in the index; AIDS gets one mention, within the context of life-challenging illnesses. Twenty years earlier, Daniel Levinson's *The Seasons of a Man's Life* (1978) set the standard for discussing the different "stages" of a man's life, but "homosexuality" was mentioned only once, with the example of two men who experienced "homosexual activity" during their youth.

More and more studies by gay social scientists are proving that gay men follow a different developmental path from nongay men. These differences are both positive and negative, but are rarely known or understood by the average gay man. Not realizing how their development differs, many gay men continue to compare themselves to nongay standards, which leads to the feelings of fear, confusion, and terror many of us feel at the mention of aging. For gay men, aging presents its own special issues and challenges, different from those of our nongay brothers. We can learn from books like the MacArthur Foundation's and Levinson's, but they don't give us the whole picture of our experience. In addition, as gay men, we have all witnessed the entitlements of the nongay world that make heterosexuality the standard by which everything is judged. One of the reasons I prefer the term "nongay" to "straight" is because it levels the playing field by making "gay" the reference point.

The few examples that do address the topic of gay aging, notably the work of pioneering psychologist Doug Kimmel and anthologies like *Gay and Gray*, have appeared in the field of gerontology, in which the focus has been gay men sixty-five and over. Work about middle-aged lesbians and gay men finally began to appear in 1991, with the publication of *Lesbians at Midlife: The Creative Transition* by Barbara Sang, Joyce Warshov, and Adrienne J. Smith, and *Gay Midlife and Maturity*, edited by John A. Lee.

Overcoming—or even voicing for the first time—our fears about aging has taken many of us a long time. But only in speaking out do we have a chance of breaking out of the trap set by negative stereotypes about older gay men. We do have the power to age well, and it is my hope that the stories and exercises that you will find in these pages will point the way toward knowledge of your own power. For many gay men, power may seem like an abstract concept. But our recent history suggests that gay men are on a journey toward power, both individually and collectively.

In the last three decades, gay men have struggled to overcome the messages of shame, self-loathing, and homophobia inherited from the nongay world in order to create a community of love, pride, acceptance, joy, and power. During the 1970s, gay men fought for and achieved liberation and set the foundation of a community of openly gay, self-loving men. In the 1980s, this fledgling community faced a life-threatening epidemic, and gay men and their allies devoted their time, energy, money, imagination, and lives toward saving one another. In the mid-1990s, the gay community came out of the despair and depression brought about by AIDS and began to fashion a new identity based on the lessons of the past and the promise of the present.

The year 2000 heralds the approach of a new millennium, and gay men stand upon the threshold of liberation—not just sexual or political, but a liberation of all arenas of our lives: mind, body, and spirit. During our twenty-year battle against AIDS, we have taught the world that we know how to take care of our sick, honor and bury our dead. Now is the time to take our lessons and use them to live and to teach one another how to live. We owe it to ourselves, as well as to the generations to follow.

FIVE PRINCIPLES FOR GAY AGING

In putting together my observations on gay men and aging, I came up with five basic principles that govern the phenomenon of gay aging. I'll list them first, then elaborate on each of them in the sections that follow.

1. By virtue of our coming out, gay men already possess the power to age well.
2. Midlife is our true adulthood.
3. The mind and the body are one.
4. Ageism causes death.
5. We can not only survive, but *thrive*.

Taken together, these concepts challenge many of the assumptions and myths around aging that American culture, and gay male culture in particular, embrace. Part of my goal here is to introduce a new vocabulary around aging that will enable gay men to understand the phenomenon of their aging and to appreciate the strength, ability, and power they possess to age successfully.

1. By virtue of our coming out, gay men already possess the power to age well.

As gay men, we create ourselves daily—with few role models, fewer social supports to gauge our development, and no universally sanctioned rituals to define us, we are free to create a life of our own choosing. Moreover, our coming out initiates a process of self-creation that extends well beyond the period in which we came out. Coming out may require five years of concentrated struggle and efforts toward self-acceptance, honesty, disclosure, and integrity. It is also a life-changing event whose aftermath can be felt decades afterward. Coming out is an opportunity to stop living our lives for other people. Coming out empowers us to create one life, *our* life.

Just as "successful aging" challenges many people's perceptions about aging, the idea that gay men have the power to age well is beyond the comprehension of most people, gay and nongay alike. Ironically, it is the very experiences that make a gay man an outcast in the nongay world that strengthen him and grant him advantages for aging successfully. If he can overcome his internalized homophobia and ageism, an openly gay man can actually become a role model on how to age well, not just for other gay men, but for everybody.

By "openly gay man," I mean a gay man who has started the process of coming out in at least one area of his life. Coming out can happen on many levels: first to ourselves, then to a friend, then to more friends, maybe to a sibling, our parents, our coworkers, our church, and ultimately, to our entire community. Since each coming out is unique, it's difficult to generalize about the entire gay male community, but coming out does give a gay man a source of integrity, power, and strength, regardless of whether he comes out when he's in his twenties, forties, or sixties. The lessons of our coming out— which we may still be learning at midlife—are our best preparation for a transition into middle age and beyond.

A central principle of this book is that the skills we have already developed in order to live our lives as openly gay men in a nongay world are the same skills that will enable us to age well, if not better, than our nongay peers.

In fact, there is a considerable body of research that reveals how the majority of older lesbians and gay men do not conform to the negative stereotypes of lonely, depressed, and asexual people. Studies conducted in the United States, Canada, Australia, The Netherlands, and Denmark have established the positive phenomenon of gay aging.

These reports do not deny that some lesbians and gay men experience old age as negatively as the worst stereotypes would suggest, but one factor that influences the experience of aging for lesbians and gay men is *the degree to which they have resisted homophobia by coming out as openly lesbian and gay people.* As a result, most of these studies attribute the positive aspects of gay aging to one or more of three skills that result from coming out: (1) crisis competence, (2) less rigid gender roles, and (3) community involvement.

Crisis competence can be defined as a way of resolving present and potential losses. This ability has been linked to successful aging as a measure of how well a person can adapt to the losses of family, friends, and physical health associated with old age (over sixty-five). In 1978, Doug Kimmel first described coming out as a potential crisis for gay men that "once resolved, may provide a perspective on life crises and a sense of crisis competence that buffers the person against later crises."

Clearly, coming out as a gay man represents an exceptional process in which adaptive coping talents are very necessary. At the same time that coming out puts at risk all familial, social, communal, and vocational relationships, it also eventually empowers gay men. Coming out is a life crisis that takes much courage to enact, even though there may only be a conscious awareness of fear and terror. Gay men often dismiss coming out as a courageous act because they focus on the anxiety of the experience and the residue of painful memories. Action with anxiety *is* courage; action without fear is like doing the laundry.

From the crisis of coming out (which may play out over many years, beginning in young adulthood, midlife, or old age itself), many gay men fulfill *less rigid gender roles* that also facilitate the transition into midlife and beyond. Many gay men develop the flexibility to play many social roles at home and in public because they live alone or with another man. Most gay men are not afraid or ashamed of their ability to take care of themselves, whether that means cooking and cleaning (traditionally "feminine" roles) or home repairs and car maintenance (traditionally "masculine" roles). In addition, a gay man's sexual identity is less likely than a nongay man's to be threatened by shifting gender roles as he ages. Daniel Levinson calls this the Masculine/Feminine polarity in which men must face "the coexistence of masculine and feminine parts of the self." Many nongay men feel emasculated in later years by having to feed and clothe themselves after their spouses have passed away, while many gay men learn how to take care of themselves from day one.

Finally, *community involvement* can be an indication of how well a gay man will age by providing a support network, role models, a sense of life purpose, and well-being in his life. Depending upon the resolution of his coming out, a gay man may or may not remain supported by his biological family. Many gay men, however, create a new family though friendships that they tend to keep throughout their lifetimes. Usually consisting of other gay men and women (both lesbian and nongay), these "chosen families" are a major source of emotional support that extends beyond any romantic partner and for many gay men, *are* their main significant other. Primary friendships among gay men usually start with a onetime sexual attraction and/or one-night stand (just as nongay men use sex to propagate and develop their families, so do gay men—but in our own way!). On the other hand, nongay men tend not to have an intimate circle of friends or other emotional support outside of their immediate family. If they are married, they usually rely upon their wives to do the emotional work, including handling any problems within the home. However, a support system is crucial when dealing with the process of aging, as well as whatever other crises may arise.

In addition to a chosen family of friends, many gay men find the gay community itself to be a source of strength and support. A recent study of racially diverse men living in San Francisco established a "positive association" between community involvement and psychological well-being. The more kinds of "nonsexualized community participation" (for example, public rallies, bars, social clubs, volunteer organizations, and outdoor recreational groups) a gay man enjoyed, the more he increased his "sense of pride and belonging," leading to "greater comfort with [himself], to overcoming internalized negative images of what it means to be gay, and to being more available for emotionally intimate relationships."

In short, upon reviewing his life history, a gay man can probably acknowledge how the experiences of coming out, developing a gay identity, and participating in the gay community have strengthened him. In the context of midlife, he can begin to appreciate his differences from nongay men as assets rather than liabilities. At midlife, a gay man begins to realize that he has already developed the skills he needs and can now access for successful aging.

In 1991, Richard A. Friend of the University of Pennsylvania proposed that older gays and lesbians can be divided into three groups: "stereotypic," "passing," and "affirmative." In Friend's model, the "stereotypic" group is composed of older lesbians and gay men who conform to the negative stereotypes: few gay friends, isolated, guilty, anxious, lonely, extreme internalized homophobia, depressed, and low sexual intimacy. The "affirmative" group is at the other end of the continuum: vibrant, well-adjusted, sexually vigorous, well-adjusted to aging, social with gay friends, and with a positive gay identity. The "passing" group is in the middle: conditional self-acceptance, marginal acceptance of homosexuality, possibly passing as heterosexual, somewhat depressed and negative, not aging well, and not involved in the gay community.

Many of my clients initially fell into the "passing" group. Some began therapy because they wanted to change their lives but were not sure in what way. Few had a sense of commitment to a gay community or were involved in public gay issues. Although some had a wide circle of gay male friends, their friendships were not necessarily intimate or nurturing. Their most intimate ongoing relationships tended to be with nongay women. Many were also dissatisfied with their lover or boyfriend relationships. Some had been celibate for years and had not taken good care of their health or bodies beyond watching their weight. In general, they had a negative sense of themselves as older gay men although some were looking for middle-aged gay role models. Not surprisingly, many mentioned an awakening spirituality as they had begun to consider their mortality. Others wanted to reexamine their value systems and felt the need to explore broader life issues. In summary, many of these gay men felt they had been passive participants in their lives—life had just happened to them.

Although they entered therapy as belonging to Friend's "passing" group, many of these men ended our work together as members of the "affirmative" group. They developed a positive gay identity, became comfortable with their age, were able to be sexual and intimate with peers, felt attractive and took care of themselves, and had a positive sense of the future. I was able to observe their transformation over time as well as be aware of the different issues that they worked on to make this successful transition. It is from these observations, my own experiences, and that of my peers that I conceptualized the developmental tasks for gay aging. Many gay men survive this transition without therapy—with the same result, but not with the same process of my clients. The issues to be resolved are the same for both sets of gay men—those who undergo therapy and those who do not—on their path to successful aging.

2. Midlife is our true adulthood.

Part of the anxiety that many gay men experience over aging is that we don't know how old we are. Yes, we were born on a certain day at a certain time, but that time is only one measure of our age. In the field of human development, many scientists believe that we don't have a single age, but a composite of several ages, along three continuum: chronological, biological, and experiential. For my work, I have added a fourth category: sexual. Understanding these four distinct ways of measuring our "age" will help clarify the confusion many gay men experience in talking about aging.

THE FOUR AGES OF GAY MEN

Chronological (an objective measure using linear time) refers simply to a man's age according to his birth date. I call this our "Clock Age," and it's what most people answer when asked how old they are. *Biological* (a physiological quotient) refers to the age a man's body is based on the way his body functions—in some cases, it may be simply the way his body looks in comparison to most men of his chronological age. I call this our "Body Age," and it is determined by (somewhat) objective standards: height, weight, heart rate, cholesterol level, flexibility, endurance, and so on. *Experiential* (the emotional component) refers to the age a man feels he is. This is his level of maturity according to his experiences and present state of mind, and I call it our "Heart Age." This concept gets to the gut, emotional level of how old he feels he is, regardless of what he looks like or his birthdate.

Finally, I have added a *sexual* age—our "Gay Age"—that measures how long a man has been practicing and preparing for the adult expression of his sexual orientation. This age can be measured many ways when talking about gay men, and is largely self-referential, with each gay man deciding his "gay birthday" for himself. Gay men may start calculating their Gay Age from when they became aware of an attraction for another male or decided to act upon that attraction. Other gay men may see their Gay Age in terms of the first time they accepted themselves as "gay" or the day they came out to their parents. Since gay men usually take longer than nongay men to express their sexual orientation openly, the idea of a "gay birthday" as an anniversary event makes a lot of sense to gay men.

For nongay men there is a socially approved, largely chronological map toward adulthood: boy/girl games ("playing doctor") in childhood, sexual awakening and experimentation in adolescence, job, college, career, marriage, children, retirement, grandchildren, and so on. But for gay men, no such road map exists. Since a full commitment to a gay sexual identity may take years (or even decades) as they struggle to overcome the shame and loathing that has been

instilled by a nongay world, gay men may be set back on the journey
to adulthood. Further, it takes longer for gay men to achieve a sense
of themselves as men since they have to do it without the usual
social supports and benchmarks that nongay men experience. The
majority of us don't get engaged and marry. We don't get gifts or
social recognition for our serious relationships. Few of us become
fathers. Not many of us join boards of directors or country clubs.
We don't send children to our alma mater. *As a result, becoming a man
is more of an internal experience for gay men because of the lack of social cues
and socially approved behaviors that can give one a sense of manhood.*

Let's look at one myth about gay men that contains an element
of truth: We are seen as perennial adolescents who refuse to grow
up. The reason for this misperception can be explained by our Gay
Age. For nongay men, adolescence is a time of sexual awakening and
exploration, as well as social development and acceptance among
peers. With this framework, gay male adolescence usually comes
much later chronologically, when a gay man is in his twenties and
thirties, or even forties if he married a woman in his youth. (Recently,
however, society's comfort level around homosexuality has risen to a
point where younger gay men are coming out earlier, with the reality
of "gay teenagers" becoming more accepted, as well as visible.) In
effect, many gay males have experienced their sexual adolescence at
a later Clock Age and after separation from the parental family
(which usually provides emotional support for the nongay teenager
during adolescence). In addition, many gay males do not find a satisfying community of gay peers until their thirties or even forties,
which further delays a gay man's adolescence.

Understanding his four ages helps a gay man clarify the confusion he feels about aging. His Clock Age may be thirty-five, but his
Body Age is thirty (doesn't smoke, runs three times a week). Meanwhile, his Heart Age is fifty (having survived the death of a lover)
and his Gay Age is fifteen (started dating men after college). No
wonder a gay man can feel young and old all at the same time! Some
of his life experiences (Body and Gay) make him feel young, while
traditional concepts of age (Clock and Heart) make him feel older.

How a gay man gauges his different ages determines his true
age, but we cannot ignore the additional effect of AIDS on gay men's
sense of aging. No matter how young they are, many gay men are
experiencing the world as their grandparents do—with many of their

friends dying and their own health a constant issue. This often makes their lives feel foreshortened, and as a result, their Heart Age will be unusually high.

American culture, and especially gay male culture, has little sense of aging as a dynamic process of growth, which can be cyclical like the seasons and nonlinear like memory and the imagination. Using the four ages to describe our experience of aging will ultimately lessen our dependence upon a rigid, linear framework of aging and give us more freedom to explore ourselves. For many gay men, the biggest stumbling block in talking about aging is their fixation on a particular number: thirty, thirty-five, forty, fifty, whichever one triggers their sense that they're getting older. Given American myths and stereotypes around aging, we all have some number in our head that signifies, "That's the crest of the hill. Before that is life. Beyond it lies death." But it's as if gay men leapfrog from young to old, without any middle passage. Many gay men feel they can lose value overnight, when the clock strikes twelve and "Cinderfella" turns forty. A 1976 study of ninety-five gay men between the ages of twenty-five and sixty-eight found that gay men felt the onset of middle age was around forty-one, and old age began at sixty-five (Berger, 1982). Twenty-five years later, many younger gay men think turning thirty is the beginning of the end.

I consider "middle-aged" a self-referential term and not specific to any particular age, whereas "midlife" is more of a cultural term to denote a significant shift in attitudes and behavior. Once a gay man grasps the concept of four ages, he realizes that he has many ages that, in the long run, do not matter that much. He has no real age except how he feels and lives his life.

But when a gay man's Clock Age strikes a culturally significant number like forty, he can begin to wonder if he's where he's supposed to be at that point in his life. American culture expects a nongay individual to have reached a level of maturity and stability—his adulthood—in his late twenties and thirties, so that by the time he reaches midlife, he is conditioned for change (the infamous "midlife crisis"), which either strengthens or redefines his adulthood. But given his late-blooming adolescence, a gay man will often hit midlife just when he feels himself becoming an adult.

As gay men, our journey is less clear than for our nongay counterparts: Since we age less linearly, our middle age (and whatever "crisis" it brings) will represent something altogether different. Even the few books on gay male development (such as Stanley Siegel's *Uncharted Lives* or Richard Isay's *Becoming Gay*) spend the majority of their emphasis on the stages leading up to coming out. Midlife gets short shrift in these books, as if a gay man's development stops when he comes out.

I would argue that coming out is the beginning of our gay lives, not the culmination. In my own life and the lives of my clients and friends, I have observed that most gay men feel their sense of manhood most strongly at the same time they are beginning to consider themselves middle-aged. I have heard gay men often say that they went from feeling like an adolescent to feeling middle-aged and seemed to have bypassed adulthood. *Because of our unique history, middle age is now our true adulthood*—a time when the internal signs of maturity (self-image and self-esteem) and the external ones (physical changes, career, relationships) come together. Adulthood is not tied to any particular age, but to a gay man's knowledge that the world operates according to a set of rules (social, economic, cultural, political) and his comfort with his place in the world. Understandably, many gay men become angry and frustrated that just when they begin to feel as if they're coming into their own, both American culture and gay male culture begin to reject them for being "over the hill."

3. The mind and the body are one.

A major goal of my work has been understanding the mind-body connection, which I define, briefly, as *the mind and body acting together as an organic whole, with each part influencing and affecting the other*. Many people (Joan Borysenko, Deepak Chopra, Candace Pert, Andrew Weil, to name a few) have written about the mind-body connection in the context of aging, and examples from my own life and the lives of my clients and friends have convinced me more and more of the power of this pathway to successful aging. Using a mind-body framework requires listening to your body and speaking with your heart, paying conscious attention to your emotions and your behaviors, sifting through memories to recognize patterns of experience, while charting the future toward your goals.

In short, this work is interior, and your tools are language, honesty, memory, reflection, and imagination. *But what about my wrinkles?*

cries a fifty-year-old man. *What about my career and my retirement?* Although many people resist change, when we do get around to changing, we crave instant results and concrete improvements. Consider the billions spent each year on weight loss tonics and products. Yet the miracle of weight loss is simple, but not easy: eat less (or better), exercise more. No mystery there. The absolutely fabulous ab, butt, and leg books offer the same "harsh" reality: the way to a firmer, leaner body is through daily exercise and taking care of yourself. At the gym, a trainer advises to do reps of weights because that is what builds muscles that last, not the sudden ballooning of steroids. *Slow and steady*, intones the tortoise, but *what about my wrinkles?* wails the rabbit.

As with maintaining the body, there is a "simple, but not easy" solution to aging: if you do the interior work, it shows up on the exterior. We're used to separating the mind from the body, categorizing "what we are thinking" from "what we are feeling" from "what we are doing"—yet all three spheres (intellect, emotions, and behavior) are connected and capable of influencing one another. I think a lot of the abuses of the body (overeating, underexercising, smoking, overdrinking, and so on) come from not feeling internally positive about yourself. In a sense, you externalize any negative feelings through an abusive behavior or relationship (even, perhaps, through an abusive relationship with your own body). Mental health and physical health combine to create *wellness*, and successful aging requires paying attention to both aspects of our health, the mind and the body.

In the early eighties, when many of my clients were getting sick with a new disease, then called Gay Related Immune Disorder (GRID), I wrote about the difference between those who survived longer and those who seemed to weaken immediately. The ones who had a sense of the future and took charge of their health care were the ones who were surviving, and I still firmly believe what studies have confirmed: *Having a positive sense of the future and control over one's life are significant factors in maintaining one's health.* In short, if you think negatively, it's going to be reflected in your body.

How, you might be asking, *can I think positive about getting older?*

Ask any gay man what he most fears, and after AIDS, most would respond: growing old, or more specifically "being alone in my old age" or "being unattractive (and alone) in my old age." When asked how aging has changed their lives, most men will immediately speak of the negatives. We don't think of changing for the better. Our immediate assumption is that change equals loss, which overshadows any gains brought about by change. When we're young, we think of aging in terms of development: going to high school, learning to drive, beginning to date, graduating from high school, and leaving home. The future beckons with all that we have to gain: independence, money, sex, power. At some point, though, our sense of time shifts, and the future looms with all that we have to lose. For so many of us, a perceived loss of power represents our harshest fear as we age.

What if we reconsider fear as a *positive* force for change, as an expression of a desire to keep what we have that's good in our lives? We are afraid of being lonely because we are not alone now. We don't want to gain weight or lose our eyesight because we value our current health. We are having a good time feeling alive and vibrant, and we want (but may have trouble imagining) a rich and joyful future. For some of us, the fear of aging is not so much a fear of losing what we have, but of never attaining what we don't have. We are single and want to be coupled. We have a stagnant job and want a thrilling career. As with adolescence, midlife exacerbates any feelings of inadequacy.

Successful aging is not simply adjusting to something negative—less flexibility in a changing body, for example—nor is it about becoming a Pollyanna who sees only the positive (a Perky Paul). Aging is about realism—accurately assessing what you have, what you want, and how to get there from here. Looking at your fears about aging as an indication of what you value in your life allows you to operate from a position of power, rather than a feeling of powerlessness fueled by negative fears. As a force of change, fear can motivate you to do what you need to do in order to take care of yourself; fear can empower both the mind and the body, propelling a gay man at midlife into action. The alternatives of passivity and negativity only strengthen the ageism within, and the consequences can be lethal.

4. Ageism causes death.

In 1969, Robert N. Butler coined the term "ageism" to describe "the systematic stereotyping of and discrimination against people because they are old." The phenomenon he was defining was not news, but the framework in which he described the treatment of older and old people was revolutionary because he linked it to the other "isms" that plague society: racism, sexism, classism, and heterosexism. By making it an "ism," Butler identified ageism as a wrong that can be corrected. His work established ageism as a form of social conditioning that, when challenged and examined, could be relearned.

Ageism works its way through American culture on many levels, from the way we regard Medicare and Social Security, to the way we get irritated at older people for driving slowly or at teenagers who talk too loudly. Whenever we judge somebody because of their age, we are engaging in ageism, and it can cut both ways: We worship youth and denigrate older people. Like the other "isms," ageism lessens both sides of the human equation—those who are older (or younger) as well as those who discriminate against them. In effect, any -ism dehumanizes, reducing some people to representations of their age or gender or color or class, while defining the only acceptable worldview to a homogenous elite. Both the young and old benefit by identifying and dismantling the age bias against people.

One principle that I've witnessed is that *ageism causes death*. I have seen many gay men who feared growing old more than actually dying. They had such a negative perception of their growing old that it was an experience to be avoided at all costs, even of their lives. Both HIV negative and positive gay men have found it difficult even to imagine growing old—in part, because of the way AIDS, ageism, and homophobia have combined to weaken and damage the gay male psyche.

Doug Kimmel has observed that "the stigma of homosexuality [has intertwined] with the stereotypes about aging in our society [so that] fears about aging as a gay person have been used to dissuade young people from accepting their homosexuality, further hindering self-acceptance." In addition, AIDS has drained many gay men of their sense of the future—when so many of their friends are dying, they fear they could be next. For some individuals, this has meant having no sense of reaching middle age or even having to deal with the whole issue of aging. Their energies have been focused on simply surviving. For others, anger and depression have led them to lives of self-destruction or unsafe sexual practices.

In a 1998 roundtable discussion on sex and HIV prevention,

Michael Weinstein, president of AIDS Healthcare Foundation, observed, "I wonder what kind of community we have if you are an invalid after the age of forty. Every community—Jewish, black, Korean—is judged by how it treats its young and how it treats its old. To me, that gives you the whole story about where our community is at in its development. We exploit the young and we disappear the old. I've heard a lot of young gay men say, 'You know, I would rather die of AIDS than grow old.'" Diagnosed as HIV positive when he was twenty-six, Tony Valenzuela, a San Diego "sex radical," admitted that he has "normalized HIV into my existence as a young gay man and somehow come to terms with a life span of thirty-five to forty years." But he resisted identifying ageism as the sole culprit: "I think that while that may be an element, it is too simplistic to say that, because we don't want to grow old, we put ourselves at risk."

Ageism isn't the whole picture; internalized homophobia also contributes to a young gay man's sense of "maybe not living a long time." In addition, the absence of role models has also complicated the situation. Part of the reason so many gay men are frightened by the prospect of aging is that no openly gay generation has survived to midlife and maturity. The death of a generation of public and openly gay elders has denied role models to younger gay men. This loss is critical as elders are essential for teaching the younger men of a community how to become adults. Many of my friends and colleagues would have been amazing role models, and it is against the invisibility caused by their absence that this book is being written.

Thankfully, in the new era of protease inhibitors, many gay men are reclaiming a sense of the future. Some have been near death, only to have their health restored with the new treatments. Many are returning to work after years of being on disability and being too exhausted to pursue a career. For the men who can afford the new treatments and for whom they work (roughly 50 percent of those who undergo them), AIDS no longer has the power it once did to destroy their faith in their future. Faced with a future, these gay men are full of anxiety and questions about what the rest of their lives will become. With a restored sense of purpose, both HIV negative and positive gay men are looking around to find role models for aging, only to confront, perhaps for the first time, their own ageism.

Gay male ageism is blatant in the sexually provocative images of youth that dominate our gay media, but we participate in ageism in less obvious ways as well. I define ageism as *using one age period as the standard of comparison for judging or describing another age period*. When we begin to measure our self-worth in terms of our age ("After fifty, no one wants you") and with even more damage, in terms of the ages of others ("He doesn't want me; I'm too old for him"), we are perpetuating negative assumptions about what it means to be attractive and sexual. Examples of ageism can be explicit ("I shouldn't go out because I'm not a kid anymore") or implicit ("You don't look forty" or "You look so young"). Implicit comments can sound like compliments ("You don't look your age") but they can be just as ageist as the more blatant examples.

Such "compliments" still use or imply another age period to make a positive statement about the person—saying "You're young at heart" *instead* of saying that the man is instrinsically active, wise, vibrant, attractive, in good shape, and so on. Also, ageism works in reverse, undercutting the abilities of the young with comments like "You're wise for your years" and "You're so mature for a twenty-one-year-old." Clearly, these qualities (maturity, appearance, intelligence, and so on) are independent of age, yet so often, we idealize another age—any age but our own—to the point where we make ourselves depressed and miserable.

If this dynamic of self-negation through constant comparison to others sounds familiar, you might be thinking of your experience with homophobia. Growing up in a nongay world, gay men absorb untold negative messages about what it means to be gay: sick, immoral, criminal, unnatural, predatory. During our development, we internalize the homophobia until we begin to believe the lies and propaganda are factual. Part of the struggle in coming out is getting rid of these negative feelings, these "voices" inside our heads that tell us to be gay is sick. By and large, we silence most of this internalized homophobia during the process of coming out. By participating in gay-positive behavior (pride activities, dating, sex—the activities that make us feel "normal"), we nourish a constant effort to eradicate our internalized homophobia so we can develop a positive gay identity.

The same dynamic operates with ageism. *Internalized ageism* occurs when the gay man accepts and incorporates into his self-definition a double dose of ageism: all the American cultural negativity as well as gay negativity about aging. But gay men are ideally suited to tackle ageism. Why? Having dealt with homophobia while coming out, gay men can use the same strategies of empowerment whenever they are confronted with internalized ageism. *Just as gay men's internalized homophobia must be eradicated in order to develop a positive gay identity, so must gay men's internalized ageism be eradicated in order to age successfully.* My goal is to empower gay men to understand and remove their internalized ageism so that they may not only enjoy but also celebrate (yes, celebrate!) getting older.

5. We can not only survive, but *thrive*.

> "I believe mankind will not only survive, but prevail."
> —*William Faulkner, Nobel acceptance speech*

When one of the characters in Tony Kushner's play *Angels in America* remarks, "I am a gay man living in New York. I am used to stress," the audience responded with laughter, but the line resonates well beyond the world of gay men in Manhattan. Gay men do undergo a tremendous amount of stress in developing and maintaining a healthy identity, in large part owing to homophobia and heterosexism, both society's and whatever they've internalized. But what inspires me, what strengthens my faith in the gay community is that we not only survive our various childhoods and coming(s) out, but we manage to come together to flourish as a community. As testimony to Faulkner's belief, gay men have prevailed over much in order to be themselves and to love one another.

In the summer of 1998, one of the leading psychological journals, *Journal of Social Issues*, devoted an entire issue to the concept of *thriving*. Through a series of articles, the editors explored what makes certain individuals not only survive a trauma, but thrive afterward. The range of potential traumas under study was wide: childhood abuse; being fired; loss of a parent, sibling, or spouse; a car wreck; a critical health diagnosis; a geographic relocation, and so on. The traditional understanding of trauma has been that an individual may succumb to the trauma, survive with some impairment, or recover to his previous condition. This new thinking adds a fourth option: thriving, which means going beyond recovery to a better-than-before lifestyle.

The factors that determine whether or not an individual will thrive are multiple (personality, worldview, social support, socioeconomic status, and so forth), but Crystal Park of Miami University observed that "probably the most consistent finding in the literature is that people possessing *higher levels of optimism and hope*—those who expect positive outcomes and who believe they have the ability to attain their goals—are more likely to report experiencing growth in response to stress" (italics added).

This concept can apply to several experiences common to gay men. I would argue that coming out and AIDS represent two opportunities for thriving that the majority of gay men have faced, are facing, and will continue to face, and our aging represents a third arena in which we can thrive.

In a sense, the clinical research has caught up to the anecdotal evidence of many older gay men. Getting older isn't easy, but there are rewards and benefits. Longtime activist Frank Kameny has observed, "Now that I am among those who are older, I do not merely *sense* that the stereotype [of the older gay man] is wrong, I *know* it from firsthand experience. My forties were better than my thirties, and my fifties better than my forties. . . . Life continues to be more rewarding, exciting, and satisfying than I could have ever imagined when I was twenty. My life is too full to permit time for misery or loneliness."

When gay men reach a deep and proud sense of themselves, it is a highly internalized and integrated identity often independent of external reinforcements. Without social approval or much encouragement (and sometimes, in the face of physical harm and emotional abuse), gay men find their rightful place in the world. Becoming an adult may require a different path or take longer for a gay man than for a nongay man, but the prize is just as precious: a life of our own.

Thriving at midlife does follow a sequence. I call them the Three C's: Consciousness, Choices, Change. The first step is becoming conscious of yourself in the present, i.e., what image you are conveying to the world. The next phase calls for acknowledging all the internalized negative images you hold about yourself: gay, short, old, African-American, Jewish, Japanese, poor—whatever part(s) of your identity that are subject to negative stereotypes. The serious thinking you put into how you want to feel internally begins to dismantle those negative images. During all this self-reflection, you begin to realize you have choices in your life about how you want to feel internally and externally. Choose a role model—whether from fantasy

(John Travolta) or real life (your father)—to create the positive image you want to convey to the world. Finally, begin the task of living out that image: the act of change. It is not as far a jump as you might think to go from trying an image "on for size" to beginning to convey and believe in that image. The main work is letting go of those negative images and embracing the positive feedback (compliments, recognition of our talents and achievements) that we have been too busy dismissing. In creating our identity as middle-aged gay men, we have the opportunity to be all that we can be, or rather, all that we're *willing* to become.

Yet as long as we are locked into a linear model of aging, with death as the natural endpoint, we will have difficulty finding anything positive or successful about the aging process. Successful aging does not deny death or even physical decline. It is a balanced approach that sees positive value in getting older with the acquisition of many skills and a deepening of awareness and control over one's life. But it does involve a recognition that physical changes can be handled more smoothly if one remains physically active and takes care of one's internal health. Successful aging means keeping oneself active, vital, adventurous, risk taking, sexual, loving, healthy, and proactive. It doesn't mean avoiding dancing because you're over forty, but it means going dancing with the recognition that you may not be out all night and will probably need to rest more before and after ("disco naps" aren't just for the young!). The important point is that if you love dancing, you should go dancing. Successful aging means continuing to do what you love to do—and never using your age as the only reason for not doing it.

Successful aging is about choices: realizing you can actively shape your life through decisions you make. It is a process of taking charge of one's life and learning to listen to one's inner voice for guidance. It is about paying more attention to spiritual issues, however you define them, so that death is an accepted part of the living process and so that quality of life becomes paramount. If you understand nothing more about successful aging than "I can make my life and it can continue to be a dynamic journey," then you've gotten it, and the rest, as they say, is commentary.

I have come to realize that the essential product from my life is me. It is not a book, nor an organization, nor an award—it is who I am now, yet also who I am becoming. I'm not finished. It means embracing my strengths and weaknesses and not denying anything about myself. It means recognizing that the aging process is, in a real sense, the development of a new performance, the creation of a new character in my own life story.

TOOLS FOR THE JOURNEY, or HOW TO USE THIS BOOK

Since aging is a state of the body, mind, and soul, the changes we face as we grow older are behavioral, mental, and emotional. Accordingly, I have divided the book into three sections, Body, Mind, and Soul. Each chapter describes a "developmental task" that represents a component of successful aging. I call these steps toward successful aging "tasks," in accordance with current human development theory that assumes the individual is active rather than passive. Aging well is work, a process that takes doing and that takes time. While recognizing a gay man is vulnerable to early social forces as well as the influence of family and peers, I make a core assumption that a gay man is the central agent in developing his identity, and he continues his self-creation over the course of his lifetime.

These tasks overlap and do not adhere to any strict timeline: Some of them may happen in a sequence or all at once. Life is never clean and tidy, and midlife can be an especially messy time. I begin by focusing on the body because our sexuality is at the core of our identity, as well as the source of much gay male anxiety around aging. From issues of physical well-being, I move into behaviors of the mind and heart: How we define our work and play, what is the nature of our relationships. Careers and relationships are two areas most affected by changes at midlife, and abrupt transitions in these areas are the hallmarks of the so-called midlife crisis, which will be discussed in depth. The final leg of the journey concerns issues of the spirit: our values, the principles by which we live, our sense of mortality, and our growing desire for spirituality. The journey begins in the root of the body and ends with the full flowering of our soul.

Exercises will be woven throughout each chapter and will focus and direct you through the shifts in perception and attitude that will bring about your successful aging. Stop and think about your answer to each exercise before continuing with the text. Ideally, you will want to keep a journal to write down your thoughts and whatever feelings come up during this process. It is also my hope that these exercises will encourage you to seek out your peers and begin a dialogue about aging. Perhaps you can advertise on a local bulletin board or on-line service to start a discussion group about gay aging. The more that groups of gay men can talk about these issues, the more successfully our community will age as a whole.

To begin this process of reflection, consider these first two exercises.

1. **When did you start considering yourself a middle-aged gay man and how did you feel about it?**

Maybe you don't feel middle-aged, but everybody says that you are since you turned forty or fifty. How does that label feel? Try to describe your true feelings, rather than what you think you "should" feel. Keep it about feelings, not about rationalizations or complicated arguments. What are you feeling? What is in your gut? What is in your heart?

2. **What are the positive and negative issues about your aging?**

Make a list—quick as a reflex—of the positive and negative associations you have around aging, both your own and generally. For example, not as much energy; financial stability; not as much sex; a lover; not enough fun; retirement. And so on. Put down as many items as you can, and don't hold back on the negativity—naming the negatives is the first step in putting them into perspective. Making this list will give you a baseline from which to assess your progress toward successful aging.

Working through these exercises, listening to your fears as well as your fantasies, talking about these concepts, absorbing new information, sharing experiences with your friends—are all parts of this journey. This process will work if undertaken alone, but doing this work in a group could deepen friendships or develop new ones from a gathering of gay men. The more we discuss these issues, the less our fears will persist around aging. There is no right or wrong way to approach these exercises or the larger tasks at hand; there is only the failure of passivity.

GOLDEN MEN: A NEW GENERATION

Ageism devalues us the same way that homophobia does, and many gay men are fed up with it. Unless we begin to tap into the power we have to age well, the antagonism, defensiveness, and cruelty among the different generations in our community will destroy us.

As with any revolution, change begins with one person refusing to participate in the status quo. The basis of my faith in gay men comes from the fact that we have already refused to protect the status quo once—when we came out as gay men—and I know we can do it again. By targeting ageism the way we did homophobia, we can dismantle the stereotype of the "lonely old queen" and begin the new millennium with a new generation of gay men: Golden Men. It's as if we were alchemists transforming the leaden dross of our fears and stereotypes into the gold of a good life.

As you undergo the transformation into a Golden Man, you will begin to:

Appreciate your body and intrinsic attractiveness as a person.

Celebrate the individual differences among your friendships.

Define and value your chosen family.

Recognize your priorities in the dance of work and play.

Nurture your ability to take care of yourself.

Become a role model for other gay men.

Speak confidently from your own voice, recognizing your sense of empowerment.

Stop trying to please others and learn to appreciate the unique values by which you live.

View your past as a dynamic history that led to the present and offers a foundation for the future.

Unearth the buried treasure of your spirituality.

The transformation *is* possible. Aging is inevitable. But thriving is a choice.

PART ONE

Body

ONE

Body Image and Sexuality

In May 1998, SAGE (Senior Action in a Gay Environment) hosted the first national conference on aging in the lesbian and gay community. Approximately four hundred people gathered at Fordham University in New York City to hear academics, social workers, therapists, and lesbian and gay members of the community discuss ageism and aging within a lesbian and gay context. The keynote speakers were Dr. Robert Butler, who first coined the word *ageism*, and Del Martin and Phyllis Lyon, the pioneering founders of the first national lesbian organization, the Daughters of Bilitis, who are now actively involved in OLOC (Old Lesbians Organizing for Change).

Perhaps the most telling moment of the entire conference came during an open discussion following the Saturday morning plenary on "Self Image and Aging." The lesbians on the panel, as well as female members of the audience, were like old-time revivalists preaching the gospel of activism. They detailed the efforts of groups like OLOC to fight ageism in general and in the gay community in particular with consciousness-raising efforts, campaigns to protect Medicare and Medicaid, boycotts, petitioning, and participation in national efforts like the White House Conference on Aging. These women were inspiring and courageous, and their energy galvanized many members of the audience, who whooped and hollered their support.

In contrast, the gay men in the audience seemed more wary,

confused, and fearful on the subject. One of the male panelists was a pioneer in the field of gay civil rights, but around the issue of aging, he seemed like a neophyte, saying he had never experienced ageism. One observer suggested that since he was relatively well-known within the gay community, the power of his celebrity had buffered him from ageism. Many men in the audience stepped up to the microphone to admit feelings of powerlessness, despair, and absolute dread over getting older. A common feeling was "Younger men don't look at me anymore, and if they do, they look away." While the lesbians were active, involved, and motivated, the gay men present generally appeared more passive, shut down, and hopeless about aging.

The differences between lesbians and gay men are many, but the gender divide has never been more visceral to me than in that discussion of ageism. Part of the disparity between how lesbians and gay men are reacting to their aging is clearly connected to the differences between how the two communities relate to their bodies and the value that each assigns to them.

In general, the majority of negatives around aging involve the body, while many of the positives about aging have nothing to do with it (such as the freedom to do as one pleases or to speak one's mind; financial stability; a strong emotional support system; a sense of finally having arrived in the world). Based on the comments made at the SAGE conference, it seems clear that these lesbians are aging better than the gay men because they assign less value to their bodies. It's not that their bodies are unimportant, it's that these lesbians tend to recognize and value a woman *in her entirety*—not just her body but also her intellect, her personality, the whole package. In contrast, gay men tend to commodify their bodies like so many packages of meat.

Gay men are deeply invested in their bodies, and many feel that their body is their best asset—not only for sex, but for feelings of attractiveness, power, and success. The more other men respond to their bodies, the more a gay man will feel good about himself (a phenomenon many nongay women experience). For many gay men, the body is a form of currency in the free market of desire, shaped by the supply and demand for sex and romance (preferably one is in demand and willing to supply). Or, as Andrew Holleran observes in his essay, "Survivors": "We're told it's what's inside, not outside, that counts, but on the street the outside is the medium of exchange," while the city operates "as a vast exercise in retail."

But by assigning so much value to the one thing that is most negatively affected by aging, many gay men are setting themselves up for a horrible experience at midlife, when their bodies begin to change. Extending the economic metaphor, aging then becomes a form of inflation, making our bodies lose value. Even when nothing else changes in his life, when a gay man reaches midlife and his body begins to go through its natural changes, his entire worldview can become jeopardized.

The task in this chapter and the next is to understand your relation to your body at midlife. Through focusing on body image and sexuality, many of us can begin to understand how our negative assumptions around aging and our perceptions about the body can affect the reality of our midlife. In the next chapter, I address both our physical and mental health in a new concept of well-being based on the facts of aging, not the fears.

OUR BODIES, OUR SELF-WORTH

For many gay men, the body is a prison of expectations. We are expected to look a certain way, dress a certain way, behave a certain way—all because we're gay men. On one level, this pressure to conform is part of a group dynamic. Every social group has requirements to belong, a "price of membership," and in many parts of the gay community, the cultural standard is set with an idealized body. So many gay men look in the mirror, only to shudder and start listing what they *should* be doing but aren't. "I should eat better, cut out the ice cream at night." "I should go to the Gap and buy a hip shirt to make me look younger." "I should get more sleep." "I should lose this belly." "I should cut my hair real short." "I should get a tattoo."

The problem is not with their bodies, but with their "shoulds"— those nagging self-criticisms which only compound low self-esteem. Whether or not they exercise regularly or eat right, many gay men experience a constant feeling that "I don't look the way I should." Yet those unrealistic expectations are the real enemy, not the body. A quick look at the gay media reveals how such expectations get reinforced, with pages and pages of images of the gay cultural ideal:

a smooth, lean torso with huge pecs, a rippling stomach, and firm thighs—all tan, toned, and hairless. Given the prevalence of this ideal in our media, it's easy to forget that it was not always this way.

THE GAY MALE IDEAL: A SURVEY

"When I first came to New York in the early seventies, your hair was very important, your butt couldn't be too big, and your only worry was affording enough nice sweaters to wear," quips Jake, a forty-five-year-old public relations executive. "But today . . ." His voice trails off in a shrug of exasperation and defeat.

Looking over the past few decades of gay male culture reveals that the gay male body has been held to many ideals.

In the fifties, the look was about conformity: charcoal suits and pink shirts, and a lot of sweaters. In the countercultural sixties, the hippies liberated everybody's sense of dress. Gays and nongays alike played with gender blending as men wore their hair long, women wore trousers, and everybody wore bell-bottoms and fringe! During the seventies, the Clone reigned among gay men, including such archetypes as the leatherman, firefighter, policemen, and Marlboro Man. In the eighties, the preppy look returned nationwide, and the wasting effects of HIV and AIDS became a common sight in our community's image of itself.

By the 1990s, the body had become a statement. The "look" is no longer about clothing, but wearing the body as a piece of armor. I agree with others who have suggested that the current "body fascism" (our rigid expectations of what a gay body should be) is partly a response to AIDS and the deterioration of the gay public body during the eighties. Though few men possess the natural genes and body structure to fit the ideal, it seems a majority of gay men are struggling, if not to become the ideal, then at least to get as close as possible. But you can't buy the right body the way you could once buy the right clothes. We put ourselves under tremendous stress in thinking about and trying to achieve such a culturally ideal body. This stress is reinforced by the images our media feeds us of "the Circuit," a quasi-organized social calendar of elaborate parties attended by men who embody the cultural ideal.

In his recent book, *Life Outside*, Michelangelo Signorile traces our current obsession with body image back to the Clone look of the seventies, when gay men began to adopt the styles of hypermasculine "types" as a way of offsetting the "crisis of masculinity" that has always haunted gay men. While his analysis draws some interesting connections between the Clone culture of the seventies and the Circuit culture of the nineties, I think there are major differences between the two phenomena. Both in their dynamics and in what they say about gay bodies, these cultures are more different than similar.

To begin with, the Circuit is limited to a very small segment of the gay male population. Granted, they are highly visible in our media, but totally out of proportion to their actual number. The structure of the Circuit is elitist and insidious as well. Attending a Circuit party usually requires a gay man to have a lifestyle that accommodates travel. He has to be willing to spend a certain amount of money, to experiment with recreational drugs, to possess a certain kind of body, and yes, be of a certain age in order to participate fully as a member. On many levels, the "price" to join the Circuit is quite high.

In contrast, the Clone phenomenon was much more widespread throughout the country, from the big cities to the smaller ones. It was more about dress and attitude than the physical body, or exposure of the body. It was also inclusive, in that many body types were considered sexy. (Lesbians, then and now, also seem to accept a wide variety of body types in their community, with no one "type" becoming the standard to which all lesbians aspire.) The Clone look was a way of representing masculinity and borrowed archetypes from the nongay world, but the larger idea was to create a fantasy around yourself. The attitude wasn't about expressing superiority over other body "types" but about pleasure and pride in the presentation of the self. The Clone culture was open to everyone who saw clothes as costume and believed that our choice of costumes conveyed our relationship to the world. It was a celebration of the male body, but not a particular male body.

The Circuit is about wearing the body like a designer piece of clothing, but for some of our emperors, the clothes don't fit. A man on the Circuit may be pumped up, yet slumped, walking hunched over, as if he were carrying heavy shopping bags. Body parts get objectified and exaggerated: while a gay man may sport a huge chest and arms, his legs may be scrawny and he may walk as if he doesn't know what to do with this body he's worked so hard for.

On a more playful note, the poster doll of the Clone culture would be G.I. Joe, while the boy toy of the Circuit is Billy. G.I. Joe's appeal is wrapped up in his uniform and the fantasies boys can create with him: the war scenarios, rescue missions, Indiana Jones capers, and the like. Billed as the world's first openly gay doll, Billy is a huge, anatomically correct Circuit boy, complete with a Caesar style haircut, smooth torso, and a penis totally out of proportion to his body. A year after Billy came out, his maker introduced Carlos, Billy's Latino boyfriend, who is also buff and tattooed, with a goatee and a gigantic "uncut" penis. Whereas G.I. Joe was sold as an action figure, Billy and Carlos are more static and a prop for accessories (though perhaps a West Hollywood Dream House is in the works).

In pursuit of this cultural ideal of a muscular gay body, many gay men join a gym, which has replaced, for some urban men, the bar as the meeting ground for sexual partners and potential boyfriends. But for many more men, I think, the gym has become a symbol for belonging to the gay "club" and for whether or not they're taking care of themselves. While many gay men may join a gym, how many of us actually go regularly? Many men tell me that whether or not they go to it, the gym hovers above them, reminding them of what they "should" be doing if they want to remain "valuable" in the gay male market.

Many gay men exhaust themselves with hours upon hours of workouts, dieting, and the discipline required to create the "perfect" body. Yet all that hard work is often not enough. A gay man might turn to steroids, the tricks of the muscle trade, to create the body he wants. Yet in doing so, he tacitly acknowledges that the goal is not attainable without assistance, that such "perfection" does not come solely from within, but must be applied.

Sadly, however, even G.I. Joe has not been able to resist the muscle culture. In December 1998, *The New York Times* reported that since 1964, each version of G.I. Joe has become "more muscular and sharply defined, or 'cut,' than the model before." G.I. Joe Extreme "possesses a waist so small and [biceps] so pronounced that no real adult could approach them without the help of potentially dangerous body enhancement therapies." As a result, G.I. Joe has become as insidious a role model for boys as Barbie is for girls.

Although the gym culture has reached its peak in the major cities of New York and Los Angeles, many of us across the country carry such cultural standards around in our heads (thanks to the ridiculous overkill of images of such bodies in our media) and end up comparing ourselves to them. We need to learn to take care of the body on its own terms, without confusing muscles with health. We need to stop making our bodies a fashion statement and more a statement about how we feel about ourselves.

Yet because we're male, we have little experience or conditioning in relating to our bodies. As boys, we are not taught to think of our bodies in the same way as girls, who are generally more conscious of their bodies because of their monthly cycle. Recent books like *Reviving Ophelia* and *Real Boys* have documented how both girls and boys are conditioned to accept rigid gender stereotypes (girls are social and emotional; boys are tough and stoic), and a boy child is taught to disregard what goes on in his body, even if it hurts—take it like a man, don't cry, be a big boy. Conditioned to be ignorant, a boy grows up unable to listen to his body.

Can you imagine a man writing a book called *Our Bodies, Our Selves?* That book was the result of years of feminist consciousness-raising among women in the early seventies. Our expression of liberation was *The Joy of Gay Sex*, which was groundbreaking in providing gay men with information about STDs and other health issues, but the knowledge had to be presented in a sexual context. Only in the last few years have books like *The Gay Man's Wellness Guide* by Robert Penn begun to treat gay bodies as whole organisms, rather than reducing them to just sexual organs. Both these books are by-products of AIDS and the sense of our health being jeopardized. It's taken gay men twenty years to get to where the feminists were in the early seventies. We are only just beginning to examine our relationship to our body as an ongoing commitment to health, and not just a reaction to an epidemic.

HOW DO I LOOK?

Body image, in psychology, is usually talked about in terms of the discrepancy between a person's body and how he feels about it. In other words, our body image is some combination of objective reality and our subjective opinions. To age successfully, a gay man needs to work toward bridging this gulf and getting a more realistic appraisal of himself. To integrate the physical reality (how he looks) with the emotional reality (how he feels) requires eliminating the distortion between the realities.

Successful aging also means not being judgmental about your body. Having love handles doesn't mean you're unattractive. Losing your hair is not a sign of weakness. Your body's natural aches are no excuse not to go dancing. Successful aging is about seeing your body and its various parts without putting value judgments on them. It's about looking at the facts of your body, not your fears.

To see your body as it truly is requires a revolution in consciousness. Gay men are not the only ones plagued by this body image dilemma, but we are the only ones who can help ourselves *because we are the ones who are creating and choosing the images by which we compare one another*. Try to consider your body only in relation to yourself, not in comparison to some anonymous face in a magazine. Try to measure your body image against how well you understand yourself.

If you find yourself struggling to separate your feelings about your body from your feelings about the gay male "ideal" you see in the media, try to remember what it was like when you began to come out. Just as we then resisted believing the negative stereotypes about being gay, we need to resist the elements of gay male culture that insult and degrade our body image, namely, our "body fascism" and our worship of youth culture. Both features of gay male culture complicate our aging process with unnecessary negativism. Security about one's body is difficult for gay men of any age, and at midlife, the issue is critical as we daily live in our changing bodies.

1. **What are the three parts of your body that you like the most? Why?**

This first exercise may startle you. We're not accustomed to naming what we like about ourselves. Our first impulse is to start listing the faults, the weaknesses, the flaws that torment our waking hours. But I want you to stay with this until you can identify three positives about your body, no matter how minor you think they are. Hair. Eyes. Chest hair. Calves. Smile. Cock. Hands. When I ask a gay man for this information, I'm persistent in getting three positives, not just because I want to know, but because I want him to know for himself and to say what he's not used to saying. Before a gay man can understand successful aging, he has to know how and when to look for positives. And the "why" is just as important as the naming.

2. **What are the three parts of your body that you like the least? Why are you so uncomfortable with them?**

This answer comes more easily for most gay men; sometimes, I have to limit them to naming just three parts. This exercise is useful because it helps to identify your priorities. It also allows you to be what you're probably more familiar with: being negative about your body. While it's important to air these feelings of discontent, remember the positives you struggled to list. Are there any connections between the two lists? As you spend more time with these exercises, the positives and the negatives will begin to balance each other out, and in that balance, you will be able to find your true body image. Successful aging is not about canceling out or denying the negatives, but recognizing that there are positives as well.

Look over your answers to this exercise and see if the parts you named are something you can change (your weight, hair style, fitness) or something you must embrace (your height or the size of your penis). Depending upon your answers, you can probably get a sense of how realistic your body image is. If you have a twenty-nine-inch waist and are six-foot-three and you say you're too fat, or if you're five-foot-ten and consider yourself "too short," think about your ability to see your own reality. If the vast majority of your physical complaints don't match what others observe, it's clear where our work lies. One key to unlocking your relationship to your body is understanding the dynamic between the self you hold to be "me" (or, what you perceive about yourself) and the self others believe to be "you" (or, what others perceive about you). Integrating our emotional and physical realities requires listening to the feedback we may hear, but often ignore.

So much of the time, when I mention this book to people, they say something along the lines of "That will be an important book; we need to adapt to aging better." But whenever I hear the phrase "well-adapted," I think, that's not what I'm asking for: to accept a negative situation or a negative consequence or to have a lukewarm acceptance. What I'm after is a *transformation*, meaning, *a shift in perception that forever changes the way you understand yourself.* Understanding your body image is not about accepting sags and wrinkles; it's about changing your relationship to your body so that you no longer perceive such things as negative. They are simply what they are, without the language of righteousness, neither "good" nor "bad," but neutral. What they mean is what we project onto them—they mean what we want them to mean.

Two examples come to mind to help explain what I mean by a perceptual shift. Once I had a speech to prepare for the annual convention of the American Psychological Association. I had planned to write my remarks during the two weeks prior to the convention, a time when I was also scheduled to visit some friends upstate at their house by a lake. Not wanting to miss the trip, I resolved to work every afternoon for the first week, and instead of rowing or swimming with my friends, would draft my remarks and then polish them on my return home.

Monday afternoon came, and I found myself setting up a work space on the porch. I had my pens; I had my pad of paper. I even had some idea of what I wanted to say. The problem was that I didn't want to work. I resented having to spend a glorious summer week struggling to articulate a few remarks that may not have been remembered a week later (even by me).

I had several rough starts, scribbling down some comments, then scratching them out. I was distracted by the sound of birds in the trees, by the wind rustling the trees along the lakeside. And I was fuming, resentful of my friends. But I continued, unwilling to stop what I had started and determined to enjoy my resentment. I got very little accomplished that day. On the second afternoon, I again found myself being angry more than being creative. Then I thought: I'm lucky to have this porch by the lake to write this speech. I wasn't locked away in a stale office or library having to do this chore. For the moment, I had a task to do and pleasant surroundings in which to get it done. Once I recognized all of this, in the space of a minute or so, I went back to the speech, and the words began to flow. Instead of hanging on to resentment and making my task more difficult, I let it go and shifted my perception of the situation. Nothing changed but my attitude, but what a difference that made!

The other example that comes to mind has to do with coming out. Many gay men become angry when their families do not accept them immediately upon their coming out. After years of struggling with the issue of their sexuality, many gay men are relieved finally to reach a point when they can tell their family. Of course, many gay men expect their families to cry, argue, shout, go into hysterics— the whole range of drama—but coming out gives us a faith that things will resolve. "It'll be tough at first, but sooner or later, all families will come around" is a core assumption of our community, and I believe this, too.

But I think we seriously underestimate the time it takes for our families to make the same adjustment that we have made in accepting our own gayness. Whenever I hear a gay man complain that his family still hasn't accepted him, I wonder a few things: how old he was when he came out to himself, how old he was when he came out to them, and what he has done (or not done) to help them through this process.

When a gay man comes out to his family, his revelation immediately isolates them from their own sources of support (just as he felt isolated when he began to become aware of his attraction to other males). They may not feel his sexuality is something they can talk about outside, or even within, the family. In many ways, a gay man's declaration to his parents, in effect, puts them into a kind of closet, where they may spend some time learning to accept many things (beginning with the reality that their child is sexual) before they come out as well.

The perceptual shift comes when I ask a gay man to reflect on how long it took him to accept himself and to give his family half that time. Many gay men take years of denying, acknowledging, figuring out, before even expressing their feelings toward other men. It doesn't seem fair to expect a family to go through that process in a few months, or even a year.

The perceptual shift occurs when a gay man can move beyond his anger or frustration to a sense of compassion about his family's reaction to his coming out. (Of course, I'm not talking about a family who kicks a gay teenager out of the home, or a parent who physically assaults a gay son for coming out. Those families do exist and are dangerous. I'm talking about your average family, which reacts with anger, confusion, tears, but not direct abuse or violence.) The facts of the situation haven't changed, but the gay man's perception of the situation has begun to shift. Once he has begun to understand their perspective, he usually finds it easier to respond to his family's confusion and questions and awkward attempts to communicate. Having compassion for what the family is going through does not mean going back into the closet or denying his sexuality, but it does mean showing the family the same level of acceptance, love, and patience that he gave himself during his coming out.

My examples of shifts in perception probably seem easier than understanding and embracing your body at midlife, but the dynamic is the same. Part of what makes such shifts in perception possible (transforming a negative body image into a realistic appreciation of your body) is our ability to process new information about any given situation. The new information may need to be repeated again and again in order for you to absorb it and stop burdening yourself with worry, resentment, anger, fear, and other emotions that paralyze. What determines the number of "repetitions" is your ability to accept feedback. Feedback is the new information you need to bring about a shift in perception. Usually, feedback is another person's response to something you said or did: an opinion, a critique, a compliment, a grade, an observation, new details or points of information which can affect not just your view of the situation, or of yourself, but of the world.

One of the major problem areas many gay men experience is the ability to process *positive feedback*. It's fairly easy for a gay man to accept negative opinions about himself, given the homophobia of the culture in which he was raised and his own internalized homophobia. But the good things? What do you do when someone compliments the shirt you're wearing? If your first impulse is to say, "I got it on sale" or "This tired thing?" or even, "It was a gift," think about what you're doing: don't negate your positive feedback by slapping it away.

If we have a negative perception of ourselves in the world (either we're too fat or we're too old or we're too hairy or we're not smart enough, whatever it is), one of the ways we maintain that negative image of ourselves is to deny anything that challenges it. Whether it be a comment about looking fit or how we're dressed or how we completed a project at work, we either negate it or qualify it. We may *hear* the compliment, but we don't *listen* in the sense of absorbing it, understanding it, and accepting it. Feedback requires not just hearing, but listening. One of the behaviors I used to work on constantly with clients is feedback. I'd say, "Anytime anyone gives you compliment, say thank you and shut up."

Try it the next time you receive a compliment. If you're throwing a dinner party, try to resist saying "It was nothing" when someone compliments the entree, or try not to say, "the chicken's a little dry" before anyone takes their first bite. If you can cut off that defensiveness, just on a physical level (literally, bite your tongue), then it permits a space for the compliment to sink in, a little bit. It may have to happen a hundred times, but it may be at your hundred and first dinner party that you actually hear the compliment. Once you begin to listen, you might be surprised by how many compliments you are receiving. The next time someone says, "Good job!" at work or "You handled that client well" or "The pride committee thanks you for your hard work this June," practice listening to them, and not just hearing them. Otherwise, you run the risk of insulting them.

Every time you qualify a compliment or deny someone's praise, you are telling that person that their judgment is weak, that they don't know what they're talking about, that their taste is mediocre. Sooner or later, people will stop giving you feedback (both positive and negative) if they don't think you're listening to them. Why bother giving a person feedback, if he can't take it? Once people stop giving you feedback, their silence begins to confirm whatever negative perceptions you were protecting all along: I can't cook, I can't dress well, I'm inefficient, I'm no good, I can't do this job, I'm ugly, I don't fit in—the whole barrage of self-criticism that so many of us wield against ourselves.

Because of its connection to our feelings of power and sexuality, our body image is especially vulnerable to feedback, and positive shifts in our perception can take time and practice. Midlife can be a tremendously upsetting time for our body image, when our body begins its natural changes. But by listening to what others tell us and by paying attention to what we know for a fact, we can begin to transform our body image into a source of power and strength.

3.   How has your body changed since adolescence until now?

Maybe it's a few gray hairs in a thick auburn set of curls or a soreness the morning after a night of dancing, a sudden creak of joints upon rising, or love handles, or those tiny etched lines around the eyes you remember your mother fretting about. But one day you feel young and invigorated by life, and the next day you want to run to the Clinique for Men counter and scream for the latest moisturizer to overcome the unwelcome but inevitable signs of aging.

Our bodies are changing organisms that have never been static. Do you remember your mother placing a ruler on your head and measuring your growth as a child, inch by inch up the doorframe? Or when your father showed you how to shave those first scraggly whiskers on your upper lip? Remember when you used to look forward to getting older because of the changes it would bring to your body?

We have been adjusting to many bodily changes our entire lifetime, though we may not recognize many of the changes along the way. Adolescence is often the first dramatic period of change we are conscious of. The rate of change during adolescence is so fast our bodies suddenly become alien to us. The growth of the body from infancy to childhood is the actual greatest concentration of physical change we go through, but we're not aware of the changes. Our consciousness of the changes is what makes adolescence (and later midlife) so traumatic.

Midlife represents a crisis for gay men because it reminds them so much of adolescence, with the reemergence of feeling like an outsider, but this time within their own community. No longer "young," gay men at midlife may begin to question if they truly belong in a gay community, especially given our media's emphasis on the young and muscular. Other adolescent feelings come up as well: experiencing rejection from peers, a changing body and sexuality, and a hundred different choices to make about the future. This time, however, the source of much of the discomfort is ageism, rather than homophobia. Small wonder that midlife is a gay man's nightmare. Who wants to go through all those feelings again?

In midlife, the feelings of inadequacy familiar to adolescence are reactivated when the physical appearance is noticeably altered. Many gay men fear midlife because it forces them to give up the previous social persona (a "young" gay man) through which they have related to the world. No longer the golden boys, we now have to adjust to a new social and personal perception of ourselves as middle-aged gay men, Golden Men.

A gay male at midlife feels conflicted between his need to feel attractive and the tendency of many gay males to equate youth with good looks. This conflict is complicated by how he *imagines* others perceive him. The discrepancies between all these needs and feelings can produce, for some, an unrelenting source of pain and anxiety. What's important is to try to figure out the ways in which we contribute to our own pain by comparing ourselves to unrealistic standards or ideals.

Do you pass mirrors without wanting to catch your reflection? Do you prefer taking an elevator, even to the second floor, because you don't like it when your knees creak or when you get winded? Do you wear loose, baggy clothes because you don't want anything tight fitting? Or do you wear the tightest jeans you can find because you want your legs to look muscular and your basket to attract attention?

Whatever discomfort you may feel at midlife has a source: your body *is* changing. But are your reactions to those changes driven more by a fear of inadequacy than the consequences of the actual changes?

As with adolescence, midlife exacerbates your reactions to the changes you're experiencing because the changes seem to be happening all at the same time. Also, as with adolescence, adjusting to your new body—physically and emotionally—can take time and work. By voicing your negative feelings, you are better able to face the changes you're going through without being overwhelmed and defeated. The first step in this process is to be clear and open about all this discomfort. Have you left anything out?

THE WHOLE YOU AND NOTHING BUT THE REAL YOU

After coming out, a gay man's relationship to his body changes, as he realizes the currency his body represents in the gay male community. But this late-blooming attention to his body and a need to solicit attention from other men can lead to an exaggerated emphasis on the body. As a result, the body becomes overvalued and the body image distorts and overshadows the self-image. As a community, we need to devalue our body currency and set a new "gold standard" of appreciation for ourselves, balancing our body image with other sources of self-worth.

Take the time and the honesty to appreciate the value of your new midlife body by re-examining your understanding of attractiveness, sex, and power. One obstacle to eliminating your adherence or comparison to community "ideals" is your own perception of how others see you. Do you feel that people pay attention only to your body (your external self), which is now aging, while the true you (your internal self) remains alive and kicking? This gulf between how we see ourselves and how others see us is particularly intense around issues of attractiveness and sexuality. Loss of sexual attractiveness initially appears to be central to our fear of being middle-aged. This is especially true for those who felt they were sexually attractive when younger and no longer feel that they are sexually desirable.

4. In what ways are you an attractive man?

As a very attractive fifty-two-year-old, Michael worked hard at maintaining his body and he usually dated younger men who were constantly amazed when they learned his Clock Age. Despite the validation these men provided, he still didn't believe he was attractive. Michael's body image was of the awkward teenager he once was, and he was unable to let go of this mental image of himself. When I asked him to list all of his attractive qualities, not just his body, he began to understand how attraction is a combination of factors on many levels: physical, intellectual, emotional, spiritual.

In considering what makes you attractive, you will come up against your own body image. If you feel that you are totally unattractive on all levels, or if you feel resistant to tackling this exercise, try to focus on identifying your redeeming qualities: ease in social situations, intelligence, sensuality, humor, health, whatever positive qualities exist in your life.

In this exercise, did you focus only in sexual terms? Or did you go beyond the sexual realm and come up with a general statement of your attractiveness? We might feel attractive, but for many gay men, feeling *sexually* attractive depends upon the kindness, or rather, the horniness of strangers.

This exercise can serve different functions. It can push you to see yourself as an attractive man without assigning any sexuality to that image, to identify your positive qualities that are beyond the physical self. It can also get you to talk about yourself in terms of sexuality if you have not done so previously.

Try to dig deep into your feelings about sexual attractiveness, your own and the other men you find attractive. As with listing the parts of your body you like, your feelings of sexual attractiveness are crucial and esteem building, no matter how inconsequential they may feel at first. Spend time listing these positive sexual feelings, instead of qualifying and rationalizing them away.

Deepen your thinking about "attractiveness" and "sexual attractiveness," which may seem like the same thing. Does adding "sexual" to your idea of attractiveness flush out contradictions and confusions? Struggling with this exercise enables you to consider, maybe for the first time, what constitutes sexual attractiveness. You might feel attractive, but not sexually desirable, or you may see yourself as merely a sex object, but not as "boyfriend material." There is no right or wrong way to answer this exercise. The main point is for you to see how you define these terms and apply them to yourself.

5. Do you feel that you once were a sex object and no longer are?

Arthur feels he was once handsome, but at forty-eight, he no longer gets the looks he used to. An investment banker, he has given up trying to look good and has begun to drink and smoke heavily. He doesn't exercise because he doesn't see the point. He still goes to the bars, though he rarely talks to anyone during the hours he spends there. He used to spend the night on the dance floor, but now he stands to the side, watching the boys turn and spin in the colored lights. Arthur has surrendered to a self-image of the Clone in Decline.

You may have answered this exercise in the negative because you still feel you are a sex object, or perhaps because you have never felt that you were a sex object. Or are you like Arthur, answering in the affirmative, while remaining convinced that aging has everything to do with diminished sexual attractiveness? Being a sex object requires someone to objectify you, and this exercise requires you to measure others' responses to you as you have aged. If, like Arthur, you have stopped taking care of yourself and picked up some habits like smoking heavily or not dancing (even though you love to dance!), maybe those qualities, and not your age, are what's diminishing your being seen as a sex object. Think about what you might actually be doing to make this fear a self-fulfilling prophecy.

As you try to identify any "loss" of sexuality, try to think of all the ways there are to look at sexual attractiveness. The depth of your sense of loss may reflect the degree to which you have been defining sexual attractiveness solely by one or two qualities (age, physique, energy level). The more you're able to expand your notion of sexual attractiveness, the less this "loss" will seem.

SEX AND THE GOLDEN GUY

At the core of our anxiety about aging is a fear of becoming asexual, unable to have sex or be approached by others for sex as we age. But in a 1990 study, Mark Pope and Richard Schulz found that sexual activity declines very little as we grow older.

Interviewing eighty-seven gay men between the ages of forty and seventy-seven in the Chicago area, Pope and Shultz reported the good news that 91 percent of the total were still sexually active. The better news is that sex for these men did not change in frequency or enjoyment. Fifty-four percent of men in their forties reported that they had sex *more than once a week*, while thirty-four percent of men in their fifties reported the same. The best news is that there is little bad news. As with so many of the myths around aging, attitude is all.

In midlife, our reawakened adolescent feelings of inadequacy trigger a need for validation, sexual and otherwise. But we are often confused by exactly what our changing body wants. We may have emotional needs that we translate into sexual needs. For example, you might feel like just *being* with other gay men, talking, listening to music, dancing, getting out of the house, cruising on the street, whatever. But since, "going out" by definition, means sex for many gay men—you may feel as if you have to score in order to justify going out at all.

Going out to socialize doesn't necessarily have to translate into sex. Since much about gay men's therapy seems to be about their sexual failures (at least initially), I always encourage gay men to listen to their bodies. There's nothing wrong with feeling like you need a hug, with wanting to snuggle with another body, or just wanting to

socialize or get out of the house. What's confusing is when we immediately transfer such desires for intimacy, social interaction, and ten-
derness into lust and the quick fix of casual sex. Sex may not have
been what they wanted, yet many gay men feel the need to justify
going to a bar by having sex. So they find themselves in a sexual
situation "going through the motions," literally, and not having a
good time.

Many gay men are often dismayed by the different feelings they
have after meeting someone and connecting quickly for sex. Four out
of five times, the sex is lousy and the experience not very satisfying
(yet the one time the sex is really good keeps him going back for
more). Is it possible that the lousy sex results from not really wanting
sex in the first place, but maybe just conversation or snuggling or
flirtation?

The good sex happens when sex is what you really want, not a
hug or a dance partner or a brunch buddy or a conversation—though
any of those things can also lead to great sex. Another variation is
the gay man who realizes he doesn't want sex and is honest about
it when he meets someone. If the other man leaves, that's okay. But
sometimes the other man just wants conversation and a hug, too.
Even if the evening culminates with their going home together, that
time spent together just talking and having a cuddle can lead to
enjoyable sex later.

Some men worry about how much they cruise guys on the street;
it seems compulsive to them to keep turning around to see if a
stranger has noticed them. If the cruise is returned and they eventually have sex, again, the result is often lousy. Usually, after examining
what they were really looking for, they realize that they didn't have
to do anything more than acknowledge the cruise. If they were not
feeling horny, or wanting to have sex with the other man, the visual
affirmation may have been all they really wanted, not the actual sex.
Cruising doesn't have to lead to sex, but to a mutual acknowledgment
of attractiveness.

When a gay man begins to hear what his body is actually saying,
the potential for a real connection increases because he is more direct
in stating and getting what he wants. He learns to appreciate the
different forms of validation available to him. He learns to distinguish
between his lust and his need for validation, between horniness and
a desire for simple social contact.

6. **List the reasons why you do or do not find men your age
    sexually attractive.**

What sort of men do you find yourself attracted to? How old
are they? Does the idea of dating a peer seem unlikely? Since our
pattern of dating and attraction shifts over time, we may find ourselves attracted to different ranges of men over our sexual life. What
this exercise concerns is determining what you think constitutes your
attraction to other men and to what degree is age a factor in that
attraction.

Usually, older men who are not attracted to men their own age
have difficulty feeling and seeing themselves as sexually attractive.
For some, this inability to see their peers as attractive reflects their
own self-image. Yet younger men who find older men sexually attractive are not necessarily denying their own attractiveness but see age
as a positive element in sexuality (an attitude that will help them in
their own aging process). Try to determine whether age is a factor
in your formula for sexual attraction.

How old was your first boyfriend? How old were you? When
you have casual sex, how old are the tricks? What excites you about
a man your age? What's off-putting? Are young guys annoying or
spellbinding?

What I'm after is how you have or have not related sexually to
men your age throughout your lifetime. Most likely, the age of your
partners has shifted as you've gotten older. No matter the direction
of the shift, try to identify a pattern to your attractions. What is
your history of choosing sexual partners? Can you identify a period
when you only went with older guys or younger guys or has there
always been a mix? Be explicit in your feelings about age and sex.
Honesty is the mandate here, regardless of whether you're expressing
negative or positive experiences.

7. **Describe the men you feel are sexually attractive. Do you differ
    from them?**

The goal is to determine exactly what you mean by sexually
attractive—what are your criteria and how do you feel about yourself
in relation to those criteria? Successful aging requires a better understanding of the ways we feel sexual, how we express our sexuality,

and how we choose our sexual partners. Whatever discrepancy emerges between the men you find sexually attractive and how you regard yourself will suggest how you may put yourself down and devalue your own attractiveness.

8. Would you cruise a man who looked like you and why?

This exercise pushes you to look upon yourself as a sex object, *without comparing yourself to others*. You may never have considered yourself from this perspective, and the goal is for you to look at yourself in the same way you cruise a man: checking out his body. His hair color. His voice and walk. His laughter. His sexy glasses. By bringing out your most basic feelings about your sexual attractiveness, this exercise implicitly reveals your general feelings about yourself. Once you give yourself the attention and generosity that you give the man on the street, you may begin to see a few aspects of yourself that you might find sexually attractive. This awareness of your own sexiness is a step toward being positive about aging and expanding your self-image to include sexual attractiveness.

9. Describe your fantasy man.

A fantasy can have many elements: a physical type, a particular attitude, a specific scene, a triggering emotion. What is a fantasy that you keep returning to, again and again, that turns you on sexually? Maybe you always had a crush on a guy at work and you imagine him snuggling up at home with a fire and a blanket (and getting under his blanket!). Or your heart pounds when a certain trainer at the gym looks your way. Or you lust after a movie star or celebrity. Or there's a figure from your past, a Scoutmaster, a coach, a teacher, a cousin, who awakened your sexuality. You remember the color of his eyes, his scent, his crooked smile, the timbre of his voice, how his body moved, how his hands looked up close.

Let yourself go with this exercise, filling in as much detail as possible. The whole point of the fantasy is to explore what you desire; only by understanding your desires can you begin to make the fantasy come true.

10. In what ways are you like your fantasy man?

Most gay men hate this part, especially after getting all hot and bothered by describing their fantasy man in the previous exercise. But this question should not be dismissed quickly with a simple answer. If you thought that fantasies are supposed to be about things you don't have, think again. Fantasies can be about wish fulfillment, but they can also express and exaggerate our own personalities. *There is always a part of the dreamer in the dream*. There are usually ways you are already like your fantasy man, but you may have a hard time getting in touch with those similarities. It's important to stay with this exercise until you can identify some similarities with your fantasy man, no matter how small or insignificant.

DO YOU SEE WHAT I SEE?

Discrepancies between how a gay man feels about himself and how others see him can emerge in many areas of his life, but those surrounding the body may be the most ingrained. A gay man may know how others see him and be aware of their attraction to him, but that awareness does not necessarily mean he *feels* it. Your mind may say, I am in good shape and attractive, but the shoulds reply, You're fat, you're skinny, you're losing your hair.

One of the guiding principles in my work is that feelings usually follow perceptions. It is more often the way we *view* our reality that affects what we *feel* about our reality. For example, if you're walking in the woods and you step on a stick, the sound might startle you. But if you perceive that stick as a snake, you'll jump back with your heart racing. Or consider a stranger on the street approaching you with his hand held out; if you perceive it as a handshake, you'll be open, friendly, but if you see it as a fist coming at you, you'll become defensive and afraid. When we respond emotionally to what we perceive, our perceptions, in effect, create our reality.

Many therapists argue the opposite, that our feelings determine what we think or how we perceive reality. And sometimes, it's true. If we feel negative and powerless about aging, our aging will be a negative and powerless experience. If we don't feel attractive, we won't encourage or absorb feedback that tells us we're attractive. Our feelings can affect not only our perceptions but our reality as well.

The challenge comes in sorting out whether our perceptions are different from other people's, as well as whether our perceptions are affected by our emotions and events in the past. Can you recognize that what you feel is different from others' perceptions? Which is the reality? Or are there many realities to comprehend?

11. Whom has an accurate perception of the way you look—you? Your friends? Strangers?

Whom do you trust to tell you how you look? Whose opinion do you value most when thinking about your physical body and your sexual attractiveness? Can you make yourself feel sexy or do you need compliments from strangers to feel that way? Is flirting a way of getting attention for the hard work you give to your looks? Will looking in a mirror do the same thing for you?

This exercise focuses on the external/internal dilemma. We may know we look a certain way, but if our friends tell us we look good, we may not believe them. We want to be validated, but on some level, we still don't believe we're attractive. If we don't get cruised on the street, then something must be wrong. When our internal assessment doesn't match our external feedback, we begin to realize that we make distortions or inaccuracies in our perceptions about ourselves. But maybe we can't stop the "shoulds" or stop dwelling on the negatives. This perceptual stalemate intensifies at midlife because our bodies are changing and we're afraid all the negative myths will come true. We don't know what we believe any more about our own attractiveness, so we choose not to believe the positive feedback we encounter. What we feel becomes the only reality, especially around the issue of visibility.

INVISIBLE MEN

"It's not that they ignore me; they don't even see me," remarks Jake, our forty-five-year-old public relations executive talking about the younger men he cruises in gay bars. "I'm not even on their radar screen; they walk by like I'm not even there." One of the hardest things to achieve as gay men has been visibility, and yet aging seems to take away that very hard-won achievement. For a group for whom visibility has been a personal as well as community struggle, to suddenly become "invisible" is a cruel aspect of gay aging.

Some young gay men are myopic and can't see anyone outside their own age group—not just as a potential sexual partner but also as a role model, friend, or mentor. What's more troubling is that some older gay men often don't even leave themselves open to being seen. At midlife, many gay men stop circulating because they don't think they'll be noticed or cruised. Instead of facing the indifference of others, many gay men may choose to stay home, rendering themselves even more invisible in the community.

Since so much of our fear of aging has to do with a fear of giving something up or losing something of value, we find it very difficult to imagine ourselves as being *seen* by others as vital and sexual older men, that is, as *having the very qualities we believe we are losing*. It's true that most of our cultural images of aging are of older, asexual persons who find their satisfactions in nonsexual ways, and that vibrancy, sexuality and risk taking are not usually associated with the older person. Yet inasmuch as we accept these negative stereotypes, we also convey our negative self-images to others and help bring about the negative responses from people so that our self-image becomes a self-fulfilling prophecy. On the other hand, if we are feeling sexually attractive and someone does not find us that way, their response can be seen as a statement about whom they find attractive rather than a negation of our feelings about ourselves. But how many of us can see rejection in those terms?

Most gay men take a physical rejection very personally and feel that it is equivalent to a negative statement about themselves. It takes a strong ego to be able to see this situation primarily as an indication about the other person (what he likes, what he finds sexually attractive), rather than a statement about the gay man in question (he's worthless, ugly, old).

12. Do you believe that if someone does not find you sexually attractive, his response is a statement about whom he finds attractive, rather than a negation of you?

This is an incredibly difficult exercise for many, many gay men, but acting "as if" you believe this statement will bring you closer to actually accepting it. The logic of the statement is clear enough, but the emotional acceptance underlying it is tough to achieve because it means rejecting what our culture, both mainstream and especially gay, teaches us from day one: it's crucial to be sexy, and gay men are about sex; if we're not sexually attractive, we have no value in our community and we become invisible and ignored. We're so used to equating not being cruised with rejection that we can't see that the person is making a choice based on whom *he* finds attractive, the same way we make choices based on whom we find attractive. Rejection feels like an insult only when we're attracted to the other person; if we're not attracted to him, it doesn't really matter that he's not attracted to us.

Since men are generally conditioned to be the sexual subject, or the one in charge in a sexual situation, most nongay men don't stop to think that maybe women look at nongay men in the same way that the men look at women; nongay men rarely see themselves as sexual objects. But gay men do realize that they are being objectified by their sexual objects *at the same time* they are objectifying them, which means that each man gets a double dose of the cultural standards and conditioning that all men apply to their sexual objects. (No wonder dating is so hard!)

This object-object dynamic determines how gay men treat one another, and thereby how they feel judged and judge themselves. This dynamic also explains why gay men seem especially vulnerable when it comes to internalized ageism, since so much of their sexual history can be seen in terms of objectification. Ageism reduces an object's value to one dimension: our Clock Age. Part of many gay men's fear around aging is being reduced to a number. On the eve of his fortieth birthday, my friend David told me, "I'm pissed off that all I have worked for, all the stuff I'm proud of, will just not matter anymore as soon as I turn forty. Guys will look at my age and not be able to see beyond it." Some guys, yes, but not all guys.

Before we can expect other men to think of us as more than our Clock Age, we have to think of ourselves that way. Many men think of their twenties and thirties as a window of sexual opportunity that begins to close when they turn forty. It's as if when they leave the closet, they enter a room of gay life, full of sexual energy and fun; they spend their twenties and thirties thriving in that room, but then are told to leave when they begin to age, exiting into another closet:

middle age. I am saying there is another room to enter, and the goal is to keep moving. Don't stay hidden in the closet of midlife; come out into a new room where sex and happiness and life satisfaction are waiting for you.

13. **If you knew for a certainty that gay men would continue to find you attractive and would continue to be interested in you sexually, do you think you would be as concerned about aging?**

In my experience, most gay men consider aging and sexual disinterest as going hand-in-hand. Beneath our fear of losing our attractiveness lies the greater fear of becoming sexually inactive. But what if sexual activity as we age were a certainty? As it is, medical studies tell us it is possible and the anecdotal evidence of older gay men also confirms it. By shifting the question of sex from an "if" to a "when," this exercise clears the water so we can see to the bottom of our fears.

I faced this fear in my early fifties, when my lover of ten years died. In 1990, I was single and fifty-four—not an easy age to begin dating again. So I withdrew from romance and shut down sexually, focusing on my grief and my work, and for a long time, I shelved my desire for any connection beyond friendship. For many gay men, grief exhausts their capacity for relationships. There's no energy left to pursue someone new or get to know anyone.

After almost two years, I began to feel like going out again, meeting some new faces, perhaps pursuing some men I had been attracted to in the past. But then I had my first major health crisis and was hospitalized twice with pneumonia. This resulted in an official diagnosis of AIDS. For another year, I was sidelined from romance and sex, as my health and recovery became my priority and consumed all of my emotional, physical, and spiritual energy.

In 1994, with my health stabilized, I was ready to date again, but I wasn't sure where to begin, what I wanted, whom I found attractive, who found me attractive. I decided to put myself out there and see what would happen. I ran some personal ads and responded to some. I made a habit of accepting invitations to parties and social events, making myself available for new experiences. But what taught me most directly about what I wanted and who wanted me was going to the baths.

My friends were dismayed by my weekly trips to a local bath-house. *How can you go there? That's so seventies. You're not going to meet a boyfriend there. What about safe sex?* I reminded them that safer sex had to do with what one did, not with how often or where or with how many partners. And yes, I didn't think I'd meet a boyfriend there, but I did find attractive gay men of all ages who were attracted to other gay men of all ages. Sometimes I would make a connection; sometimes not. Sometimes with men my age, sometimes with younger men, and sometimes with men older than I was. I would also see incredibly handsome men, the kind that stop you in your tracks at the gym or at a club, and they would not be talking to anybody and would usually leave without connecting. All in all, not much had changed since the seventies.

Part of my strategy in going to the baths was to force myself to feel sexual again, after almost three years of grief and getting my health back. I wasn't sure I could even have sex or could attract a partner. I had maintained myself and not gained weight, but I was not a gym goer. I was an older man who took care of his body, plain and simple. What I found was that people responded to the way that I took care of myself, rather than to my age or my physique only. I became a sexual being again, and the renewal of my sexual feelings started a process of exploration. I began to go to HIV posi-tive tea dances, I started circulating more in places where I could meet new people. I knew that when I was ready, I would meet someone, and it would be when I wasn't looking and feeling as if I *had* to look so hard.

Based on my experience and that of others I have spoken with, I believe that when a gay man perceives that men will continue to find him attractive and want to have sex with him as he ages, his vision of his future will brighten and his concerns about aging will fall away. It's an example of perception creating feelings and reality. *We have to perceive ourselves as sexual beings in order to attract sexual interest.* If we're locked into a negative framework that equates our Clock Age with our sexual worth, we're not sending out a positive message. Perhaps we're not even putting ourselves in circulation because we are projecting our feeling that other people won't find us attractive. We sabotage ourselves when we project rejection; if we get out there and make ourselves visible as sexual, middle-aged men, we are telling the world we're ready, willing, and able to prove ageism wrong.

YOUR BODY, YOUR LIFE

Body image is not just how you think about your body. It's the kind of relationship you have with your body in terms of caring for it. How do you see yourself using your body? Do you use your body to get attention? Or is it something you use to get close to people emotionally? Or just physically? Think of your body as an extension of yourself, what you're trying to convey to the world, rather than a tool to manipulate the world. Your body tells the world who you are before you can say it verbally. Is your body sending the message you want?

My client Mike was a tall, handsome, broad man. He rarely connected with anyone even though he desperately wanted to. He would spend hours alone in a bar or gym because his body made others see him as unapproachable. He knew once he got a man into bed, his body would do the talking. But he felt unable to approach or to engage anyone. He stood there with what he felt was a blank face, but his attitude conveyed "Don't come near me." My first thought was simple: Learn to smile. There are no quick fixes in therapy, but that's the closest thing I know to one. It gives someone an opening, a way into getting to know you. Without having to go through a long, involved process of "learning to love himself first before expecting others to love him," he learned just to smile and actually found himself connecting. Once he was connecting with other men, we could then focus on other issues, and yes, he could begin to love himself. When he was depressed about his loneliness, there was no room for progress in other areas. Learning to smile jump-started his social life, which then boosted his ability to work on other areas of his life.

We develop our sense of ourselves through social action, through constant interaction with others. We don't develop in a vacuum, independent of our relationships to other people; we need interaction to build our sense of who we are. For many of us, our self-image has been damaged by growing up gay in a nongay world. After we come out, we have to reconstruct our self-image, working through and letting go of negative assumptions, fears, and doubts about ourselves. One of the first ways we begin this reconditioning to like and love ourselves is to take in new information—from the people around us, especially.

So listen to the feedback, take in the compliments and the criticisms, balance the positives with the negatives, but don't allow any one opinion to outweigh the others. You can develop a new relationship with yourself by taking a fresh look at your social interactions. In order to get a realistic body image, you also have to know yourself. A voice inside you may say, *I want to look hot*—yes, but why? And for whom? Yourself or a stranger? Try to discover what's motivating your behavior. I'm not crusading against working out or eating right—those are goals of maintaining your body and nurturing yourself. Nor is this a crusade against romance, of preparing yourself for your knight in shining armor—*as long as you also see yourself as a knight in your own shining armor*. One good knight deserves another.

14. What qualities would you like other gay men to see in you?

Be honest. Be specific. What do you want others to notice about you? Your strength? Sense of humor? Virility? Smarts? Independence? Be concrete. No false modesty, but no exaggeration either. Be real.

15. What do you have to do to make this a reality?

Depending upon your goals, it is pretty likely that you know what you have to do to make your wishes come true. You are beginning to learn that there are things you can do, say, and think that will bring you closer to your goal. Exercise by exercise, you have been realizing that change is possible and that change has to start with *you*, not with some dramatic event in the external world. A major step requires just accurately hearing and accepting the positive things people say about you. Another major shift is in acknowledging your own attractiveness and when others find you attractive.

Our physicality is only one component of this attractiveness, just as our Clock Age is but one component of our aging. As we age, our sexual experience, maturity, adult body, and rich history become additional dimensions of our attractiveness. As you work to take in the feedback from your peers, you will begin to see how attraction is not a momentary, fleeting image but a construction in time, over time. Change does not require miracles, but it does take work. When someone compliments you by saying, "You don't look that old," try to reply, "Yes, I do." To paraphrase Gloria Steinem, try saying "This is what a man my age looks like." Chances are, you look better than you think.

Jonathan's Story

Jonathan came to me with one of the worst body images possible. Not only because he is short (he's probably five-foot-four), but also because he's on the slight side and came out late. He felt totally inadequate sexually, experientially, every which way. Though he was an architect and had incredible social skills, he felt he was ugly, short, awkward, out of shape, and worst of all (in his mind), he possessed a very small cock.

When we started working together, he was in his late thirties and considered himself bisexual. He was seeing a nongay psychiatrist with whom he did not feel comfortable, so he joined a gay men's group I was facilitating as a way of evaluating whether he wanted to start working with an openly gay therapist, his first after many years of therapy. In addition, when we met, he was overmedicated: dependent upon drugs, alcohol, and cigarettes, and taking antianxiety medication and antidepressants as well. He eventually reduced his consumption of most of these substances after joining the group I was leading. He realized that he couldn't express himself or even know what his true feelings were under the influence of so much medication, both prescriptive and recreational. By the time he decided to start individual therapy with me, he was clearly beginning to think of himself as a gay man. He felt strong enough to switch to a nonmedical therapist who would not be able to prescribe medications.

His sense of physical inadequacy was pathologically great, dominating everything. It was partly a reflection of how he felt in the gay world and partly because he was not a Clone, did not come with the "proper" gay male body.

The two years he spent in that group was a time of exploration for him and transition into a gay identity from a bisexual life (he had dated women, but had only had anonymous encounters with men). He felt extremely isolated from the gay world: not knowing how to act, where to go, how to dress, what to do. Much of the work was getting him to have experiences in the gay world and then for us to talk about his reactions. I encouraged him to get involved in gay social events, so he began to volunteer at our local gay health clinic. He also pursued dating with a vengeance, using a dating service to make initial contact with potential boyfriends. Because of his experience with women, he knew *how* to date, so as a result, he had more ongoing dates with men than any other gay man I knew.

Jonathan found it incredibly hard to accept the positive feedback that he was receiving from other gay men, both from within and outside of the group. This resistance to compliments made it difficult to evaluate his experiences realistically—he kept rejecting any positive comments that contradicted his negative self-image. It was only with constant persistence from me and others that he began to accept a minimum of compliments. After many months, he was able to accept that he knew how to socialize and be engaging. It was amazing to see how once he actually accepted one solid piece of positive feedback, he slowly began to accept others. The first was actually the most difficult and the most important.

One of his difficulties was that much of what he felt he lacked was reinforced by the culture of the gay community. It was especially difficult for him, as he was so well socialized in the nongay world where his body size and body image were not highly important. His intellect, professional standing, social skills, and appearance established him as an equal participant. Now he had to reject *that* positive feedback for the gay world to which he was attracted but, in his thinking, did not value what he had to offer and only valued what he did not have. And of course, there was a reality to his perceptions. Some gay men do value height and cock size, but many more do not.

It was not that he had no problems in the nongay world—he was just better able to cover them over by adopting and performing the necessary social behaviors. One of his strengths was that he was one of the best socialized gay men I'd ever met. He was completely comfortable in all kinds of nongay social situations and was extremely articulate, perceptive, and well mannered. But he didn't always use these strengths when interacting with other gay men. He was so afraid of coming across as crazy in our group therapy sessions that he would not join the discussion, but he acted out in other ways, withdrawing, disrupting the session, clamoring for attention, and so on. An important turning point for him in group came when he realized that the behavior he exhibited when he withheld his opinions was crazier than what he was feeling. Whenever he just expressed himself, he was marvelous, honest, and articulate. The more everybody supported him by identifying with similar feelings, the more he began to feel like a gay man, rather than an outsider. By working with the group and interacting with his gay peers, he realized that he could move into a gay world while still rejecting some of what it had to offer—its intense body image standards.

This shift continued when he met Bob, his current lover, at a public gay event. Bob is an old-time activist and a teacher who's been around forever, knows everybody, lived through the seventies and survived the eighties. What's contributed to their relationship (they've been together seven years now) was that Jonathan recognized that though he had missed many experiences by staying in the closet for so long, he was clearly seen as a peer by this very experienced gay man. His unique challenge at midlife was accepting that he was not ever going to be a Clone, nor would he have the same history that a lot of gay men had.

Jonathan was one of those people who are "born" middle-aged. He never had a gay adolescence. His chronological peers had the baths, the Mineshaft, political activism, and years of cruising. Jonathan didn't have a lot of the experiences that he felt would make him an adequate gay man. So for him, his struggle with body image was about whether or not he conformed to some Clone standard. In a sense, Jonathan experienced a very heightened example of what many gay men constantly feel, especially as they get older: the sense of not living up to a community standard. By the time he met Bob, Jonathan had arrived at the point where the size of his body and cock weren't as important as they once had been. He had had enough sex with enough men who really enjoyed sex with him that he no longer perceived himself as inadequate. Clearly, his body and penis did not change, but his perception of them did.

TWO

Dipping into the Wellness: Physical Health and HIV/AIDS

When asked about their health, most gay men will typically think of HIV and AIDS first, then their weight, and maybe then their bodies (whether or not they're fit or muscled). Ever since HIV was identified in the early eighties, many gay men can measure their health only in terms of the virus's presence or absence in their lives. In addition, the rise of muscle culture and the Circuit (again, a small number of gay men, yet culturally omnipresent) has contributed to the confusion of muscles with health and the mind-set that "If I don't look sick, then I can't be sick."

But our health is more than our HIV status, our weight, or our body shape—it's an overall sense of being well, both mentally and physically. This "wellness" can appear in all areas of our lives, since how we feel about ourselves, how "well" we feel, can affect how we interact with others, how we regard the future, and how we give value to our lives.

The physical changes that a body undergoes as it ages are probably the number one source of fear and anxiety about aging. Recent genetic research doesn't make people feel as if they have much power over what their body will go through as it ages; high blood pressure, cancer, arthritis, back problems, Alzheimer's, strokes, etc., all seem to "run in families" because of genetic similarities. But new research, published in *Successful Aging*, funded by the MacArthur Foundation, suggests that "lifestyle choices" more than genetics or family medical history determine how a person will age. Rather than focusing on "disease prevention," a new direction in aging is "health promotion," which goes beyond maintaining good health to trying to reverse some negative effects of choices made earlier in life.

TO BE WELL, OR NOT TO BE WELL

Wellness is a state of the mind and the body. The relationship between our mental health and our physical health is a powerful one. At midlife, confronted with a changing body, many men experience a loss of motivation to take care of themselves. As a result of these feelings of helplessness or even depression, many stop making healthy choices in regard to their diet and exercise and let themselves go. In contrast, other men may find themselves renewed at midlife and determined not to let their health deteriorate.

What determines whether you survive or thrive at midlife is the degree to which you feel you have control over your physical health. While genetics, family history, income, and environment are significant factors affecting your physical health, what's important is that at midlife, you begin to realize that physical health is often a *choice*. Your current health reflects the choices you made in the past about your body, while your longevity will depend upon the choices you make today. By midlife, we can no longer ignore our relationship to our body and health, since the consequences can be life shortening.

During our youth and early adulthood, we often abuse or ignore our bodies. We don't sleep right, we don't eat right, we don't exercise, we may overindulge tobacco, alcohol, and recreational drugs, and we often seem to have a sense that we have time before we have to change our habits. In short, we take our bodies for granted.

Too often, we ignore early warning signs or the advice of our health-care practitioners and put off making changes. If we're under stress and unwilling to reduce our anxiety level, the stress manifests itself in aches and pains, which we ignore. Then come the headaches, the shortness of breath, but we don't pay attention to those either. When the stress and diet and headaches finally all combine to produce a heart attack, we feel ambushed and wonder what happened.

We can stop that process at many stages, but it's usually not until the final stages of a health condition when we wake up to what our body has been telling us for years. After all, potbellies don't appear overnight. Instead, we often need a slap in the face to pay attention to our health. (In fact, it took a health crisis like AIDS for the gay community as a whole to begin to take its health seriously.)

While we cannot deny the physical changes that become more obvious internally and externally at midlife, we can decide our response to the changes. Do we take control of our health care or do we drift along, hopeless and going to seed? That's what I mean by health as a choice. Moreover, the degree to which we maintain our health is an accurate measure of how we feel about our bodies. To be well, or not to be well, that is indeed the question.

A successful advertising executive, Michael is a handsome man, but at fifty, he feels that his glory days are over. Once part of the "A" crowd, he lived at the center of the Gay Universe, spending his summers on Fire Island and his winters in the discos and saunas of Manhattan. Now he feels invisible in his old haunts and complains that younger men don't respond to him anymore. As a result, he's let himself gain weight and stopped his regular gym schedule. He now rides the stationary bike once every two weeks, and has begun smoking heavily again, a habit he kicked in his late twenties. He's also drinking more, during the week as well as on the weekends. He indulges his life-long sweet tooth and has stopped minding the calories. His breath quickens more easily now, and his doctor has warned him about his cholesterol and high blood pressure.

My partner Friedrich and I just returned from a scuba diving trip off the coast of Honduras. When I met Friedrich, he was turning fifty-three and had just stopped hang-gliding two years earlier. We chose scuba diving as a sport to pursue together because it fulfilled several of our physical needs. We wanted something we could do together in a warm climate, that would be new for both of us, had a small element of excitement or danger, was interactive, and finally, that we could do regardless of age. Scuba diving met all these conditions and more. And under water, the body behaves differently; our present ages (fifty-five and sixty-two) are not a factor at all in our performance.

Michael and Friedrich reflect different approaches to their physical well-being, and again, I'm not talking about gym memberships and steroids and 3 percent body fat. Michael's anxiety over turning fifty has affected his health-care choices, and to those who knew him before, he seems to have given up taking care of himself. He still looks to the social fast lane he once belonged to for validation, but because of his frame of reference, he has created his own hell. By "frame of reference," I'm speaking of the standards by which he judges, values, and makes decisions for himself. I'm not talking about what's physically appropriate for a man his age, but what's *emotionally* appropriate. At fifty, Michael needs to develop enough awareness and maturity not to look to a twenty-five-year-old—who has different values, different priorities—for validation. Would that twenty-five-year-old look to a fifteen-year-old for validation? I hope not, since they are at different stages in their lives and what's appropriate for one is probably not appropriate for the other.

Often, when we come out as gay men, we reject the community we were born into—at least temporarily—and find our way into a new community. Coming into your own as a middle-aged gay man involves the same dynamic: the recognition that you no longer belong to one age group, and in fact, may need to reject that group, in order to come into a new body of peers.

Michael's attitude is not unusual, nor is it easy to change. Learning to be neutral and nonjudgmental about your body is difficult at any age, but especially at midlife, when the rate of change your body undergoes can be frightening. But, again, there are choices to make. When Friedrich realized he wasn't as flexible as he needed to be to hang-glide safely (plus the insurance rates had skyrocketed because of his age), he decided to withdraw from the sport. But he didn't then begin to overeat and give up exercising. He looked for another activity that could challenge, excite, and benefit him. He is willing to try a new sport like scuba diving and undertake the lessons, training, and practice the sport requires to do it well.

In the previous chapter, we dealt with how we feel about our bodies, our body image, and how we see ourselves as we age. This chapter focuses more concretely on the body itself: what physical changes we face at midlife, but more important, what we do with our bodies in the face of such physical changes. My focus on health is not about specific diets, skin creams, exercise routines, and the like. It's about getting you to *do* something—you decide what changes make sense to you.

1. What physical changes in aging are you most afraid of?

If you're used to an active lifestyle, you will want to maintain that energy level. If you enjoy reading or listening to music, you will be concerned with your eyes and ears, the sensory ability to experience what you enjoy. If you enjoy sex, you will fear impotency. If you like working long hours on a project or even playing long hours, you will want to keep your endurance. If you enjoy dancing or gardening, you'll want to stay flexible, able to move as your heart desires. If you've got a sweet tooth, you'll want to be able to have dessert, at least on special occasions.

When we first discussed common fears surrounding our getting older, I suggested that your fears give clues about what's important in your life, to your self-definition. In the context of our bodies, the physical changes we most fear will indicate what we value in our bodies. Your answers to this exercise will help identify your frame of reference as well as your priorities for health maintenance.

The body is like a machine that is subject to a certain amount of wear and tear, and the real issue is *maintenance*. Many of the changes at midlife that we experience as "negative" are only the cumulative effects of our previous choices about living. If we drank a lot in our youth, we can expect liver damage. If we baked ourselves at the beach without sunscreen protection, our skin will show it. A high-fat, high-sugar, high-meat diet will affect the digestive system over the course of a life. Like any piece of hardware, the body can take only so much. The "negative" physical qualities we fear so much at midlife are not so much a function of age, but of behavior. Of course, we possess an incredible amount of power over our own behavior.

2. What kind of physical activities can you no longer do because of your aging?

Staying up all night, not watching your diet, being able to come more than once during sex, keeping an erection for hours, being "on the go" all the time, keeping up with your coworkers with manual labor, gardening all day, dancing all night, overdoing it with drinking and drugging (including nicotine, alcohol, sugar, and caffeine): do any of these activities come to mind?

There's an old joke about a man who goes into a bar with a cast on his arm. As the bartender pours him a scotch, he tells about the car accident that broke his arm. "That's too bad," the bartender consoles him. "And you know what the worst thing is? I can't even play the violin," the man adds. "That's really horrible," the bartender says. "How long did you play?" "Oh, I've never played, but I can't now, that's for sure."

When you begin to list activities you can no longer do, are they related to actual physical changes in your body that you've noticed or are they what you expect you can't do anymore? Has your energy level really changed or do you think that people over forty aren't supposed to stay up late? How much are your activities affected by what you're "supposed" to do for a man your age? How many of what you describe are *activities that you* actually *did regularly* or are you more worried that you've missed a window of opportunity? Be realistic. What did you really do before that you can no longer do? How many of these physical changes are about what you wished you could have done and did not do and think you cannot do now?

It's very easy to use aging as an excuse for what you have not done ("I'm too old to start ice-skating lessons. I'll break a hip!") or as an excuse to stop doing what you were actually considering stopping (like Friedrich and his hang-gliding, he's more realistic about what he can do properly). We can do much of what we want to do, *if* we prepare ourselves properly.

Why do some people run marathons in their sixties while others bask in the Florida sunshine? Of course some people may have innate physical gifts, but I'm not talking about setting world records. I'm talking about an active lifestyle that improves circulation, blood pressure, metabolism. Walking, swimming, bicycling invigorates the body, but also the mind; you have to believe "I can do this, I am not powerless." Just as we use the "shoulds" to beat ourselves up, we often use the "can'ts" to keep us from taking an action. Both the "shoulds" and the "can'ts" need to disappear from our vocabulary, especially around heath and well-being.

3. **What can you do for yourself to balance these physical changes, both mentally and externally?**

At midlife, you may have to make adjustments with regard to diet, exercise, frequency of medical examinations, changes in energy level, weight, medications, substance use, etc. In effect, the sins of our twenties are visited upon us in our forties. As Wordsworth said, the child is father of the man, and the decisions you make early on will determine the health of that older self. *But the decisions you make at midlife can determine the rest of the journey.*

Given my busy schedule, I was very worried about my energy level as I aged. My friend Doris taught me that we don't really lose our energy, it just comes from another source. Did you ever notice how older people seem more peaceful and relaxed? Less concerned with what used to consume them? As we age, we let go of many of the anxieties that fuel our youth with energy and drive. But what anxiety actually produces is adrenaline, not real energy. As we learn to deal with anxieties differently, the adrenaline, the source of so much of our energy in our youth, disappears. As a result, we have to pull from another energy source; we have to gain access to our energy in a more disciplined, conscious way: getting proper rest, drinking adequate amounts of water, and following a good nutrition plan gives us the energy that adrenaline formerly did. Others like Doris have echoed and confirmed my experience with this change in energy. Recognizing this "energy shift" made all the difference when I reached midlife, and I find I'm able to maintain as busy a schedule as before, but with less stress and more health.

If you find you can't stay out dancing the way you used to, consider resting before going out. Or perhaps if you get a headache after an hour of reading, when you used to read an entire book in a day, maybe you need reading glasses. If you're unusually sore after riding a bike or lifting weights, consider more stretching after your workout as a way of loosening up the muscles. If you feel too sedentary, try walking to some appointments instead of driving or riding the subway or bus. If you find yourself stressed out by your schedule, consider putting less on the list of things to do each day. If you always put down more than you can possibly accomplish in a single day, look at what that says: you're setting yourself up for failure, for not meeting a goal, and sooner or later, for beating yourself up. List making is an essential tool for living (not just aging), and it takes practice to create a list that you can accomplish, rather than a list that depresses you because you can never finish it.

These sorts of changes can be simple, but their emotional and symbolic weight may be significant. Naps are for old people. Glasses are for nerds or librarians. Basically, what you might need conflicts with how you see yourself. Or more crucially, how others see you. Are you afraid of being judged for making these new choices? Making changes isn't defeatist—it's acknowledging a new reality and making different decisions in response.

What's essential is that you become aware that you have power in regard to aging. Yes, aging is a physical phenomenon the body undergoes, but how we experience that process, what meaning we ascribe to it, is very much a social and cultural and personal phenomenon. Are you like Michael, who feels powerless and defeated by aging? Or are you like Friedrich, who adjusts to his body to define its new, shifting limits? Or are you, like most of us, a mixture of the two? Some days we are ready to take on the world, while other days we feel invisible, listless, unwanted—we experience such mood changes all our lives, but only in middle age do we begin to attribute them to our age. Some twenty-two-year-olds can feel invisible, tired, and undesirable, while some forty-five-year-olds strut their stuff like everybody's favorite boy toy.

The crucial keys are motivation and purpose: an active approach to living versus a passive response to life around and in you.

4. Are there any physical advantages to growing older?

Advantages? You must be joking, you might be saying. It's all downhill after thirty. Let's see, I can't bend, I can't breathe, I can't dance, I can't eat what I want, I can't drink what I want, I can't fuck as long as I want.

But honestly, when you can come up with even one positive aspect of growing older, your attitude toward aging will begin to shift. The more you can think of, the less fear you will experience. This exercise is meant as an exploration. Take a look around you and see what you find.

One area of change that frightens many men, gay and nongay alike, is sexual ability. Many men fear impotence or diminished performance as they get older, but often, the changes you experience are what you make of them. In *Sex Over Forty*, Dr. Saul Rosenthal observes, "Men begin to worry so much about not living up to [sexual] expectations that that in itself causes genuine sexual dysfunction." He goes on to list four consequences of aging upon sex: (1) you'll need more direct stimulation in order to get erect; (2) you may not be quite as firm; (3) you'll need to climax less often; and (4) waiting time between erections will increase.

While many men would see all of these changes as negative, Dr. Rosenthal explains how many of these changes can make your lovemaking better, not worse. Not having spontaneous erections encourages your partner to get more involved and stimulate you directly. Having fewer orgasms means you can last longer and enjoy the sex more. You won't have to wait as long as you might have earlier before your sexual desire returns. He spends some time discussing the treatments available for actual physical dysfunction, but most of his advice is about overcoming the mental blocks we create for ourselves that prevent us from enjoying "sex over forty."

These mental blocks can be simple distractions ("I have to go to the bathroom"); insecurity thoughts ("I'm too fat"); concern about your sexual performance ("My penis isn't hard enough"); putting sex last in your priorities ("I don't have time for this"); holding on to irritations and resentments ("I'm mad at him; I'm just doing this because he wants to"); and worry about other problems (business, unpaid bills).

Attitude and mental outlook are the keys to sexual wellness (and your health overall). Dr. Rosenthal suggests you reconsider priorities (be clear in your own mind that having the pleasure, intimacy, and satisfaction of good lovemaking is something you desire); put aside resentments (holding on to them strongly interferes with your ability to respond sexually and to enjoy the experience); focus your thoughts on your actual physical sensations: softness, roughness, warmth, etc.; tell each other about your feelings and sensations; fantasize; help each other overcome distractions (learn to tell your partner and ask for help).

His approach to sex makes sense to me, and it helps to flesh out the results of a recent survey by the National Council on Aging that found that nearly fifty percent of people over sixty are sexually active. Of the sexually active, seventy-four percent of the men (and seventy percent of the women) reported that they were "as satisfied, or even more satisfied, with their sex lives as they were in their forties."

When Viagra was released in 1997, it quickly became the best-selling prescription of all time, and it was even reported that men of all ages were trying to get some in order to enhance their sexual performance. In a few of the articles, gay men were cited as a potential market for the drug and some gay journalists took the pill as an experiment and reported the results. Since my sex life with Friedrich has been overwhelmingly satisfying, I didn't really feel the need for the drug. But one night last summer we were curious and split half a dose. As promised, the physiological effects were strong: we were both erect longer and harder. But the more significant effect was psychological: without the anxiety of wondering how long I could last, I let myself go. We experienced one of the hottest times we had ever had, and I felt like a door had opened into our lovemaking. But what was significant is that the door didn't close once the drug had worn off. The next morning, we had another incredible experience, without any prescriptive assistance. It was as if the pill had given us permission to be as sexual and energetic as we wanted to be, and we were able to keep that momentum, not only after the drug was out of our system, but even to this day.

After considering any changes in your sexual life, continue to record other physical changes you're experiencing at midlife; feel free to air your negativity, but don't stop there. Go beyond the reflex to be pessimistic about getting older, and try to discover what positive changes you have experienced. Less anxiety. More play. Less work. An energy shift. The ability to give to yourself more. A sexual shift from a totally genital experience to a more full-body sensation; as we age, our entire body becomes an erogenous zone, not just our genitals. No crazy hormonal horniness as in our adolescence, but a sustainable erotic response to direct stimulus.

Perhaps my most radical assumption is that there is a benefit to aging, a reward for reaching midlife. This may seem like a contradiction, but that is because we are so locked into a negative framework around aging that equates change with loss, as opposed to change on its own terms. Aging is not just about positives either. Aging is a process of change that has consequences, to which we assign meaning. We choose which of the consequences to prioritize, and all too often, it's the "negative" changes we choose to dwell upon and they create a negative framework around aging.

This negative framework makes the last exercise particularly difficult. We do not hear or witness any of the "positive" changes with aging because they challenge our negative assumptions about midlife.

If you hear somebody admitting to actually enjoying being or getting older, we dismiss him as crazy, out-of-touch, a Perky Paul.

Maybe he is loony, but maybe he's just in touch with a reality that's different from the one you're experiencing. When we hear only the voices of ageism ("old gay men are asexual," "men over forty are boring," and so on), everything, and I mean *everything*, about aging becomes negative.

5. **In comparison to men your age, both gay and nongay, how would you rate your physical health?**

Are you as active as your gay peers? For a man your age, what's the average weight and cholesterol and blood pressure? Do you have a sense of what your actual health goals might be? To whom are you comparing yourself? Real people you know? Or images from *Vanity Fair* and *The Advocate*? *Entertainment Weekly* or *People*? *Poz* or *Reader's Digest*?

In short, what's your frame of reference? If you're constantly comparing yourself to the Chelsea/West Hollywood/Castro "boy" ideal, you're doing the same thing that women do when they look at Kate Moss and think they're too fat. (And I have two words for that: FEED HER!) This "compare/despair" dynamic is not just a gay thing or a male thing or a female thing. It's a sad feature of our entire culture that we must constantly compare ourselves to others and despair over our falling short.

Ask yourself, whose critical voice am I using to judge myself? A trainer at the gym? A deceased parent? A boss? It's so important to identify your frame of reference when figuring out your priorities, not only for health, but for life. Throughout this book, identifying your frame of reference will be a constant goal.

Now consider your nongay peers, your coworkers or family members. Do you feel more or less healthy in comparison? Do you share anecdotes about your health with one another? There might be a family history that affects your health. Diabetes. High blood pressure. Arthritis. Poor vision. Or if you do manual work, there could be environmental factors that affect your overall health. What do the men you know do to take care of themselves? Given our gay consciousness about our bodies, you'll probably sense that you're in better shape, both mentally and physically, than your nongay peers.

Practically every gay man I know has returned home for a class reunion to find the "top" athletes from high school or college gone to seed. Gay men are the ones who've stayed physically active into midlife and kept our health a priority.

Most likely, as gay men we are more attuned to our health primarily because we are at the epicenter of an epidemic. But as men, especially, we are generally less inclined to pay attention to what our bodies are telling us. As I pointed out in our discussion about body image, men and women develop vastly different relationships with their bodies. On the most basic level, women's monthly cycle keeps them in tune with what's going on with their bodies, while men tend to remain clueless unless there's a major injury or condition. But even then, men are notorious for not knowing what to ask their doctors, or putting off going to a doctor for as long as possible. For a nongay man, undergoing an anal exam for prostate cancer can be an extremely painful and embarassing experience. As a result, a majority of prostate cancer in nongay men goes undetected until it's too late for treatment. Clearly, gay men have some advantage in this arena, since we tend to be more open and conscious about all areas of our body (including our ass).

Neglect is a choice. Aging is not. There's a major difference. In the former case, we are giving up the power we have to affect the aging process, while in the latter, we are recognizing the changes we go through as part of life, as the consequence of living. And as the saying goes, "Aging is not great, but the alternative is worse."

6. **Talk about the gay men that you admire who have aged well physically and who have taken good care of their health.**

When you hear the phrase "aged well," what do you think of? A pumped-up, tanned body? A hot daddy? A man who has beaten the statistics? Are you thinking of men who "don't look their age"?

Describe the physical characteristics of aging well. How much of what you list is seen (the externals: muscles, sleek abdomen, tight skin, wrinkles, full head of hair) versus what's unseen (the internals: flexibility, normal blood pressure, low cholesterol, good circulation, good digestive system)? Your areas of concern will suggest a frame of reference. Are you limiting your definition of health to just the exterior, rather than both interior and exterior?

What's crucial for this exercise is to make a distinction between health and good looks. An attractive gay man may also be a chain smoker or an alcoholic or a binge eater—not exactly healthy choices! The gulf between how we look (physical features) and how we feel (health) can be wide, but we can build a bridge across it, with honesty and commitment.

Over the years, I've struggled to define a concept of health for myself that does not rely upon external factors only, such as what others think of me or how they respond to my "looks." Like any gay man, I've faced a preoccupation with how I look to other men, but I've come to accept that health is how I feel, not how I look.

7. What has been your regime to maintain your health?

Okay, now, be honest—this is for yourself, not to impress anybody else. Have your decisions about health care been about how you look or how you feel? Good health just doesn't happen. A willingness to educate oneself and to choose health actively makes all the difference. Have you compared yourself to the standard measures of health for men your age, your height, and your body size? Do you know much about your family history, if certain conditions run in your family? What is your actual experience of good health? When have you felt healthy? When have you felt like you were taking care of yourself? Do you realize you can develop a regime to maintain your health? That a series of choices awaits you?

A "regime" is a concept similar to lifestyle: a pattern of behavior that you create and adopt for yourself in which the goal is health (whereas the goal of a lifestyle is happiness). Again, it's a list based in reality, not fantasy. Eat more vegetables. Bicycle to work instead of driving. Take a long walk over the weekend.

At first, this may sound like just another list of New Year's resolutions: stop smoking, watch what I eat, go to gym more. A friend of mine once said that he started his New Year's resolutions in mid-December, so that by January, he had a chance of actually continuing them into the New Year. It's extremely important to keep the list grounded in reality: not the "shoulds," but the things you have actually done, or could actually do. This is a "positive" list and measures your commitment to yourself.

You may never have had a regime for health. That's okay. The point of this exercise is not to beat yourself up for eating badly all those years, though you will probably want to do that, since it's easier to make yourself feel bad than it is to make yourself feel good. By accepting what you could have done differently or what you could have avoided, you will begin to understand the relationship between choice and health. By acknowledging what you have done in the past, you will start to take some responsibility for where you are now. More to the point, you can begin to consider what you can do in the present for your future.

What must you do now to begin the road to health? Be concrete. Be specific. Watch what I eat. Okay, but how about: eat more vegetables. Better, but what kind of vegetables? Not the kinds you hate, but feel compelled to eat because they're good for you. Vegetables you actually *like*. Broccoli? Carrots? Beets? Cabbage?

Don't make an extreme list. Don't make it "ideal," make it real. It's better to have lower expectations that are possible to meet—two concrete actions that you can actually take—than to have high ideals that you can't keep. You are not going to impress anybody by listing all the things you're going to do. You will impress yourself by sticking to a reasonable list of changes.

Also, try not to think only in negatives (such as no cheesecake). It's not about deprivation and pain. It's about balancing your goal of health with your behavior and that doesn't have to translate into white-knuckling your sugar intake. Have cheesecake if you want it, but don't have it every week if you want to lower your cholesterol. Make having cheesecake a special occasion. Or have a smaller piece each time, instead of two pieces. The goal is not to set up rigid standards you can't meet; that only sets you up for failure and beating yourself up, without getting you any closer to health. The important thing is to take the steps, make the choices, be proactive. If you want to keep your teeth twenty years down the road, you better brush daily and floss regularly.

The most important concept to incorporate into your regime of health is the idea of *balance*. Say you've committed to a low-dairy, low-fat diet. You go out to celebrate a friend's birthday and he chooses a really swank Italian restaurant. You have shrimp, you have goat cheese drizzled with olive oil, you have roast lamb, red wine, tiramisù, and cappuccino.

Don't, I repeat, don't think of this as breaking your diet, an infraction to punish yourself with. Try to recognize it as the truly fabulous meal it was and then balance it. If you know you're going out for a rich meal, make the meal before and the meal after especially low fat and low dairy. Don't judge indulgence as wrong because it's not—*as long as you balance it with maintenance.*

It's the same with the gym. Don't commit to a routine that's too exhausting (a two-hour workout involving all the major muscle groups) because you won't want to stick with it. You'll miss workouts, then try to make it up in one huge session that leaves you sore and vulnerable to injuries. A shorter workout three times a week is less intimidating and more sustainable in the long run.

There are many ways to get exercise (walking, hiking, rollerblading, dancing), and joining a gym is not the only answer. I used to go to the gym, but not anymore. I found that I was better disciplined if I worked out at home, as opposed to fitting a trip to the gym into my day. I don't have a lot of equipment either. I work with hand weights, do some sit-ups and push-ups, walk up nine flights of stairs in my apartment building at least twice a day (on Sundays I treat myself to taking the elevator!), and plenty of yoga, a form of exercise and discipline I've enjoyed using for twenty years. *Health does not have to be expensive to be real.*

It's okay if you have a wish list of actions and plenty of self-condemnations. What's more important is to recognize the path of health that lies ahead. Some people put off making changes in their lifestyle because they believe it's too late, the damage has been done. But the MacArthur Foundation research shows that "it is almost never too late to begin healthy habits such as smoking cessation, sensible diet, exercise and the like."

The news around cigarette smoking is especially good. Studies show that the risk of heart disease begins to fall almost as soon as a person quits smoking. "In five years, an ex-smoker is not much more likely to have heart disease than a person who has never smoked!" In addition, the MacArthur Foundation found that "among people aged thirty-four to fifty-five, those who stopped smoking within the past two to four years were no more at risk for stroke than those who had never smoked at all." The risk of lung cancer is harder to reduce, since it takes at least "fifteen years after quitting for a smoker's risk of cancer to become as low as that of a lifetime non-smoker." But the best news is that upon stopping smoking, the lungs begin to heal immediately, and thus, there's less risk for a whole range of illnesses. For some people, stopping smoking is a difficult step to take, but the long-range health benefits are enormous.

STAYING MOTIVATED

At this point, you're probably feeling overwhelmed by the choices you may need to make. You want to change, but you've tried before and haven't been able to keep a regime of health going.

It's important to air all the concerns and fears you can think of. We've talked about certain fears: not being able to run as far as before, becoming winded on the stairs at work, the bald spot up top has become a dome. Go ahead. Plumb the depths of what you fear. It's the only way to take control. By not talking about the negatives, you give them more strength.

Behind these fears can be real despair, fueled by a sense that we're powerless over aging, so why bother? Why watch what we eat or go for walks—it doesn't matter in the long run, we're all going to get old and die.

Yes, we are going to die, but we're not dead yet. And the question we have to answer is do we want to speed up that process or slow it down? Do we want to enjoy our life or do we want to spend our days in fear and loathing? Do we want to live until we die, or do we want to spend our entire life dying?

Attitude affects every choice we make. As children and as adolescents, we longed to become adults because they got to make their own decisions and have all the fun. We looked forward to getting older because we saw aging in terms of what it would enable us to do. Now that we're here, we need to remember that attitude of *possibility*. The more we can embrace change (by recognizing how good change has been in the past for us), the more we will be able to think about the future as brimming with positive possibilities as well as negative ones.

To taste the clear, cool water of good health, you need to dig a deep well, beneath the rocks of these fears, below the roots of our culture's ageism, to find the natural spring of your own well-being.

REACTIVE VERSUS PROACTIVE:
WHO'S IN CHARGE OF YOUR HEALTH?

This core dynamic (being reactive versus proactive) appears in multiple forms throughout the midlife years—I'll come back to this essential difference many times in the course of this book. Being reactive to a stimulus (a health condition, a relationship, and so forth) usually entails operating from past pattern of behavior: doing what you always did, without thinking. Being proactive to a stimulus is about being in the present, taking in new information, and making a conscious response to the present situation (your own cancer as opposed to how your father reacted to his cancer). No matter the context, understanding this difference will result in major changes in your attitudes about aging over time.

Our health is one arena where issues of power and control come up again and again. Since AIDS emerged, many of us have felt powerless over our health, and between taking care of our friends and ourselves, we faced multiple decisions on health treatment. Faced with a health crisis, how have you reacted to the situation? Have you been able to make informed decisions or did you rely upon the advice of doctors and other patients?

Contrary to popular belief, physicians are not God, though we often treat them that way in our health-care decisions. The way all of us were raised, hospitals were sanctified and a doctor's word was gospel. He (always a "he") knew best. Always. No questions. For most people, it's still the same.

In the age of HIV and AIDS, gay white middle-class males finally learned what people of color, women, and poor people have long known: Health care is not always accessible, affordable, or a right. When traditional medicine and physicians weren't treating gay men with a curious new disease called GRID, many of us struggled to find our own answers. AIDS activists joined the fold of health-care activists, who had been working for years to expand health care to all people. Many of us expanded our understanding of health care to include many different kinds of practitioners (herbalists, acupuncturists, massage therapists, nutritionists, and so forth), whom we could consider as consultants in our health-care decisions.

8. How comfortable are you in making health-care decisions? Do
    you feel in charge of your health care?

Faced with a range of choices of care (assuming there is care available), you will have to make decisions. And while the patient may listen
to many opinions, it's important to distinguish between the person(s)
relaying information and the individual who must make a decision
based on that information. More and more, the patient himself must
make the final decision. You have to educate yourself and listen to
your body, as well as your intuition. You owe it to yourself to gather
all the information and come up with the best answer, the best
approximation, the best course of action. No one treatment can heal
everybody, and you'll soon learn that the best treatment represents
an estimation, the art of the healer, rather than the product of an
exact science. Each body is different, and each treatment unique.

An acquaintance of mine, Jose, is short (five feet five inches) and
highly sensitive to certain kinds of medicine. When he begins a new
medication, he often has to educate his physician on what the proper
dosage should be. Given Jose's stature and unique metabolism, the
necessary and effective amount is often less than what the physician
would typically prescribe. But Jose developed this approach only after
trial and error, gathering enough information about his medications,
and learning to pay attention to his own body. In a way, "learning
your body" is like learning a new language: What is it saying to you,
what does your treatment of it say?

When you have an ache or stomach problem, do you ignore it
and hope it goes away? Or do you prefer to take a Tums and never
investigate the cause of the discomfort? Do you take a friend with
you to important meetings with your health-care practitioners?
Friends not only provide emotional support but they're also another
set of eyes and ears to help you understand what your physician
might be telling you. They can help you remember what was said
and what was not.

Do you know what to ask your physician? Make a list of questions to ask before your appointment, then write down her or his
answers. Keep a journal about your health and a file of all your tests
and records. After going through the work of getting such valuable
information, you don't want to misplace it.

Do you get second opinions? A second opinion is not when two physicians with the same training make a similar diagnosis, but when two different types of physicians explore different sources of your condition. If you have strong feelings about invasive procedures such as surgery, perhaps you could see a physician who might take a nonsurgical approach. Are you willing to explore alternative treatments?

Of course, your ability to make decisions partially rests upon the amount and quality of the information you receive, including details about possible effects of any medication. At times, I find fault with the language of medicine, and I think the whole notion of "side effects" is dangerous. "Side" effects are actually negative effects, but the phrase minimizes the risk by making the effects sound incidental, off to the side, not front and center. If a drug's effects were classified as positive and negative, then a patient could tally up the drug's potential as with a balance sheet and make an informed decision. When I first considered taking AZT, I weighed the potential boost in my T4 cells against the potential for permanent liver and bone marrow damage. Based on both the positive and negative effects of the drug, I chose not to take it. But I wouldn't have been able to make such a decision if I didn't have all the information. If your health-care provider resists answering questions or doesn't give you much information, then leave. This is not someone you want involved in your health-care decisions. You want someone who respects you—it's a mutual relationship, and both of you are invested in your well-being.

9. **Do see a difference between doing things to save your life and actively choosing to be healthy?**

This first approach is based on fear and negativism and as such, doesn't feel like a choice, but an ultimatum. The second approach is based on positive goals (health) and taking charge of one's life. In the first mind-set, we avoid a feared outcome (if I don't have radiation treatment, the lung cancer will spread), and in the second, we actively choose a goal (I will decrease my caffeine intake over the next six months and stop drinking coffee by my next birthday). Both lead to actions, but the motivation for the decisions makes all the difference.

I have also witnessed a similarity in attitude between those who are successfully handling AIDS and those who take confident charge of their health. Even when the disease was called GRID, there were those who were desperately trying everything in order to save their lives and those who were actively choosing to be healthy. The former would change their treatments often, rushing from trend to trend, trying to find the "magic bullet" to cure themselves. Their desire to live was so intense that no single measure seemed enough, and when their health improved, it was often impossible to tell the source of the change.

The latter group tried to gather as much information as possible before making any decisions, and they often felt better emotionally and physically because they had positively taken charge of their health. They saw themselves as the primary decision maker who used health-care workers as consultants and learned to listen to what their bodies were telling them.

AIDS has highlighted the tension between reactive and proactive approaches, not just to our health, but to our lives. Every gay man must have thoughts about AIDS and his own health. Such awareness is an inevitable consequence of living during an epidemic, and there are now whole generations of gay men who know only a world with AIDS as part of the landscape. As we age, our pre-AIDS history and awareness are disappearing.

10. In what ways has AIDS changed your approach to your health care?

Whether you have done anything directly or not, you have responded to what you know about AIDS and made some choices, whether it was getting tested for HIV, not thinking about it, not doing anything differently, caretaking, or volunteering as a buddy. It's important to acknowledge and verbalize your thoughts on health, AIDS, choices, and responsibility. Talking about AIDS can get you to focus on changes that you can make, or have made. You may have begun to change without realizing it, and this discussion on AIDS may bring that change to the foreground. Spend time reviewing the changes you've made, no matter how subtle. Anything that gives you the sense that you have done something positive or taken action will better prepare you for future actions.

Consider safer sex. When the health establishment began insisting that gay men incorporate condoms and "no fluid exchange" into our sexual behavior, many within the gay community resisted and rebelled. Most of the early education around AIDS was moralistic (focusing on promiscuity, closing the bathhouses) rather than informative about what to do and the art of negotiation. To use a condom, a gay man has to learn how to negotiate sex, a skill that most gay men didn't (and still don't) have. We learned that safer sex is not "all or nothing," but a series of limits and "acceptable risks" that each gay man decides for himself. Is oral sex without a condom a behavior you're willing to perform? Are you nervous about anal sex even with a condom?

As our friends continued to get sick and we feared for our own health, we made changes in our behavior that seemed to protect us. Today, safer sex still invites controversy, even though it has proven effective in limiting the spread of the HIV virus and other STDs. The simple act of putting on a condom is a positive action you can take, and perhaps it has become a reflex, a part of your regime to be healthy that you're not even conscious of anymore.

BECOMING CONSCIOUS, BECOMING EXCEPTIONAL

My late lover Jim was the "eternal Peter Pan," who could never see himself becoming an older man. And that self-image affected his outlook on health. When he was fifty, he was diagnosed with a hernia, and his recovery from the surgery took much longer than he had expected. For Jim, it was the beginning of the end, and his health went downhill after that. Asymptomatic for years, he died from complications from AIDS when he was fifty-four.

In 1986, Bernie S. Siegel, M.D., published *Love, Medicine, and Miracles*, a moving and compelling account of his work with patients facing cancer and other life-threatening illnesses. Despite a negative prognosis, many of his patients survived their illness and lived well beyond the expectations of the medical establishment. Siegel cited his patients' ability to become exceptional in the face of illness as crucial to their recovery:

Exceptional patients refuse to be victims. They educate themselves and become specialists in their own care. They question their doctor because they want to understand their treatment and participate in it. They demand dignity, personhood, and control, no matter what the course of the disease.

Rather than citing his role as physician as the source of their healing, he acknowledges his patients' own courage and hope in handling their health. He observes, "Refusal to hope is nothing more than a decision to die."

AIDS has made many of us exceptional patients. In terms of maintaining good physical and mental health, I have seen a significant difference between those who have a definite sense of the future and take central responsibility for their health care, and those gay men who have no sense of growing old and/or let others take responsibility for their health-care decisions.

My observations about developing a positive sense of growing old have come from my personal experience and my work with persons who were HIV positive or diagnosed with AIDS. My experience of caretaking with Jim persuaded me more than ever that there was a parallel process for both middle-aged gay men dealing with aging and persons dealing with HIV-AIDS health-care maintenance. Both groups become conscious not only of their relationship to their bodies, but how their daily decisions can affect the well-being of those bodies.

Once testing for HIV was available, many in the gay community debated the need for testing, when was it appropriate, did it really tell us much that would help, especially in the days when few or no treatments were available? That reality has changed. There are many treatments available, both traditional and alternative, and early detection of HIV and subsequent treatment can significantly improve the longevity and wellness of a person living with HIV. Don't wait for an HIV diagnosis to give yourself permission to take care of yourself. Our focus should be health and well-being, regardless of our HIV status.

11. In what ways have aging and AIDS made positive changes in your life?

It can be difficult to look for the cloud's silver lining, but like aging, AIDS is a fact of life that we ascribe meaning to; it is neither inherently positive or negative. Since death is usually projected as the result for both AIDS and aging, coming up with positives may seem like a form of denial, but we need to break free of an exclusively negative framework around both AIDS and aging. In a sense, gay men suffer from a "ghetto" experience—not the ghetto of Dupont Circle or the Castro, but the Warsaw ghetto of World War II. As a community, we have been under siege in battling this illness and we need to be reminded that there's life not only within our walls, but outside. In fighting AIDS, it's tempting to become myopic and forget to reach out for help. Some gay men find it hard to believe that nongay people care about them or AIDS, but we do have allies, especially as the epidemic crosses racial and social boundaries and the possibility of coalitions of health care becomes real.

What positives come to mind when you think of aging and AIDS? They're both a wake-up call about our behavior. Health care becomes a priority, especially if we haven't given it much thought. We learn to appreciate our friends and our loved ones. Both offer avenues of activism for us to be engaged with the larger world around us. In both experiences, we find ourselves struggling with homophobia and visibility, and the work we do in these areas strengthens our self-esteem and self-worth.

12. What kind of picture do you have of yourself as a much older man?

How do you see yourself in ten years? Gray-haired? No hair? Happy? With glasses? With a walker? Lonely? Brunched out? Snorkeling in the Florida Keys? Rock climbing? As the Shuffleboard Champ of South Beach? Honestly, what sense do you have of how you will change over the next ten years? Is it your impulse to focus on the physical or the emotional or both?

I hope that you are beginning to have a new picture of yourself instead of the old, negative one. All is not written in stone. Maybe now you're starting to substitute a new picture of yourself at forty, fifty, and sixty for the old negative stereotypes. An active, vibrant you—at any age. This is a first step in a continual process of substitution—whether it be of pictures, attitudes, or ideas. Think about fantasies you've had about attractive older men. Sean Connery. Denzel Washington. Armistead Maupin. George C. Wolfe. Armand Assanti. Tom Bianci. David Geffen. Harrison Ford. Barry Diller. Sexy older men who lead vibrant lives. Try some of those images on for size and see where you need to make alterations.

Even wishful thinking (running a marathon even though you've never run farther than a half-mile) can be beneficial at this stage. Such a fantasy can be a doorway to a new way of thinking.

There is a difference, however, between wishful thinking and visualization. The former is about daydreams ("I wish I had a million dollars."), while the latter takes the wish more seriously, pulling it toward the realm of possibility. Visualization requires sitting and thinking deeply, putting your whole body and mind into the experience of the fantasy. Using the total experience of seeing yourself in the fantasy, you can actually visualize the steps you need to take to make it real.

13. What concrete steps would you have to take to make this a positive reality?

I want to push you to come up with something concrete that you can do, no matter how seemingly inconsequential. No step is too small. No habit is too insignificant to change. The first step is action, regardless of the content of the action. This is an important distinction you'll witness throughout this book: action versus content. My concern is with motivating you to take action; you decide what actions to take.

By identifying areas of change, whether it be diet or exercise or even getting an annual physical, you will begin to tie together the ideas of positive aging, concrete action, and a new picture of yourself.

Even if you approach this exercise thinking "I'll do this pretending that I believe it will work, even though I'm not convinced it will," whatever changes you make will be a big step in this process. Acting "as if" is a definite precursor to doing it with conviction. Even if it is all fantasy, it is fantasy in a constructive direction, the first movement toward changing your health and well-being.

Friedrich's Story

Friedrich is now fifty-five years old and in good physical health. He was born in Dusselfdorf, Germany, but now lives in Munich, where he has been in the interior design business most of his adult life. For some unexplained reason, he has always believed that good health meant having to take continual care of himself. It was not something that he learned at home though his mother always stressed eating healthfully, by German standards. As a result of this attitude, he has taken good care of his body over the years and has continued to go to the gym regularly. He rides his bike for many miles during good weather and goes to the gym three times a week. He also keeps fit through his construction work when he is redesigning rooms and kitchens.

Once he started realizing he was approaching middle age, he made sure he exercised regularly as a way of maintaining his health and body. As a European, his diet is definitely different from that of people in the United States. The higher fat content (meat and dairy) and wine do not seem to affect his health or his weight negatively. He is surprised by the constant focus of Americans on diets and low-fat meals—he believes in the concept of moderation and not sacrificing good taste. (He has taught me how to have smaller, tasty portions!)

For many years, one of his passions was hang-gliding, which he enjoyed because of its excitement and physical exhilaration. He stopped just a few years ago, when his insurance rates went up, and he felt that his body was not as limber as it had been and he could be susceptible to more serious injuries. For himself, he does not think that certain activities are limited by age unless there is a clear-cut connection between age and accidents, as in his decision about hang-gliding. In general, he sees nothing limiting him physically because of his age, except that he has to rest and sleep much more than he did when he was younger. When I suggested our learning how to scuba dive together, he took to the suggestion immediately, and we have traveled to Turkey, Puerto Rico, and Honduras on some amazing diving trips.

When he found out he was HIV positive, he immediately began to investigate the relevant medicines that are available in Germany. He has avoided those medications that he considers too toxic for his body and supplements his medicines with vitamins and minerals.

In terms of his aging, he has been comfortable with getting older and has had no illusions about his looks or being "younger than his years." He has always felt that he has looked his age, probably since he started losing his hair when he was in his early twenties. He has also always been interested in men close to his age and has only briefly and disastrously had one boyfriend younger than him. He looks for maturity in the men that he is with and is totally comfortable with men who look their age. Clearly, since he is my partner, he can see a sixty-two-year-old man as being attractive and sexy. It wasn't until he was in his forties that he started thinking of himself as a "hot" man—he defines this by how much he enjoys sex and knows that his sexual partner is having a good time, too.

On a recent scuba diving trip, Friedrich and I spent a week off the coast of Turkey with two other German families. During the course of the week, the seventeen-year-old son of one of the families struck up a friendship with Friedrich, and they spent hours talking about diving and life in Germany. At the end of the week, as we all said our goodbyes, the teenager shook Friedrich's hand and said, "I hope I'm like you when I'm fifty-five." Friedrich's humility keeps him from telling this story, but I think it's incredible that a young, nongay man would look to a middle-aged gay man as a role model.

THREE

A Different Kind of Mirror: Role Models and You

JAMES: How long have you two been together?
PERRY: Fourteen years. We're role models. It's very stressful.
—*Love! Valor! Compassion!*

What's stressful about being a gay role model is that we don't know what to do: We make it up as we go along. To be a role model requires having a sense of what it means to be an adult and to be a man, but unfortunately, most gay men grow up questioning their manhood because of our culture's homophobia. Another way to look at this would be to say, *We are born male; we become men.* The terms are not interchangeable because each carries its own meaning, separate from the individual and unique to the culture. Small wonder that Paul Monette entitled one of his books *Becoming a Man.* That memoir narrated his escape from the closet of his youth, and only told "half a life," the life before he met his lover, Roger, and before he came into his own as a gay man.

An integral part of every culture is its process of socialization, that is, a process whereby an individual learns through social interaction with his elders how to become an adult. These elders have many names (relatives, teachers, mentors, therapists, community leaders, and so on), but they all serve as role models, providing a model of behavior and illustrating the role of an adult in our society.

Our interaction with role models and their "welcoming" us into adulthood is critical to our development of self-esteem and stability. In many cultures, the socialization process from adolescent to adulthood requires a single ritual or ceremony—a rite of passage. The Jewish faith has its bar/bas mitzvah, the Catholics have Confirmation, a debutante has a coming-out ball. At one extreme, this process of socialization can be very formal and institutionalized. It may also be more unstructured and informal (like buying your first car or buying your first home), but it still confers adulthood, in our case, manhood, on an individual. A ritual's meaning is not limited to a specific event that transforms the individual into an adult, but includes the preparation beforehand and the learning of what the ritual means to the culture.

Our culture is full of such rites of passage, yet most are related to the institution of heterosexuality. From early childhood, the adolescent male is expected to be nongay and antagonistic to all homosexual manifestations. All familial, educational, and social learning is geared toward that expectation. He is given social support and reinforcement ("he's all boy" versus "a mama's boy") when he engages in "appropriate" nongay behaviors and achievements like dating, marriage, fatherhood, vocational and financial success, military service, and sports prowess.

In many cultures, the male adolescent is expected to father a child; in the United States, the high rate of teenage pregnancy may be fueled in part by homophobia (with teenagers having sex in order to "prove" to themselves and to their families that they're not gay), as well as low self-esteem (with teenagers desperate to be validated by the public display of parenthood). This phenomenon is cross-cultural. Both boys and girls, black and white and Latino, of all classes, feel pressure to produce offspring as a sign of adulthood.

Such cultural pressure to express heterosexuality continues past adolescence into young adulthood, when most males and females feel compelled to marry. Adrienne Rich once described these social reinforcements as steps toward "compulsory heterosexuality." With the institution of marriage comes a host of financial supports as well: gifts of cash and household goods, tax breaks, and insurance benefits. Although the economic landscapes differ for gay and nongay individuals and couples, it's clear that heterosexuality has financial "mileposts" (mortgages, college tuition for children, and so forth) that can adversely affect many gay men's sense of themselves as adults.

Where are the gay role models for gay adolescents? Mostly invisible or out-of-reach, unavailable. Direct interaction with role models, as well as the internal preparation and training to become adults—the process of *anticipatory socialization*—is missing for lesbians and gay adolescents. Our lack of communication with gay adults complicates our coming out, not only as gay men but as adult men. The lack of mentoring within the gay community increases the isolation of the coming-out process for many teens, while the image of the adult gay community beckons with its freedoms. If it weren't for sex, gay community centers, or the few social agencies that address the needs of gay and lesbian teenagers (like the Hetrick-Martin Institute in New York), there would be very little exchange between gay youth and gay adults. In addition, this generation gap perpetuates itself with further isolation between gay adults of various ages (twenties, thirties, forties, fifties, and so on) because of our community's ageism. Role models can change that dynamic of exploitation and avoidance.

MALE SEE, MALE DO

Though women in general, and mothers in particular, are expected to provide more nurturing to a child in its earliest years, by early adolescence, males are expected to find their role models among their own sex. As the anthropologist Margaret Mead observed, "Women, perhaps, make a human being, but it takes men to make men." By interacting with his father, an older brother, or an uncle, the young male becomes aware of what he is to become, and the path to developing an adult ego is set. A variety of male role models outside of the family (a coach, a Scoutmaster, a pastor, a TV or film actor, and so on) expands the younger male's instruction on how to feel, perceive, respond, and behave as a man.

As a role model, an older man nurtures the young male emotionally, awakening his manhood as a component of the emerging adult. The transformation of boy into man necessitates this male-to-male involvement and would be incomplete without it. Just as the female gives physical birth and nurturing to a child, the male-male relationship is a rebirthing by the male of another male. In some cultures, at puberty there is even a bloodletting, symbolizing this rebirth, ranging from a cut of the flesh, scarification, to a full circumcision. (Some scholars believe circumcision was once part of the covenant that Jewish males undertook at thirteen and was a symbolic cut, not a full circumcision at birth as we know it.)

Obviously, few gay teenagers receive this sort of bonding with older men. Often, the little mentoring we have takes a sexual expression. A gay teen might have sex with an older man, but there are many factors that affect the significance of the interaction. Is the adult openly gay or married and closeted? Is there any verbal communication or is the encounter anonymous? There is a tradition of older men supporting younger men with money, access, and culture in exchange for sex and possibly affection. Based on different forms of power each man possesses, this relationship can benefit both and serve as a true mentoring. If the interest is only sexual, however, with the "kept boy" and the "sugar daddy" barely communicating except through lust and money, the experience is clearly exploitative rather than mentoring.

Sometimes, what looks like exploitation may in fact be a form of class mobility. Since anybody, from a senator to a waiter, can be found in a gay bar, there is the potential for many romances and connections among the classes. Often, in return for sharing his youth and beauty with an older man, the younger gay man can quickly learn about and come to assume a middle-class urban lifestyle. But it is usually the degree to which the older man actually wants to teach the younger man about the world, or merely play with a boy toy, that determines the degree of mentoring or exploitation within the relationship.

In general, gay teens become gay adults by aping the culture around them, and in learning to be masculine, we inherit the full baggage of maleness in this patriarchal culture: misogyny, one-upmanship, competition, relationships defined in terms of power, racism, classism, and homophobia. Even though these qualities may seem alien, some of us may feel as if we must possess them in order to be recognized as men in this culture. If we look to our political and business leaders, our religious figures, even our own families, we find that the men who embody these characteristics often possess the most power in our society—regardless of the inherently negative nature of such qualities.

Even if we manage to reject the baggage of patriarchy, we may reach midlife with a sense of feeling like a second-class male. Not really a man. Well into our adulthood, many of us continue to refer to each other as gay *boys*, not gay *men*. Even as we come out in as many areas of our lives as possible, we maintain the mental equations of patriarchy and homophobia: to be a man is to be masculine, to be gay is to be effeminate, therefore, to be gay is not being a "real man." If you need the adjective "gay" to describe yourself ("I'm a gay man," as opposed to a "I'm a man"), you may be unconsciously putting yourself into a second-class category because of our culture's in-grained homophobia, as well as your own internalized homophobia.

The problem is that most gay men measure themselves against the larger society's idea of a man and judge themselves as inadequate, not masculine, not manly. Gay men negate themselves with such comparisons and produce real psychological harm. We need to un-derstand ourselves and celebrate our selves as men. Gay men need to appreciate one another as men the same way that some nongay men are learning to appreciate themselves. Our accomplishments and skills are rarely considered equally as valuable as those of nongay men. We are still men, though we usually don't feel like it. Because our transition into adulthood is not the same as that of nongay men, we need to expand the definition of masculinity to include our differ-ent expressions of maleness and manhood.

Why is a cabaret singer of show tunes considered feminine but a jazz artist who may sing or play the same music regarded as mascu-line? Why is a decorator considered feminine and an architect consid-ered masculine? Why are doctors assumed to be masculine and nurses feminine—when both roles involve nurturing and healing? Why must a gay man be less of a man if he doesn't like sports? For that matter, I know gay men who are passionate about sports (football, baseball, basketball—the sports "real" men watch and obsess about), but who hide their interest from their gay friends because they expect to be ridiculed for being "straight." Both gay and nongay men buy into the stereotypes of each other, making it difficult for both groups to recognize the similarities between them or appreciate the differences each brings to a new definition of manhood. *What few gay men or nongay men believe is that gay men can teach nongay men what it means to be a man.*

What keeps gay and nongay men from accepting each other as equals are the forces of misogyny and homophobia, two sides of the same coin of patriarchy. Each force finds its power by devaluing the "feminine." To be a man in patriarchy is to reject what's feminine or "womanly" or "girlish" or "effeminate." Luckily, over the past few decades, feminism has begun to dismantle this dynamic, but clearly our culture has a long row to hoe in changing how we value women and men who are perceived as feminine.

Ultimately, the distinctions between what is "gender appropriate" for men and women will drop away, as the qualities our culture admires become genderless. Strength, courage, perseverance, determination, independence, imagination, creativity, flexibility, and the ability to nurture and to communicate and express oneself—these qualities are to be admired in one another, regardless of gender or color or class.

To feel like a man—not just a label, but a genuine feeling—requires recognizing your strengths as an individual. But too often we don't recognize the strengths *we gain by coming out* and continue to measure our manhood against nongay standards. We haven't married. We don't know how to fix a car. We haven't fathered a child. We don't watch the Superbowl. We haven't become president of the firm. We don't participate in our college alumni program. We don't own homes. Unfortunately, the focus of these rituals of manhood is on behavior, not feelings. These socially sanctioned "accomplishments" emphasize the external over the internal—how a life looks on the outside, rather than expressing how it feels on the inside. As a result, the emotional component of adulthood remains underdeveloped for many nongay men. Just as boys are taught to ignore what's going on with their bodies or their emotions ("take it like a man"), nongay adult men are conditioned to repress any feelings of inadequacy or pain or depression.

Some nongay men take the underutilized route of therapy to pursue and develop an integrated, mature adult ego. Psychotherapy is one of a few arenas where men are permitted to develop and strengthen their emotional body. It also remains one of the few socially sanctioned professions in which men may emotionally nurture other men. Therapist and client are permitted to have this emotional relationship without aspersions of homosexual or "unmasculine" behavior. In the recent film *Good Will Hunting*, the characters portrayed by Matt Damon (Will Hunting) and Robin Williams (Will's therapist) are not portrayed as less manly for talking to each other deeply about their emotional histories. Even their loving hug at the end of their work together is seen as appropriate, "as long as you don't squeeze my ass," qualifies Robin Williams with a homophobic joke that reinforces stereotypes about male-male affection.

At the same time, this aside is revealing about what our culture suspects of the therapeutic relationship between men. I doubt this film would have had the same impact if the relationship between Will Hunting and a young British woman were not central to the plot. What if Will Hunting and his therapist were gay, with other men as their love interests? Would a nongay audience value their emotional communication as much? Would their intimacy be as compelling? Or would a nongay audience sexualize it? And how many gay viewers would also expect their relationship to turn sexual since we don't expect gay men to be capable of anything more intimate than sex?

The men who enter therapy—gay and nongay alike—do so in order to solve a problem they have or keep having. My experience with gay therapy groups suggests that the group also provides an additional level of support for a man who is coming out and looking for a peer community. The work of a coming-out support group focuses on what might be described as adolescent issues: becoming comfortable with yourself and your peers. I've often thought of therapy as a type of "finishing school" for gay men that satisfies an emotional need they never had met during adolescence.

In groups of nongay men, the work of therapy is usually focused on how to be more mature emotionally: learning to express their emotions, learning how to listen. Again, these are skills they could have learned as adolescents, except that patriarchy limits nongay male development in this area. Since we are not exempt from this baggage, gay males also need to work on their communication skills, but the process is different. Whereas both gay and nongay men must reject old behavior and incorporate new ways of feeling and thinking and acting into their mature, adult identity, usually the nongay male doesn't feel as compelled to reject as much as the gay male. Homophobia haunts gay men throughout their lives and reinforces a desire to reject themselves. Coming out, therapy, interaction with peers, both gay and nongay—are all tools for reversing the effects of homophobia.

Sadly, we don't yet live in a world where gay and nongay men can easily interact and learn from each other. As members of separate cultures, both groups of men are deprived of this socialization process in any formal way. As gay men, we have to seek out our elders and those who will guide us in the steps we have to take toward adulthood. Along the way, we must resist the subtle and not-so-subtle expectations about male behavior as we define ourselves as gay men.

THE LEGACY OF EXCLUSION

Excluded from our culture's primary socialization process, gay adolescents and young adults do not prepare themselves for adulthood. If we do not expect to be accepted and treated as valid adults, we may resist becoming adults. The avoidance of interaction with the "adult" world can affect everything in gay men's lives, from our relationships (we can't marry so why have committed relationships) to our economics (underearning, a lack of financial planning, and so on). Two of the major psychological consequences of our exclusion from adult socialization are what some describe as our emotional adolescence and our internalized homophobia.

If there were social rituals through which a gay man could be accepted by the larger society, we would prepare ourselves for adulthood more rigorously, starting in adolescence (strictly defined by our Clock Age, rather than the experiences that contribute to our Heart and Gay Ages). Without the anticipatory socialization nongays experience, we don't possess the same chronological map toward adulthood (sexual awakening, dating, college, marriage, career, children, retirement, grandchildren) and can remain adolescent in behavior and self-image far longer than our nongay peers. This observation is not meant to blame or shame gay men because this adolescence isn't "perpetual" or "delayed" or "arrested." It is real for gay men, given our different developmental path. The "adolescent" behavior the nongay world tries to pathologize is actually a natural response to a social phenomenon. To characterize a gay man as an "emotional adolescent" is to apply nongay standards whose chronology not only doesn't apply to him, but also insults his development.

Complicating our transition into adulthood is a desire to maintain our integrity as gay males. Though we may ridicule the nongay standards of adulthood, we cannot deny their influence upon our ability to define ourselves. Out of the conflict between gay and nongay expressions of maturity comes confusion, insecurity, and instability. Many gay adult males usually feel that they do not deserve to be treated as adult men, and usually do not feel confident being authority figures, regardless of their vocational and/or academic success. In terms of career advancement, gay men may be subject to discrimination in the form of a "lavender ceiling," but we can also limit ourselves psychologically by not pursuing executive positions or not "going for it" in our jobs, whether in a factory or an office.

The second legacy of exclusion is even more insidious and destructive—the internalized homophobia that is an inescapable result of being raised in this homophobic culture. Internalized homophobia is a *cultural* phenomenon often misperceived in terms of *individual* psychopathology. Manifested in feelings of immaturity, powerlessness, effeminacy, inferiority, pretense, social ineptness, isolation, shame, and self-loathing, this internalized homophobia can be so profound that many gay males believe they deserve the condemnation that they perceive to be directed toward them.

If he can't drown out his shame and self-loathing, a gay man may come to accept misery as his birthright: "Maybe being fucked up is the only way for me." Once a gay man reaches this point it is very difficult to value himself. We need only look at the addiction and suicide rates for our community (and the teens entering it) to realize the devastation internalized homophobia can produce. Two responses are clear, but most of us spend our lives veering between the two. We can surrender to homophobia (both our culture's and our own) by attempting to become "real" men and negate our gayness, or we can actively dismantle our own and our culture's homophobia and come out as openly gay men, but perhaps feel less manly in relation to our nongay peers. Understanding and resolving this conflict is crucial to our growth as men.

GAY SOCIALIZATION, GAY RITUALS

Since the process by which society initiates its members—involving role models, mentors, and elders—is usually not accessible to us, we often have to take a more active role in our own development. In response to its cultural exclusion from socialization, the gay community created Gay Pride. One beginning of this celebration of ourselves as gay was Harry Hay's proclamation that "Gay Is Good" in the fifties. Long before Stonewall, organizations of lesbians (The Daughters of Bilitis) and gay men (The Mattachine Society) waged

war against the monolithic nongay culture. In the three decades since
Stonewall, our community has made tremendous strides in liberating
itself from internalized homophobia. One way of doing this has been
to bring to light the history that's been suppressed. We also began
to fight institutionalized homophobia on the legal front through the
repeal of sodomy laws and the passage of civil rights protection.
Another sign of growth was the national institution building we accomplished during the seventies; luckily, this infrastructure was in
place when AIDS emerged. Our response to AIDS has also brought
our community together in a manner we hadn't imagined.

In many ways, we have created an *alternate route to socialization
through our own institutions and networks*. We have community centers,
gay bars/clubs, gay restaurants, bookstores, newspapers, professional
networking associations, health clinics, AIDS service organizations,
sports leagues, and political and activist groups. This constellation of
gay organizations can create a self-contained community (the gay
ghetto) in our larger cities, while for the majority of the gay men
across the country, the gay community consists of a bar or two,
maybe a newspaper or a bookstore. The gay presence on the Internet
has changed all this to a degree; but while there are more resources
available on-line, there may be less actual interaction with one
another.

As part of our gay socialization and our rituals of gay pride, we
have discovered our own coming-of-age rituals. In *Kitchen Table Wisdom*, Dr. Rachel Naomi Remen observes, "Ritual is one of the oldest
ways to mobilize the power of community for healing. It makes the
caring of the community visible, tangible, real." In recent history, two
experiences might be considered rituals of gay adulthood: coming out
publicly as openly gay and facing the early death of friends and
lovers. However, these experiences are not universal, and not necessarily recognized or honored by the larger nongay mainstream.

For a gay man, the first ritual toward adulthood is coming out.
Coming out is a life experience that forever changes the way we feel
about ourselves and how we relate to the world. Once we are able
to identify as gay (even if only to ourselves, before coming out to
anyone else), we begin to undo the damage wrought by shame,
persecution, and self-loathing. *Coming out activates the socialization process
by which we begin to come into our own as gay adults in the gay community*.
Once a gay man initiates his coming-out process, he begins to live

in relation to the gay community's myths and ideas about what it means to be gay, which replaces the nongay anticipatory socialization from which he was excluded as an adolescent. Regardless of when you began to come out (whether it was your twenties or forties), you soon learned that there are norms and rituals for gay people, just as there are for nongay people.

Coming out is first and foremost a choice; some men remain closeted for a variety of reasons. There are generations of gay men who have lived in the closet all their lives and for whom the pain of coming out remains too unbearable, too threatening. Our culture's homophobia has forever silenced these men and what they could teach us. In addition, homophobia has produced what I call "invisible lifestyles," which prevent communication between the generations in our community. As gay men age and commit to relationships, many move to the suburbs, where they lose contact with the larger gay community. Sadly, gay couples and gay singles don't mix that much either, so that neither can serve the other as a role model. Since there are benefits to being single as well as to being part of a couple, both groups could teach the other a thing or two.

Each experience of coming out builds self-esteem and empowers the individual, who assigns different meanings to each stage. One male may feel like an adult the first time he has sex with another male, while another gay male might feel like an adult once he has come out to his parents and siblings or professionally. Also, a gay male may have sex with men for a long time before he thinks of himself as gay. In short, no single stage of coming out represents a true sign of adulthood.

In recent history, another ritual for gay adulthood has been the early experience of grief. Like coming out, grieving is a choice, as well as a process of indefinite length and intensity. Some gay males are fortunate (or isolated or in denial) enough to escape the ravages of AIDS, and do not see grieving as part of their life. For others, depending upon the nature of the relationship (friend, sibling, lover), grief takes many forms and can resurface at unexpected times. The first time someone you love dies, you may feel as if you've reached a threshold of adulthood, or perhaps it is only when you've experienced multiple deaths that you begin to feel as if you are an adult, capable of emotional strength and resiliency. Grieving also enables many gay males to recognize and work through their fear of commitment. After experiencing many deaths, a gay male may begin to believe that he will survive, that love and life are possible in the face of death, and in fact, can be made more precious by coexisting with illness and death. Surviving the death of loved ones makes you more able to love fully because you realize love transcends death.

In addition, we have lost a significant number of our potential elders to AIDS. The deaths of so many men have numbed, then angered, then numbed again our people and drained our community of resources, energy, and talent. The grief has alternately overwhelmed us, motivated us, and changed us, irrevocably. *Our community's survival is the greatest gift we continue to give one another, and our endurance has been heroic.*

Although AIDS has robbed us of older gay men who could have acted as role models for younger generations, the invisibility of older gay men in our community and in our media further complicates our search for elders. How can we interact with those we don't see? We don't usually have contact with gay adults when we're adolescents or even later when we're coming out, so maybe we don't recognize the need for them. We don't know how to talk across the generation divide, and sadly, the desire for such interaction usually isn't even present. In some ways, AIDS has exacerbated these divisions: Younger gays who've grown up with AIDS, whose world has always been shaped by the disease, may feel they have little in common with men over forty who not only remember but long for the world before AIDS. As with most communication gaps, the barriers are internal, not external. We circulate among one another through our extensive social structure, but real conversations are all too rare.

THE ROLE OF ROLE MODELS

Such generational isolation could be prevented if we recognized the need for role models in our community. In the same way that role models pave the way to maturity for an adolescent or young man struggling with identity, when we approach midlife—our true adulthood, the end of our gay adolescence—role models again become an important resource. But even the words *role model* trigger a lot of fear and resistance. People imagine role models to be smug goody-two-shoes or nerdy professors or hell-fire and brimstone religious figures or judgmental parent figures.

Identification with the role model is what's key. The person does not have to become exactly like the role model for the role model to be influential. The role model is a stimulus for the person to develop to his fullest. You don't even have to like the person, although he or she must have some characteristic that you desire for yourself. You may admire a coworker who can make people laugh easily. Your uncle may be a fiscally conservative Republican but a fabulous romantic who keeps his relationship alive and passionate. Maybe there's a guy with salt-and-pepper hair at your gym who swims daily.

Each gay man must find his own way to his genuine self, but role models illuminate the many paths available. Just as there are many "worlds within worlds" in the gay community, there are a wealth of role models to choose from. *The role model should be symbolic of what you can successfully work toward or attain.* You choose the goal; the role model offers *one* way, but not *the* way, to reach it. Role models offer a different kind of mirror: an image of yourself that has yet to emerge.

Over the course of your life, different role models will be necessary. For example, a supportive, loving, nongay therapist can be a positive role model for a gay person who is establishing his identity. This is not a role model with whom the gay man identifies directly, but one who functions more as a significant person giving the gay man support and permission to continue in his unique development (being himself, learning who he is).

At another stage, it can be equally important to have a positive gay role model to counter the negative gay stereotypes and homophobic attitudes that may have become internalized and thereby limited a gay man's self-expectations. Of importance here are openly gay men who are successful in their vocation and have integrated their social, professional, and personal lives. In addition, as many gay men have guarded interaction with their families, it is beneficial for us to see openly gay men who have loving and open interactions with their own blood families.

Though our focus is on finding role models among our gay peers, I realized that some of my most effective role models have been women. An early role model for me was Bernice Neugarten, a professor at the University of Chicago, where I completed my graduate work. Though the term was not yet coined, she was the first feminist I encountered. She became my advisor and mentor for most of the time I was in graduate school, and our friendship has continued to this day. What impressed me early on was the way she saw people in a social context—she never let her students forget the effects of culture and the political milieu. She was especially focused on the prejudices against women and older people and she recognized how people responded to such bias in ways that destroyed their integrity and sense of self. Throughout her life and career, she has combined intelligence, integrity, warmth, scholarship, and empathy in an outstanding way. What women like Bernice reveal to me is not so much how to be feminine or what it means to be a woman, but what strengths of character I admire, what type of individual I can become, what paths I can take.

Gay and nongay, male and female, blood relative or total stranger, role models can come in many forms, and come in handy at various times in our development. In our discussion of body image, I stressed finding men your age whom you consider attractive. In our discussion of physical well-being, I encouraged you to identify men who maintained a regime for health. The same dynamic is at work here with role models and self-image. In a later discussion, we will look toward our social relationships as a way of working on our self image. As our focus shifts from Body Image to Self Image to Social Image, we will continue to draw upon role models to guide us.

HOW MUCH IS THAT ROLE MODEL IN THE WINDOW?

It's not easy to find gay role models given our community's treatment of the middle-aged. Half the struggle is wanting to look, the other half is knowing where.

Gay athletic leagues, from volleyball to bowling, swimming to billiards, offer an opportunity to meet other gay men in a nonsexual atmosphere so that relationships, not just romantic ones, can develop. Volunteering for a gay organization, union organizing, political campaigning, networking within one's profession—all these forms of community activism offer an integral component of mental health. In all these areas, of course, there can be sexual intrigue and romantic possibilities, but they are integrated with other activities as part of the landscape, rather than the defining feature.

It's important to distinguish among different kinds of elders. There are men, like me, who came out pre-Stonewall and "grew up" in the community, during the institution-building of the seventies, the response to AIDS in the eighties, and the "mainstream" moment of the nineties. As our leaders, these men have lived life mostly out of the closet and have contributed directly to our community. Sadly, a huge percentage of these men have died.

Then there are men who entered the gay community at a later age, possibly through a social service agency like SAGE (Senior Action in a Gay Environment). These men have incredible histories to share, and their life stories are valuable and necessary to our collective experience. What can these men teach us about living? Being an elder is not about age, but experience.

When I reached my forties, I thought I had very few good models for being a middle-aged, vibrant, and sexy gay man. There were colleagues and activists I admired and who inspired me professionally, but I didn't really know anyone over forty who inspired me the same way. One weekend I went on a spiritual retreat. Also attending was my best friend's boyfriend, Andrew, who was in his midfifties. I enjoyed Andrew's company but didn't find him physically or sexually attractive. Even though I knew he had sex, I found it hard to imagine him as a sexual person.

At various times during the weekend, Andrew talked about how excited he was at being in his fifties. He kept referring to all the newfound pleasures he was now experiencing (joy at being able to go dancing more, doing what he wanted, not being as concerned about what others thought of him). My ageism made it difficult for me to understand his genuinely upbeat attitude.

Unbelievably, Andrew was actually looking forward to getting older and would even rattle off advantages to his aging. I was thoroughly confused by the disparity between my negative attitude and his clearly positive one. By the second day of the retreat and after much reflection, I had a very elementary insight: *I feared aging because I had only negative images of myself aging.* Further reflection enabled me to ask the question: *Since I had learned these negative images, why could I not relearn a new set of images and, this time, make them positive ones?*

1. What images do you have of yourself as you age?

Before you can identify a potential role model, you need to take
a look at your self-image as an aging gay man. Do you see yourself
as old and lonely, or vibrant and fulfilled? Jogging three miles a day
or hobbling along with a walker? The images we have of ourselves
as we age significantly influence our motivation and drive to live life
to the fullest. When I realized the connection between my fears of
aging and my negative images of myself, my next step was to look
carefully at the images I had created: Where did they come from?
Did they have a basis in reality or were they fueled by our culture's
ageism? Finally, how could I eliminate or change them?

In this exercise, really examine where your imagination is leading
you. What do these images of an older gay man suggest about your
priorities? An acquaintance of mine, Will, is terrified of being a "mean
old queen" (his words) and asked if I could write a chapter for this
book called "How Not to Get Bitter." When I asked him to think
about what's going to make him so bitter, the real fears emerged:
less sex, less energy, less fun, more hair on his back, more aches in
his joints, more rejection from younger men. If the majority of your
images are about sexual attractiveness and rejection, you know where
your work lies.

Some of Will's fears are specific to his body (hair, aches), but
most of them are the negative stereotypes many of us hold about
aging. Clearly, Will has met gay men who personify these negative
images. These men serve as negative role models for Will because
they make the aging process seem like a potentially negative experience for him. We may not even be aware that we already have
negative role models in our thinking. All we may recognize is that
we are fearful of getting older.

2. Talk about the older gay men that you don't like.

The drunks at the bars. The sad-faced men wearing baggy khakis
at the community center. The opera queen who knows it all. The
snob who prefers Lake Tahoe over the Russian River. The lecher you
encounter at every charity reception who gropes you every chance
he gets. The asexual men who seem despondent. The former marathon runner who let himself go and has a potbelly now.

By identifying the older gay men you don't like, you begin to name and visualize your own fears about aging. The more clear you are about what characteristics or behaviors you don't like about these men, the better able you will be to find a role model who inspires you and who can challenge the negative images of aging you've inherited from our culture. When you begin to look in the mirror, you may only see a blur of negativity. As you begin to look around for positive images of aging gay men, your own potential for successful aging will come into focus.

3. Talk about the older gay men that you admire.

Just as there are older gay men who operate as negative role models, there are older gay men whose behavior suggests aging can be a positive experience. Interaction with positive role models helps to expand the boundaries of self-expectations. People who have clearly extended their own limits encourage others to do the same.

Dancing is one of my lifelong passions, and when I was an adolescent, I took many classes and even briefly considered it as a possible career. One of my personal fears about aging was that I would not be able to dance as much or for as long as I did during my thirties. I turned forty in 1976, during the heyday of disco, and I spent many Saturday nights in New York City dancing nonstop at 12 West, Flamingo, the Garage, though the Saint was my ultimate favorite. Often my friend Jack and I would dance all night at the Saint, then go the next morning to the board meeting for the National Gay and Lesbian Health Foundation, which we had helped to found.

When I reached midlife, I was determined to keep dancing. Not being able to dance would have been death for me. Luckily, I began to notice older gay men on the dance floor around me and the positive images I had of them began to substitute for the negative images I had of my own aging. Once when I was attending a Gay Academic Union conference, one of the participants was a very tanned and vibrant man from Hawaii who was in his late sixties. He loved to dance and never seemed to tire, and his boundless energy and positive attitude impressed me incredibly. He was the first significantly older gay man I had met who conveyed that kind of energy.

Another positive role model for me was Pat Kelley, one of the first openly gay therapists in New York City. When we met, he was in his mid-forties, ten years my senior, and known for his love of dance and his wicked sense of humor. As our friendship developed, we'd go dancing at Studio 54, where he was admitted immediately ahead of the long lines because of his reputation on the dance floor. He helped make the party. He was quite aware of the impression he made—with his white hair, handsome face, cowboy outfit (it was Studio 54, after all), and his excellent dancing.

I go into so much detail about dancing because it serves two crucial functions for me: as pure physical and emotional enjoyment and as a spiritual connection with the other gay men on the dance floor. A night at the Saint was a tribal experience predating (and *very* different from) today's Circuit, though clearly both represent a new form of ritual for gay men that has been possible only after Stonewall. When gay men began dancing in discos, they were finally able to feel and express their masculinity in a public arena. Dancing became so essential for me because it was one area in which I felt like a man. For years, my internalized homophobia made me feel less a man than a nongay man, but on the dance floor with other gay men, I learned to express myself physically and enjoy my masculinity.

Continuing to dance is symbolic of my staying alive. I may not be able to dance as long as I could in the past but my enjoyment is even more intense. I now choose not to spend all night at a club dancing until dawn and needing to recover the next day. If it is an all-night party, I get a good night's sleep and go in the morning when there's plenty of room to dance, and treat it like an aerobic workout. When I was younger, I was too self-conscious to start dancing immediately—I had to warm up to it (usually with a little herbal motivation). Since I am fully aware that I do not have time to wait, I put my all into the dance without wasting time. I always dance to my fullest, regardless of how much time there is (but only as long as the music is good!).

4. **Talk about positive role models among men that you know, both gay and nongay.**

After spending all this time trying to persuade you not to measure yourself against a nongay standard of manhood, you're probably shocked that I'm asking you to consider positive role models among nongay men. The motivation is to get you to talk about your experience beyond the gay male community, but it's also to highlight the ageism of our entire culture that makes it difficult to find *any* positive role models, gay or nongay. Ageism is by no means limited to gay culture, though we do seem to have perfected it!

Another anecdote about dancing illustrates how role models can turn up in even the most nongay of environments. When I was thirty-one and an intern, my supervisor invited me and another intern to attend his wife's sorority dance. It wasn't until we got to his home that I learned that my supervisor, who was white, was married to an African-American woman. So when we got to the dance, there were only five white people in a dance hall of four hundred African American men and women of all ages.

Though I had been in the minority at functions before, they were usually of a political or religious nature. This was my first such party and it was magnificent. Throughout the night, what kept impressing me was that everyone was dancing. I have never forgotten one older man who was confined to a wheelchair and still danced with others. I was quite envious because I was still at the stage when I had to "warm up" before dancing. I never forgot my reaction to everyone partying: they knew something I didn't. Age or physique had no relevance to grooving on a dance floor. The people attending that party were role models for me, even though they were strangers to me and I never saw them again. As nongay role models, they helped me to reconnect with my passion for dancing.

Role models are often real-life figures, but sometimes they can be fantasy persons or celebrities who make a significant impression on us. They can also be figures that we have either a positive or negative reaction to, whom we either want to be like or unlike. It is from role models that we begin to develop an image of how we want to be in the world. The goal is to become aware of how these images—both positive and negative—affect our self-perceptions.

In my active search for role models, I started looking at the various public images of older men who were seen as vibrant, attractive, sophisticated, and energetic. The first man who came to mind was Cary Grant, who provided a clear example of a successfully aging man who was seen as sophisticated and capable of celebrating his good life. His image worked for me for a while, until I realized that he didn't convey the kind of sexuality that I wanted to feel and communicate. I then decided to adopt Sean Connery as a role model because he was simple, concrete proof that it was possible to be an older, sexually attractive man. As a role model, if he could be virile, so could I. In my mid-forties, I had no problem seeing men my own age as virile and attractive, but I tended to have a negative attitude about the men I identified as middle-aged and older. Sean Connery helped me to realize that physical attraction was independent of age; the "yukky" men I had identified as middle-aged were those men who had let themselves go and given up taking care of themselves.

Although Sean Connery provided a good nongay role model for me, I continued to refine his image in a gay context. At the time, I was ending a relationship with a man ten years younger than me. This relationship was the last of a series of relationships with younger men I had begun in my mid-thirties (a new development at the time since previously I had been involved only with men older than me or with peers). I had decided to reenter psychotherapy in order to rework part of my past and to learn not to repeat self-destructive relationships. I decided that, besides being an excellent therapist, I wanted someone who I thought was aging gracefully, someone who would be a good role model for me. I chose Frank Donnelly, a man ten years older than I was at the time (I was forty-three). An incredible therapist, Frank was also heavily involved in community activities, a vibrant and sexual man who had a whirl of social life. He was a composite of all I wanted to be.

As an openly gay therapist who was also comfortable with being a middle-aged gay man, Frank provided me with an excellent role model. Over the years, I have tried to recreate that same dynamic with my own clients. As I self-disclose when it is clinically appropriate, my client has a chance to engage in a direct dialogue with a potential role model. I am a member of the same community, and my understanding has developed by going through many of the same experiences. Being professionally and personally out, I provide a living example from which he can learn, but by no means the only role model available to him.

The therapist is a special kind of teacher to the client. For many gay males, psychotherapy with a gay male therapist and/or group is the first experience that can help them make the transition to adult manhood. The therapist, teacher, or mentor may use different means but the broadest goals are the same—teaching the other how to function at optimum capacity and to realize his potential. Explicit in the best therapeutic relationship is the expectation that the client can achieve the same level of development as the therapist. And the therapist cannot take a client beyond where he is himself or where he's afraid to go. I fully believe therapists teach others what we need to learn ourselves.

5. What are the specific characteristics of the role models you can identify?

You have picked these men out of all the possible choices, and there is a reason why these men stood out for you. Something about their personality or behavior or lifestyle must have tapped something within you, and this exercise is for you to get in touch with whatever these men trigger for you. Are they witty? Serious? Virile? Empathetic? Able to handle a crisis smoothly and calmly? A hilarious host of parties? An aggressive salesman? Well-organized and always planning ahead? Close to his family? A saint of volunteer work?

The more specific you can be in identifying the qualities you admire in a role model, the more clearly you can identify what's important to you and to your future. You may see a pattern emerge among these men that will suggest what you're really searching for. Maybe they're all in relationships. Maybe they're all single. Maybe they are all entrepreneurs or they all work in areas of public service. Maybe they're all sexually active. Maybe each considers himself a "family man," with children or a close relationship to his parents and siblings.

This exercise is another step in clarifying priorities and goal setting. By looking deep into the reflections of these men, you will better understand the kind of person you want to be.

6. How do you see yourself as being like them?

You may feel as if you have nothing in common with your role models. They're A list, you're the B-team. They're successful professionally, while you've been drifting from job to job over the last few years. You imagine they have sex all the time; you haven't been laid in months. It's easy to start listing the negatives because we have so little faith in ourselves. As with our work on the physical advantages of aging, it takes only a few similarities for you to start the identification process with your role models.

It's important to stick with this exercise until you find one or two similarities, no matter how insignificant they seem. Maybe you went to the same school or college, so you have a similar education. Maybe you live in the same neighborhood, so you have similar incomes. Maybe you like the same kinds of clothes or social functions. The goal is to see yourself in the same category as these men even though you may put yourself on the bottom of the list—it's important to place yourself on the list at the very least.

7. What do you have to do to be more like them?

Do you need to assess your career and switch gears professionally? Do you need to lose some weight, get a new haircut and some new clothes so you can feel sexual again? Do you need to mend some bridges with your family, so you can experience their love and warmth? Do you want to volunteer more in the community, so you can be a part of something larger than you?

As you begin to ponder the various actions you can take or ways of thinking differently you can practice, you will continue to identify your similarities with these men. This process shifts the focus of your energy away from feeling rejected and not part of a desired group and toward taking action. At this point, you're *thinking* about actions, rather than *taking* them, but it's preparing you for change. Putting yourself into action mode and creating a list of possible changes to make might seem like baby steps, but you have to start somewhere. The problem is when you can't even imagine starting.

8. What kind of picture do you have of yourself ten years from now?

As you've been working on these exercises, certain images may have emerged for you, and this is an opportunity to flesh out that shadowy, older you on the horizon. It's not a mirage. Change will come, and you will survive.

The specificity of "ten years" may make some difference in how you responded to the first exercise, and the goal is to look at what you conjure up. Will you be working or retired? Single or coupled?

In good health or in a wheelchair? Running a marathon or swimming laps at the community center? What are your main preoccupations? Financial security? Popularity? Sexuality? General health?

It's important to acknowledge what negative elements may have disappeared and what positive features may have emerged in your self-image. This exercise allows you to measure the changes in attitude or thinking you may have experienced while working through the exercises so far. Do you feel less fear about aging? Or more? What sort of shifts are you observing?

9. **Picture the most positive image of yourself as a successfully aging gay man that you can.**

In ten years, you will be a successful businessman who devotes himself to good causes. You will perform your first solo in a community orchestra. You will have lost ten pounds and minimized your wrinkles. You will have two boyfriends on two separate continents. You will compete in the Gay Games. You will be elected to the City Council. You will be a buddy to a gay teenager. You will publish your first novel. You and your lover will be celebrating five years of the most cherished relationship of your lives. You will not be bitter.

Expand on what you came up with in the previous exercise. This does not mean coming up with a totally positive image of yourself. Resist feeling guilty if you cannot come up with an "ideal" image. The important part of this exercise is to give serious consideration to your future image.

10. **Think about what steps you are going to take to make this ideal image a reality in your life.**

It's time to look in the mirror. Making this image of your future real is not simple or easily done.

If your ten-year goal is to publish a first novel, begin by creating a schedule that allows you writing time. Model yourself after writers you admire (another kind of role model), then begin to tell your own story in your own voice. Once you have written a chunk of material, share it with another writer for some feedback and constructive criticism. Once you feel it has reached a certain polished quality, investigate the process of publishing: how to find an agent, how to find a publisher, how to promote a book upon publication. There are many steps toward getting a book published, and resources are available to guide you. Taking incremental actions is the surest way to realizing the goal, even if it takes ten years.

It's the same with rescuing your health. If you're diabetic or have high blood pressure or are HIV positive, there are steps to take to maintain and restore health so that you're still here in ten years.

Getting to the point where you can identify actions to take requires courage and honesty and strength. The actions become building blocks in constructing your image of successful aging. You may not be ready to use all of these blocks right away or in the near future, but you will be constantly reminding yourself as opportunities arise to put them into place. At some point, you will take the necessary action. Allow yourself to set a comfortable pace, but don't get caught in procrastination ("I'll do it tomorrow.") or denial ("I don't need to change a thing.").

What will make picking up these building blocks easier is keeping it real. Just as when you put together a regime for your health, keep the list short and sweet and in the realm of possibility. Role models are gentle reminders of what is possible and may offer avenues of development you may not have considered. As you begin to identify the steps to make your ideal image real, you may find yourself illuminating the path of change for someone else.

11. In what ways are you a good role model of an aging gay man, for both nongay and gay men?

At this point in our work together, you can probably identify qualities in being gay that make you a good role model for a nongay man. You may be more independent, more flexible about gender roles, better able to communicate your feelings, able to reach out for support, or have a sense of humor and irony about the world and your place in it.

This idea is not about competition or to suggest that gays are better than nongays. A sense of your own power comes from within, not from putting someone else down. Having probably spoken of your aging only in the negative, you need to recognize your strengths in the aging process. Even if you're only repeating what your friends tell you, it's important to feel less helpless and hopeless about this process.

Looking in your own community, what kind of role model do you provide? Regardless of whether or not you want to be a role model, your life is a living mirror for other gay men, just as their lives are for you. What qualities do you feel most proud about?

Are you openly gay? Are you active in the community? Are you close to your family? Are you a good listener and friend? In what ways do you commune with your peers? What could a gay adolescent learn from you? What could you learn from a gay elder?

In trying on the label "role model," you need to recognize all your accomplishments, both internal and external. You've probably never considered yourself a role model, especially around the subject of aging, so it may seem like a stretch, but it's a necessary part of being honest with yourself. Honesty does not apply only to negative criticism; being honest about "the good stuff" is probably harder than listing "the bad stuff."

Looking in the mirror means not just seeing the work to be done, but catching sight of your own beauty.

Joe's Story

Joe was an all-important man in my life. I was blessed in having such a positive role model of a gay man as my first lover. He truly taught me what a gay man could be. I can honestly say that he probably had more positive influence on my life than any other person, other than my sister, who took care of me when I was younger.

Joe was thirty when we met, and I was seventeen. He managed a record store owned by my father's best friend. I had been sent to live with my father in Chicago because my family in California had found out that I was seeing a new boyfriend (after my arrest at fourteen, I had stopped being sexual for a couple of years, but then resumed). In Chicago, I had a job with an afternoon break for three hours, and I was sent to spend time with Joe, a relative of my father's neighbors. My father didn't know Joe was gay; all he knew was that Joe was a "nice Jewish boy."

Joe was very kind to me and introduced me to classical music in which he was an expert since he had studied to be a pianist. He was a very gentle man who was clearly a well loved and respected person in his community. He was soft spoken and best friends with the manager of the other store owned by my father's friend. Both managers were gay and made no bones about it. Over the summer, as I spent more and more time with Joe, I found myself wanting to be with him. I finally realized that I was in love with him and told him so. He was shocked since he had had very little sex (six times) and then it was not lovemaking. We arranged to have sex in which I made love to him. He was clearly the more inexperienced of us. He claimed he was in love with me and we told my father, who became incensed. He drove me through the slums of Chicago and told me I'd end up there, if I "chose" this lifestyle. My father sent me back to California, but Joe and I planned for him to come to L.A. at the end of the year. I sensed he wouldn't come since he still lived at home and it would have been too much of a change for him. So I waited a month until I turned eighteen (I was still a ward of the court until eighteen) and left for Chicago—I had saved my money as a dishwasher. I arrived in Chicago with a book, pillow, and one suitcase. I obviously surprised Joe by this—I lived temporarily in a rooming house until we found a studio apartment and moved in together.

We lived together for three years until I left to study at the University of Chicago. From the very beginning, he treated me with respect and did not try to make me into anything other than the best of what I could be. I took a job in a record shipping company and handled mail orders. Though I thought I was too stupid to go to college, Joe encouraged me to pursue my dream of being a psychiatrist. I eventually did start school and found that I did very well. In my English class, I had one of Joe's closest friends as my teacher. For one of the writing assignments, I wrote about Joe and how he was such a good example of someone who had adjusted beautifully in the world. Joe had apparently been diagnosed as a schizophrenic when he was younger because of his extreme timidity, fears, and shyness. He had undergone intensive psychoanalysis with a psychiatrist who eventually ended up being a close friend of his. Joe was that kind of person. I wrote about how Joe had dealt so successfully with three worlds—the internal, intrapsychic one; the world of friends and family; and the world of work and position in the general world.

He had seriously looked at himself, was unafraid to see who he was, and was comfortable with himself. He was very realistic about his strengths and weaknesses and saw himself as having a good life. He had established a loving relationship with his family and was quite respected by them. He was a loyal family member but did not let anyone walk over him. He was totally comfortable bringing me into the family as his lover and I was totally accepted by them. (Over forty years later, I am still close to his niece, whom I first met when she was two.) Joe was politically interested in the world and had a definite leftist orientation. He was equally comfortable with gay and nongay peers though he did not have much tolerance for prejudiced or unmannered people. His ability to respect others was one of his most important characteristics since it made him a person whom people liked to be around.

Since I was so desperate for someone to see me as a person, Joe was a godsend when we met. I am sure that I chose him because I sensed that I could grow with him. He was so comfortable with himself that he could easily allow others to be themselves. I am sure the nongay world saw him as not manly because he was quiet, gentle, and not pushy. But no one could push him around—he stood his ground if challenged. So for the first time, I was meeting an intelligent, thoughtful, sensitive, cultured, respectful, insightful, and gentle gay man—the perfect role model for a young, struggling adolescent who had a lot of sexual experience but no emotional experience with this kind of man.

Our romantic relationship lasted for three years, but we were close friends until his premature death when he was in his early fifties. He was undergoing a simple operation to install a pacemaker, when complications arose. The hospital didn't respond properly, and their negligence resulted in severe brain damage which caused him to be institutionalized for the rest of his life. I think of him often and realize what a special man the world has lost.

PART TWO

Mind

FOUR

Work/Play:
A New Paradigm of Purpose and Pleasure

Many gay men are surprised when I bring up the subject of work and play in the context of aging. "What's work got to do with this?" they ask. "I'm worried about losing my looks and my sexuality, and you want to know how I spend my leisure time."

Just as many people have a conditioned response about aging (with ideas and expectations about age-appropriate behavior, what being "old" looks like, and so forth), many people approach work the same way. At first, neither area seems open to change: We don't think we can change aging; we don't think we can change our work patterns or how work fits into our lives.

Our relationship to work is a critical factor in our aging process because it contributes to our sense of satisfaction with our lives. The more satisfied we are with our lives, the better we will age. Examining your attitudes around work and play can lead to a shift in priorities, enhancing not only our mental outlook, but our physical health as well. In chapter 2, we explored the connection between mental health and disease. By midlife, work attitudes are a major factor in our mental health. But instead of focusing on "job satisfaction," we need to look at our "life satisfaction."

In the early seventies Bernice Neugarten, one of the founders of the field of gerontology and my mentor at the University of Chicago, developed a concept of "life satisfaction" to describe the experience of people who aged well. The higher an individual's sense of satisfac-

tion with his life, the longer and better he lived. The five criteria
for this source of longevity were:

1.   Takes pleasure from daily activities;
2.   Regards his life as meaningful;
3.   Feels he has achieved his major goals;
4.   Holds a positive self-image and regards himself as worthwhile;
5.   Is optimistic.

Notice that none of these criteria are about how much money an
individual earns, but about attitudes and abilities he develops over
the course of a lifetime: his adaptability, independence, autonomy,
and self-sufficiency.

Our American and male emphasis on using work to define ourselves puts extraordinary pressure on our mental states. Any negative
feelings about work (underearning, underappreciation, being fired,
downsized, or disabled) can lead to poor health. Andrew Weil, Joan
Borysenko, Bernie Siegel, Deepak Chopra, and others have written
extensively about the connection between thinking and health, and
it's well-documented that a depressed mental state can lead to the
production of biochemicals in the body that create disease. Sadly,
the group most pressured to define their personal identity through
their work—men—is the same group most conditioned to ignore
what their bodies are telling them. When speaking about work and
pressures, I'm not surprised that one of the most frequently used
terms in the language of work is *deadline*. Overworking can lead to
high blood pressure, heart attacks, a stroke, depression—all factors
leading to death. But few people on their deathbeds wish they had
two more weeks to work. (An exception would be someone fueled
by a positive sense of work, such as the artist like Howard Crabtree,
who was working on the costumes for his show, *When Pigs Fly*, during
the final stages of his AIDS illness in the hospital.)

The American workforce is working harder than ever, despite
the promise of technology to make our lives easier and less stressful.
In January 1999, the *Utne Reader* reported that "88 percent of workers
said their jobs require them to work longer" and "68 percent com-
plained of having to work at greater speeds." The most alarming
statistic is that "as many as 80 percent of workers in our society feel
their jobs, however fast and furious, are 'meaningless.'" At midlife,

many of us begin to question why we are working so hard and to what end? One of the reasons career shifts happen at midlife is that it is the time for reevaluation of prior decisions and the developing importance of enjoying one's life. It is a time for expanding the definition of success to mean more than success in a career—success becomes satisfaction with one's total lifestyle in which work and play are both necessary components.

SO WHAT DO YOU DO? WORK AS IDENTITY

At cocktail parties, people tend to ask one another, "What do you do?" so often because they think it will tell them a lot about a stranger. Although it gives a person an opening in which to describe himself, the question tells us more about the expectations of the questioner. A feminist joke tells the story of a man at a formal dinner party who asks the woman sitting next to him, "So, my dear, what does your husband do?" His assumptions about women and work ignore her as a person and reveal his sexism. When we ask somebody what he does for a living, the response ("I'm a plumber" or "I'm a banker") gives us a category, an occupation, but doesn't really tell us much about him as a person. We fill in the blanks with our fantasy of what a plumber or banker does and rarely choose to go beyond the label (unless, of course, we want to go into that field, and the conversation turns into a networking opportunity!). As a social gambit, asking "What line of work are you in?" doesn't really foster communication, but gives us a sense of the other person's place in the social hierarchy in relation to us.

In the past, when I would begin a gay men's therapy group, I would allow each member to ask the other members any and as many questions as he wanted, with just one restriction: you couldn't ask what another man did for a living or how he earned his money. And you couldn't volunteer that information about yourself either, until weeks later and only when it was relevant during the course of that particular discussion.

Typically, the men balked at this restriction and found it incredibly difficult not to ask the question or not to share that information about themselves. Their discomfort over not being able to use a socially approved of way of communicating, as well as their curiosity about the other men's occupations, is totally understandable. Work occupies a central place in our self-definition as men, and our job is usually how we males go about identifying ourselves. Since we were little boys, we have been conditioned to become a worker, a bread-winner, a money tree, a mover and a shaker. (While little girls were conditioned to play house or go into "helping" professions.)

Work is very much integrated into the American character. Work is considered mandatory, patriotic, and moral, part of what it means to be an adult. America has inherited its work ethic from many sources, perhaps beginning with the Puritans who settled New England. Survival in Colonial America was not a given, and work was required to explore, settle, and harvest the wilderness. Facing a harsh winter and unknown elements, Captain John Smith of Jamestown was known for proclaiming, "If you don't work, you don't eat," forever linking work with survival in the New World. In addition to the Puritans, waves of immigrants have also shaped America's work ethic by translating hard work and money into the quickest means of assimilation in the new country. Then there's Horatio Alger, spinning the classic rags-to-riches story to sustain the myth of economic equality: since everyone has an equal chance in this country, there are no "fixed" classes; if you don't "get ahead" and make tons of money, there's something wrong with you.

These American myths surrounding money, work, and leisure condition us to participate in the workforce in a certain way. The current paradigm is that work and play are antagonistic. Work is often seen one of two ways: as a "job" that earns money to pay bills or as a personally chosen "career" that grows and expands with responsibility, rewards, and satisfaction. Jobs are part time, with a limited time commitment (eight hours a day), while careers are full time, with an open-ended time commitment (working late and on weekends). You leave a job at 5 P.M.; a career requires more sacrifices in time, with the assumption that it will bring more money, advance-ment, and satisfaction. In short, a job will pay your rent; a career will finance buying a vacation home.

In contrast to work, which is a necessity, play is seen as a luxury, something to be "bought" if you can afford it. A popular saying puts it bluntly: "You got to pay to play." Moreover, *play* is not a word we are supposed to use to describe our behavior once we reach adulthood. Play is for children, carefree and without responsibility.

As adults, we might have a hobby, like photography or traveling, but we don't consider it play. Calling it play makes it sound silly or immature, and we are grown up. Adults work and have leisure-time activities—but only if they have earned them! Children play. It's that simple.

Well, yes and no. It's that simple if you're locked into a frame of reference that always operates in terms of opposites. Good or Bad. Man or Woman. Nongay or Gay. Work or Play. But if you're honest about the complexity of the world, such bipolar definitions and concepts break down.

We need a new paradigm about work and play: Work/Play, or a seamless life where work and play become merged and there is no distinction between the two. This new thinking doesn't equate work with disliking your job (but paying the bills) and doesn't equate play with a lost pleasure of childhood. This new thinking also doesn't mean relegating play to an activity requiring money beforehand (and therefore, not generating any). It doesn't see work and play in conflict, but as the same thing: both enrich our lives, though in different ways. Your whole life can be spent doing things you like to do, for some of which you get money! The guiding principle is not letting the outside world define your Work/Play, but looking inward to find out what gives you pleasure and satisfaction and the courage to pursue it.

Work/Play is really about lifestyle and not only about having enough play (enjoyment) to balance work (often seen as drudgery and/or money-making activities). It's a lifestyle in which pleasure and purpose are merged. What gay men at midlife need to think about is what they want for a lifestyle that would bring them the most happiness and how to accomplish that today—not to think it will magically happen when they have accumulated enough money or stopped working (later on, you'll see how our ideas about retirement are crucial to understanding Work/Play).

WORK: TRADEOFF OR TREADMILL?

Dan works as a clerk in his state's Department of Health, processing Medicare and Medicaid forms, insurance claims, and billing. The hours are regular, the salary is modest, the benefits are generous, and as a state employee for almost twenty years, he will have a decent pension. About ten years ago, when he was in his late thirties, he began to pursue a dream of becoming a painter. He had always loved art and museums, and he wanted to explore his creativity. He enrolled in a few art classes at a local community college and set up a space in his apartment as a studio. He began to paint after work and on weekends, slowly learning his craft and experimenting with subject matter, color, and style. He went to local art galleries and got to know the dealers and collectors. A few times a year, he would go to an art show in another state to see what the artists in his region were up to.

His plan was to begin showing his art around town at restaurants and cafés before approaching a dealer. Although he planned to retire at fifty-five with a pension that would cover his basic living expenses, he wanted to support himself with his painting eventually. The year he turned forty-eight, he approached a gallery that agreed to show his work. He also began traveling to the regional art shows, not just as an observer, but as a presenter, reserving space to show his paintings. He made an artist's card with contact information and began to gather names for a mailing list of his "fans" so he could send postcards whenever he had a new show.

During all this creative planning and effort, he never stopped showing up for his day job. He felt bored sometimes, but dealing with different people and sorting out their problems kept the job interesting. His job had always been a means to an end: initially, it allowed him material comforts like a car, an apartment, savings, and vacations with his lover. Later on, it became a way to afford art classes and painting supplies, canvases, frames, and travel to art shows. He knew he did a good job, a necessary job, and when he retired, he planned to be established enough as a painter to augment his pension. Now, with three years to go before retirement, he has a following in place for his artwork, his paintings sell at different galleries across the Midwest and fetch anywhere from $800 to $1,500. He is watching his dream come true and waits patiently until he can devote himself to his artwork full time.

A lawyer in a large firm, Scott is still waiting for his dream to find him. A typical work week for him consists of more than sixty hours, with some of that time spent in his home office. A few years ago, his lover and he bought and renovated a condominium in a prewar building in Chicago. He was proud that he could afford a mortgage, but he never got to enjoy the experience of working on their first home together. His lover was the one who handled the carpenters, the plumber, and the decorator, while Scott worked even longer hours to insure they had enough money to cover the cost of the work.

Scott looks forward to retirement because he hopes it will give him the time he needs to find out where his creativity lies. He's always loved pottery, and he's been wanting to take a class. But there's always something preventing him from pursuing it, whether it's a new case or a social commitment. When he's not working, he's usually too tired to do much of anything else. He hopes once he makes partner in the firm, his workload will decrease a bit, but he and his lover have been discussing a second home in the country, so it's unclear when he'll stop pushing himself to make more and more money.

Dan and Scott share some similarities: both have jobs that are a means to an end, both have creative impulses and dreams. But their essential attitudes toward work and play differ greatly. Dan makes less money, but has more time to pursue his art. Scott makes more money, but has no enjoyment. Both have made conscious decisions about how to earn their money and how to spend their time. Dan was able to tolerate the occasional boredom of his job by focusing on his painting, while Scott felt embattled at the office and exhausted at home. To some degree, both men approach their jobs as trade-offs.

Whether the trade-off is positive (Dan) or negative (Scott) depends on your attitude, whether you are able to think creatively about how you want to live. In the new paradigm of Work/Play, we reverse the usual thinking: Decide what you want the money for, then work to earn it—don't work to earn money and then decide what to do with it. Decide what you want your life to look like (your lifestyle), then create it. No matter its shape or characteristics, your lifestyle is about choice and proactivity. It is something that has to be "worked" at and "played" at simultaneously.

THE TRUE GAY LIFESTYLE

When anti-gay forces describe homosexuality as a "lifestyle" that's chosen, the popular response in the gay community has been, "It's a life, not a lifestyle." True, but what nongay people and the media are picking up on has some basis in reality. We *do* have a lifestyle. From their perspective, they see an identifiable lifestyle in which all gay people are white and middle-class, all gay people are men, and all gay people have more money than the average American. But most of us think, "Who's got that money? Not me!" What the nongay world calls our "lifestyle" is distorted, but they're not the only ones distorting it.

Writers like Sarah Schulman and Michael Bronski have written eloquently about the "gay market" and the myths we perpetuate about gay men and money. In truth, the figures about gay men having higher amounts of disposable income are part of a strategy of predominantly gay marketing executives and entrepreneurs to persuade the nongay world to invest ("share") their advertising dollars with our community. Other economic studies have shown that gay men actually make less than nongay men, and lesbians make even less since they are already undercompensated as women. Also, the images of the "gay lifestyle" in our media distort many gay men's sense of economic security and reinforce their sense of being have-nots or outsiders, deprived from the huge economic advantages other gay men supposedly enjoy.

1. **In what ways do you feel you are more or less successful than other gay men your age?**

Do you fit the image of a gay man with a large amount of disposable income? Or do you barely make ends meet each month? Are you able to save any money after you cover your living expenses? Do you economize in order to treat yourself well at other times, say, with a vacation or a down payment on a home? Do you feel that you make an amount of money similar to your friends? Do you socialize with men of the same class or profession? Do you feel as if you need to keep up with the gay Joneses?

It's no news that gay men judge one another; after appearance, how much money you earn or spend is a prime target for gossip and criticism. When looking at your history of employment, it's easy to fall into the trap of comparing yourself only negatively to other gay men. Be honest, but don't count yourself short.

While there are economic forces that affect each of us, most likely there have been moments when you made a critical decision about a job or a field of work. Again, since work is so essential to a man's self-definition, we often link our self-esteem to what we do. For many gay men, this link may be especially strong since other factors like homophobia weaken our self-esteem. Faced with the cultural message that to be gay is wrong, many of us find salvation in our work. We hope to avoid discrimination for being gay by being a success at work, thinking, "If I'm the best salesman (or welder or teacher, etc.), they can't fire me if they find out later I'm also gay." Although mainstream culture often paints gay men as adolescents, carefree and decadent in our pursuit of pleasure, the reality is that many more of us are overachievers, the good, steady workers who can always be depended upon to put in extra hours.

Or, possibly, a gay man may have chosen another route, a low-profile job that allows him the most privacy for his personal life. Hoping to fly under the radar screen of homophobia, he does a good job, with little interaction with his coworkers. He has consciously decided not to pursue a career in which his private life may be exposed, and he keeps his professional life separate from his personal life. Success in either arena is not related to success in the other.

In evaluating your work history, be realistic about your achievements, not just your regrets. How do you feel about your work, not only your chosen occupation, but also your level of success? Have you reached the career goals you intended to? Has your occupation undergone unexpected changes? When looking at one's history, it's always tempting to dwell on our missteps along the way (want ads we could have answered, interviews we could have prepared for better, underearning in a rut of a job), but there are probably just as many moments of good decisions, preparation, and dedication in that history. We have to remember them, and we have to take pride in them. Taking responsibility for one's work history is a good place to begin to recognize your strengths and to see where change is needed and possible. You might be surprised to find that as a gay man, you have had some distinct advantages over nongay men.

THE GAY ADVANTAGE AT WORK

In the context of Work/Play and our ideas around time and money, gay men tend to be better off than nongay men. We have incredible potential to create a lifestyle in which work and play are merged and in which time and money are harmonious, rather than in conflict. In addition, because of AIDS, gay men have an advantage over nongay men in reevaluating patterns of work and play. With disability and loss of income looming as real possibilities in our lives, we have probably learned earlier than midlife where work and play fall in our priorities. A diagnosis of HIV positive or AIDS changes many gay men's worldview, and we begin to pay attention to how we are living when we have to contemplate how long we might live. With the advent of AIDS, gay men have generally become more focused on how good we can make each day rather than how many good days we have.

Work is an area where significant differences between gay men and nongay men emerge, and in *Gay Money*, Per Larson has written about the "gay balance sheet," in which the economic assets and liabilities of being gay are compared. Among the assets he lists:

1. High discretionary income, early in life;
2. Entrepreneurial characteristics, with few children to compete with career;
3. Networking, offering access to all levels of society;
4. Mobility, adaptability, and portability, all of which the nineties economy seems to require.

Among the liabilities, he cites:

1. Illegality (in the form of sodomy laws);
2. Marriage barriers (religious beliefs aside, we are prevented from enjoying the legal and financial benefits of marriage);
3. Discrimination (only nine states have some form of legislation protecting us from job discrimination: Wisconsin, Massachusetts, Hawaii, New Jersey, Connecticut, Vermont, California, Minnesota, Rhode Island);
4. Violence (verbal abuse, physical assaults, and sexual harassment).

Larson's analysis is generally excellent, although he occasionally falls into the trap Schulman describes in overestimating our disposable income.

Since most of us are typically responsible only for our own fiscal well-being, without the additional expense of children, we have more leisure time. Also, many gay men have moved away from home and their biological families and may have fewer family obligations. As adult gay men, our obligations are more by choice (whether it's work or relationships or activism), rather than family pressure.

If we are part of a couple, the double incomes are an advantage. But Larson clarifies that this "high discretionary income" appears largely during our twenties and thirties, when we are less likely to save it. After we reach midlife, much of the disposable income gay marketers hype and profit from vanishes, usually into mortgages and retirement plans.

The asset that Larson describes as "entrepreneurial characteristics" is particularly important in challenging the current paradigm of work and play. As I see it, psychologically we are mold breakers. We have gone against society by coming out, so we're freer to move toward what we want, whether in our relationships or jobs or play. By coming out as gay men, we have shown ourselves that other people's expectations don't rule us as much as they once did. We took risks to come out, both personal and professional, and we have probably left home in order to be ourselves, so we can see alternative paths. Larson suggests that this willingness to take risks generates a financial flexibility that allows many gay men to start their own businesses; this entrepreneurial energy invigorates our community.

While some gay men may not pursue a particular career because of homophobia (both projected and real in the form of a lavender ceiling), many gay men do challenge the stereotypes of what constitutes "acceptable" or "gender appropriate" work. We are teachers, electricians, police officers, doctors, carpenters, politicians, nurses, welders, athletes, union organizers, firemen (we don't just dress up like them on the weekends!).

If we just did what we wanted (what gives us pleasure, purpose, and satisfaction), without questioning whether or not it's appropriate work, imagine how many gay carpenters or stock brokers or bakers or French teachers we'd have? How many of our artists, writers, or painters have been told by their families to get "real" jobs? How many of us sought jobs in the public sector because our families taught us that to work for the government was safe and stable? How many of us have remained "good little boys" and become the teacher or businessman or postal worker or doctor or lawyer or architect our parents wanted us to be, only to realize it's not what *we* want? Too often, we don't even ask ourselves what we want. That is, until midlife.

Once we're able to wade through our own myths surrounding the gay lifestyle, we will learn to appreciate our lives more. A goal at midlife is to be conscious of your lifestyle and make it more uniquely yours. When I meet someone new, I don't ask him how old he is or what he does for a living. I want to know what he does for fun, what his lifestyle is like. I want to know what gay men are passionate about, whether it's politics or sex, food or painting. Learning how a gay man enjoys himself tells me much more than how he makes a living. How many of us really think of our jobs and careers as "living"?

A lot of my work has been about helping middle-aged gay men move into lifestyles they really want, some of which often require a change in career. A career change at midlife has become one of the clichés of the so-called midlife crisis. But changing careers and creating a new lifestyle at midlife is not a crisis in the sense that something is wrong with the person or he's trying to avoid the aging process—it's much more often a healthy recognition of who he is now and what he wants.

The need to make career decisions in our late teens and early twenties prevents many of us from finding out what we truly want to do with our lives. We are forced into making decisions too soon, and then are expected to stick with that decision no matter what. But the world no longer exists in which staying at the same job for twenty-five or thirty years is a virtue. People are expected to change jobs every five years. As Larson has noted, the most valuable work skills in today's economy are flexibility and mobility, qualities gay men tend to have in abundance.

The midlife crisis is basically about redoing decisions that were made when we didn't know enough about the world or ourselves to choose what we wanted our lives to be. Instead, we followed societal and parental expectations and hoped that our lives would turn out right. Some of those decisions turned out all right, while some of them did not. The so-called crisis occurs when somebody actually says, as an adult, "This is what I now want." I'm not talking about the free-floating, impulsive desire of a child to grab after anything shiny that catches his eye, but the decision of a grown man to decide for himself what he wants to be doing with his life, with his relationships, with his energy and imagination and passion.

So many of the gay men I meet seem to be putting off their happiness until later in life. Or they feel they had their happiness when they were younger, and now they're getting older and it's no longer about fun. Stuck in past or future thinking, they seem unable to enjoy their lives *today*.

Few of us are taught to think about today. During our school years, the emphasis is on the future, who we will become, what we will do with our lives. But when we get to be older, the focus switches and we endure the present by distracting ourselves with nostalgia and/or worries about old age. So we may be locked into jobs we don't like or committed to careers we love but which exhaust us. We aren't always able to make a dramatic shift into another career, but often the attitudinal changes are the more important shifts—moving from negative feelings around our work patterns (feeling trapped in a job, not making enough money, no sense of security for the future, etc.) to learning to play more, recognizing other priorities in our lives rather than the simple myth that equates money and time. More money does not always bring more time, in fact, usually just the opposite.

Redefining success on our own terms is a crucial component of aging well. But it takes time to figure out what we want to do, and sometimes, we know more about what we *don't* want, than what we do want.

2.   In what ways has your definition of success changed over time?

Success is not static. And our definition of it changes over the course of a lifetime. When we're children, we think success is being able to stay up to watch television. In high school, success may mean getting a car or becoming a National Merit semifinalist or being elected to student government. Obviously, as we move out to be on our own and begin working, success can mean having a first apartment, a first or new car, or the newest model computer available.

As we age, many of us begin to expand our definition of success to mean more than material goods. Success can be a friendship that's lasted ten years or still being friends with a boyfriend after you've broken up. Success can be a sense of giving back to the community by contributing your time to an organization or cause, or pampering yourself after years of devoted activism. Success can be going back to college to study a language or literature you once loved. Success can be starting a men's group to discuss politics and issues relevant to your life. Only you can define success for yourself.

Ben came from an educated, moneyed, and sophisticated family in Detroit. His mother was a schoolteacher, and later principal, while his father was a highly successful business executive. Ben was a college graduate and had an excellent training in music and literature. When Ben moved to New York, he joined the NYC Gay Men's Chorus, where he met my lover Jim. They became best friends, and it became a joke since Ben was Black and Jim's last name was Black, so they became known as the Black Twins.

For over twenty years, Ben has worked at the Strand Book Store, one of the premier bookstores in New York for old, used, and hard-to-find books. Ben is revered by his clients, many of whom will only work with him. Everyone turns to Ben to answer questions, and he is often brought in to appraise an estate's collection of books. He clearly loves working there though he has gotten a lot of flack from friends for his "underachievement." To some observers, he is a very intelligent, highly educated, and sophisticated man who has "wasted" his education because he is just a book-clerk who does not make a lot of money. He is quite happy at his job, where he is given much respect for his knowledge, and has developed intense, personal relationships with his clients (even to the point that he was remembered in the will of one).

By Ben's standards, however, he is not underachieving; he is doing what he loves doing—using his intelligence, education, and personality to work at a job that gives him personal and intellectual satisfaction. He did not let others' expectations guide him into making career decisions that were antithetical to his nature. He is not caught up in the New York rat race—and he is exercising his musical training and interests by singing in both the NYC Gay Men's Chorus as well as its smaller chamber group. He has created a lifestyle that meets his needs—though he would like to have more available cash, he feels that this is a small sacrifice to pay for having a life in which he is content.

Just as your ideas about success have probably evolved as you've aged, what you think of today as success may not be the same five years from now and certainly not in ten years. How do you measure success today? When you start to list your priorities, the characteristics of your life that define "success," where does work emerge? Where does the fun begin?

3. Does play have a strong priority in your life?

Play is an activity as well as a state of mind. To me, it is an activity that recharges my batteries in some way. Play is not necessarily the opposite of work. Making a piece of art, baking a pie, doing yoga, composing a poem, taking a memorable hike in the woods, listening to music, exercising, pulling off a stunning drag performance, or engaging in an afternoon of hot sex. Dancing, scuba diving, travel, and activism are all forms of play that I enjoy. In these activities, I am engaged with my body, with my imagination, and with my sense of joy in living, while satisfying my need to feel productive as a citizen of the world. Although it may entail some hard work, my activism is really a form of play, recharging my batteries by making me feel connected to other gay men and the gay community.

Believe it or not, work can also be about recharging your battery. Remember: work is not solely what you get paid for, while play is not solely what you don't get paid for. Also, one man's work could be another man's play. In fact, some forms of play (cooking an exquisite meal, competing in a triathlon, traveling in a foreign country) can require a lot of work and effort, time, and planning. Indeed, writing this book was a form of play, fulfilling a desire for a more active discussion of aging within my community, bringing me a new relationship with my co-author.

I once met a man at a cocktail party whose calendar was the busiest I've ever seen: not just a forty-five-hour work week as an accountant, but brunches, a book group, museum visits, the gym four times a week, volunteering for two organizations, a boyfriend, and on and on. When I asked him when he had fun, he looked at me like I was speaking another language. "Well," he answered somewhat sheepishly, "sometimes it's all fun, but sometimes I feel like none of it's fun. I don't have any time for myself because I'm running around all the time." As we spoke further, I found out he wanted to be a writer. He loved reading and talking about books, and had been an English major in college, as well as a math major. "Math was practical. I loved problem solving, and I knew I could use those skills to make a reasonable living." Instead of trying to write the Great American Novel, he filled up his spare time with social events—which don't pay the bills either, by the way—and kept his dream up on a shelf.

Only you can define what play means to you and how you will pursue it. You can have fun alone or in a group, but you may feel too burdened by work to put much energy into playing. In reviewing how and when you play, you might also find yourself becoming resentful of other gay men who seem to be having more fun than you do. All those men on the Circuit, marching in the Pride parade, going dancing every weekend, eating dinner out all the time, traveling to exotic places—these are the kind of images that perpetuate the stereotype of gay men as carefree, rich, and privileged. Yet very few gay men lead the life our advertising and magazines portray.

Try not to hold on to the resentment, but start to consider how you spend your time when you're not working. How do your friends spend their time? What pleases and relaxes you—regardless of what other people around you might like to do. Do you like scary movies? Science fiction thrillers? Do you enjoy running? Getting up early and doing laundry? Each person has to come up with his own definition of play; there really is no universalizing about this or work, for that matter. Most likely, there are activities you enjoy doing alone and those you enjoy doing with your friends. What's most important is that you have fun in your life. Having a sense of play and pursuing fun create a good feeling about your life (dare I call it "happiness"?). As I've mentioned, if you're satisfied with your life, you'll have an easier time with aging.

Play is another arena in which many gay men have an advantage over nongay men. Generally, gay men know how to have more fun than their nongay peers. We tend to do it more regularly—not just Halloween or the company picnic or holiday party. Play is more a part of our lives, and we value our sense of play. From the camp of drag to the public celebration of June Pride marches, we tell the nongay world: we have different rules on how to live and your rules don't fit us. Our ability to socialize with peers and create strong friendship networks allows us to create a space of more freedom and less judgment, a space that exposes the phony rigid blankness of the mainstream.

Part of our reality is our lower economic stake (we usually earn less, but we don't need as much either), but also, because of the difference of our Gay Age and Clock Age, we can explore the impulses of adolescence but with the economics of being an older, working adult. Having survived coming out, gay men also display a willingness to play and rebel against "age-appropriate" or "gender-appropriate" forms of play. Obviously, drag falls into this category, but also many gay men's involvement in the theater, dancing, singing, events planning, nursing, teaching, and so on. Usually, nongay men need a specific structure or occasion to cross a gender line, like dressing up for Halloween or an Elk's Club skit. They have to have external permission in order to let themselves play, in order to do what gay men do for and by themselves. For many gay men, drag means playing a part, with certain drag for certain situations (a business suit as "corporate drag"), and for some gay men, all clothes come to represent a form of drag.

Sex, of course, can be a form of play as well. Many nongay men (and the nongay culture at large) believe that gay men have more fun than they do simply because they assume that we have more sex than they do. The evidence is only anecdotal, but the sixties and Stonewall did liberate gay men to approach sex as a liberating and valid form of play. The sexual liberation of the seventies was meant to liberate everybody, gay and nongay alike, resulting in swinger's clubs, the "Playboy lifestyle," lesbian sex shops, nongay s/m clubs, and the greatest seventies invention for sex: the hot tub! Thirty years after Stonewall, some gay men may take the freedom to have as much sex as we want for granted, but it is one of the ways they can play differently from nongay men.

By looking at how your nongay peers play (or don't play), you are most likely going to get a glimmer of the different resources available to you for play. By stretching your definitions of work and play to see how, where, and when you play, you can begin to see some more advantages of being gay—a further step in the development of a positive gay identity.

Learning to play requires learning to accept what gives you pleasure. This acceptance is dependent upon your sense of entitlement, which may be fragile for a gay man. Once you can accept that you are entitled to pleasure, fun, and a good life, you can begin to take advantage of the many social outlets in the community. Play becomes pleasurable involvement in an activity of your choice, and you become more comfortable having a good time.

4. **In what ways is pleasure (having fun) a factor in your career decisions?**

This may be the first time you have truly considered fun and pleasure in the same breath as work. If so, this is the beginning of rethinking the relationship between work and play. If you have already taken "play" into account in your "work" decisions, and their interrelationship has become clear to you, you probably enjoy work more if it's more like your play. Maybe you decided to take a job in a field you've always loved, even though your family pushed you in another direction. Or maybe you took a lower-paying job in order to have more time to spend with your lover. Making a career decision based on a hunch about the work conditions or the nature of the work or how we would feel at the end of the day is practical and fair. Having fun is a legitimate category when looking at the benefits of a career decision.

Career decisions are multifaceted, and the impact they will have on our relationships is usually an important factor. This is another area in which gay men may have an advantage over nongay men, who may not consult their family in making a major career change. Many nongay men put work first, believing that more earning power will be better for the family in the long run, but such an attitude can underestimate the disruptions that can occur if the family has to move or accept less involvement from him.

In contrast, if a gay man considers his lover's needs or asks his lover's opinion about a possible job change, he is acknowledging the value of that relationship, as well as his understanding that work is not everything. Even friendships can influence a career decision, if the gay man values having his friends enough not to spend less time with them. At midlife, many gay men extend the boundaries on factors that can influence their career decisions, especially if they have made relationships a priority in their lives.

5. **How important a factor is your significant other and/or friends in making career decisions?**

Do you think of your friends or lover when faced with a decision to take on a big project at work? Do you see the way your work life is structured as allowing you to spend more time with your friends or lover, or does work take you away from your social life? Is there a balance? Do you think of your friends or lover when contemplating a transfer at work or going back to school to retrain for a new career? How do you weigh all the different factors in making a decision about work?

In a 1995 study, psychological researchers Kimmel and Sang found that many middle-aged gay men do not reach for higher-level jobs for personal reasons. This is not because of a "glass ceiling" but owing to a different balance between career and personal relationships, in which emotional satisfaction and love relations are a significant part of a career decision. This is especially apparent if both men in a relationship are career oriented. Two friends of mine from Chicago, Bob and Philip, are both professionals but in different fields. Ten years ago, Bob was offered a huge promotion and position in New York City. After discussing it together, they agreed to make the move from Chicago, and they agreed that if Philip's career took off, it would be his "turn." Four years later, Philip was offered a position with a big company in Maine. Again they discussed their situation, and they moved to Maine, although Bob commuted twice a week to New York to maintain his position. Ultimately, after more company changes, they ended up with satisfying jobs in the same city.

Like many gay men, I have always been a worker bee, getting my first job when I was eleven. At eighteen, I left home to begin a gay lifestyle (this was in 1954!) and have supported myself ever since. I put myself through school with part-time jobs, scholarships, and fellowships. Since all the men on my mother's side of the family were physicians, I felt I had to be a Professional, with a capital *P*. I had internalized my family's expectations and priorities to the point that I wouldn't have been able to consider myself a person if I didn't have a medical degree. (My first toy at age four was a play doctor's kit!) It didn't matter what kind of physician. It was all about status and prestige. When I later decided to go for a Ph.D. rather than an

M.D., it was a real shift away from my family's idea of "success." So I did become a doctor, but in my own way.

But it was when I was fired that I really began to transform my approach to work. I had been serving as director of the day hospital program at a community health clinic in Brooklyn, and antagonized my department head because I did not follow administrative procedure, nor did I see myself as the traditional authority figure. I treated the staff as egalitarianly as possible, partly because of my own internalized homophobia (who was I to lead?), partly because I was trying to be a different kind of authority figure. After a series of miscommunications (I had planned an event in another building and didn't inform him) and administrative disagreements (I made a clinical decision he disagreed with), I was let go.

Prior to being fired when I was in my early forties, I had reached a pinnacle of success for a psychologist in community mental health, and since there were not many jobs available, several friends urged me to start a private practice. For years, I had been politically against the idea of a private practice—I always felt that mental health was best served through community programs available to everyone. When I was still in graduate school, my fantasy had been someday to work for the United Nations in community health projects around the world. I've always been fascinated by how every culture defines its own concept of mental health, and my goal upon graduation was to go to New York to get training in community mental health, and ultimately, to get a position with the United Nations. I wanted to use my skills to help develop programs around the world using indigenous concepts of mental health.

Getting fired motivated me to think about going back to school, getting a master's in public health and start pursuing my United Nations dream. While I was applying to graduate school, I went from my full-time position in a public facility to a full-time private practice in a little over four months (my community activism had immediately brought me many referrals). My practice was a stop-gap until I went back to school. However, when I was accepted into graduate school, I faced a decision. I loved the private practice and the time and freedom it granted and so felt torn about giving it up. I decided to do it for another year. I deferred my enrollment, and a weight immediately lifted from my shoulders. I felt free in a way I never had before.

A few years later, I was working mostly with gay men, when I made a connection between what I was doing and my former goal of working with the United Nations. I was using my skills in mental health with an indigenous community using their ideas of mental well-being—but it was my own community! In the sixties, when I was in graduate school, there was no liberation movement, no identifiable gay community to speak of, so how could I envision what I would end up doing? My private practice allowed my fantasy to become reality, but in a form I didn't know was possible when I set my career goals.

Other gay men have experienced this as well: we often can't predict the details of how our lives will turn out, but the substance of that life, the overall picture of our lives (again, our lifestyle) is very much within our means. I felt exhilarated by my discovery, and I worked to create a practice that allowed me the lifestyle I wanted. In addition, conversations with my friends helped me to continue to shape my lifestyle and to learn the value of Work/Play.

One of my best friends, Sam, is a video artist, painter, and writer who still doesn't know how he is going to pay the next month's rent. He's fifty-two now, but he's been "retired" (by most people's standards) since he was twenty-seven. By the age of twenty-six, he was living in Australia, had bought a house and had a tenured teaching position, which he gave up when he realized his life would be set, now and forever. Not wanting to be in a rut the rest of his life, he sold the house and began traveling. He hasn't held a steady job since then, but has always found teaching positions and curating work and continues to flourish and make art in Australia, where he now lives.

Once when we talked, he remarked how no one he knows in New York has the time to enjoy life, although their salaries could give them a good life. Always anxious over time, every New Yorker seems to lead a life of stress and heartache. I replied, "I don't know how you live like you do. I would be so anxious about money all the time, where the next rent check would come from, I just couldn't do it." He responded, "I do have anxiety about the rent check, but I don't have anxiety about having enough time to do my art. My time is my own. I decided I wanted control over how I spend my time, so I let my anxiety be about money, not my art."

That conversation brought about the beginning of a perceptional shift for me. I realized that my anxiety was a choice—the result of

my priorities. I could choose which kind of anxiety I wanted—it's
not automatic that having a job or making money to pay the rent is
a top priority. Having time to do what one wants can be a priority,
too, above job and money!

My attitude toward work continued to shift as I thought of my
longtime friend, Jacques, a designer (now deceased). He never held
a full-time job, but had simultaneous projects—sometimes only last-
ing a couple of months, maybe a year—that earned him money. .
When I told him once that he had been a role model for me, he
was genuinely surprised, since he was only a high school graduate
and lived modestly in a fifth-floor walk-up. I had known him since I
was seventeen, when I was working as a parking lot attendant. Our
friendship stayed strong as I moved on to college and a career. He
was always a role model for me because he loved his life and did what
he wanted. He always had enough and even managed to save money.

What these conversations with Sam and Jacques helped to con-
vince me of was *when you make play a priority in your life, you become
psychologically freer to earn money at what you enjoy.* Earning money is no
longer what distinguishes work from play. At midlife, the distinction
lies in whose rules are being followed: one's own or others. It's the
point at which many gay men begin to follow their own rules in
terms of work and play. This independent attitude is really an extension of how we broke the "rules" when we came out. At midlife, we
realize we can continue to break these constrictive social conventions
around work and play. Perhaps the most difficult obstacle to merging
work and play is the myth of retirement.

RETIREMENT: MYTH OR LIFESTYLE?

Like Work/Play, retirement is about one's lifestyle, not the end of
employment. It is about having control over one's time and a feeling
that one is doing what one wants. Even if we do not make much
money or have savings enough to think of quitting work, we can
think about retirement in a new way—as a lifestyle we can create in
the present, no matter what our age or financial position.

Retirement? Why should a thirty-five-year-old care about retirement? I can hear the cries of anguish: *I'm only forty-five, I'm nowhere
close to retiring, How could I retire so young? I don't have enough money to*

retire yet! We need to begin to think about our retirement in our thirties and forties since the financial reality of today is that few people will have saved in the same way or as much as their parents and grandparents did. Most of us will need to work longer (which is legal now that there's no longer mandatory retirement) before we retire.

Culturally, retirement has meant that your productive life is all over, and you're coasting to death—but you can't coast for twenty years! Another cultural notion around retirement is that you retire "from" a profession, the "end" of your career, rather than that you retire "to" a lifestyle or "into" a new phase of life. Instead of thinking of retirement as an "ending," imagine it as a "beginning" of a new lifestyle.

Another myth of retirement is that we will finally have all the time we want to do the things we like: play golf or tennis, read, travel, sing, garden, go to flea markets, and so on. Retirement is the time for "fun," for all the things we would do if only we had more time, if only we didn't have to work so hard. Another myth is that retirement is only for the middle class, or for those who've been able to afford financial planning. Also, many gay men think retirement is what nongays do, along with children, college tuition, and station wagons. But what are we as gay men working toward?

The whole notion of retirement reflects our history of Puritanism: if we work hard enough, we will earn our rest and pleasure. If we don't work hard or long enough, these things will be denied us. This Puritan work ethic echoes the promise in Christianity: If we work hard not to sin, we will reach "heaven" in retirement. Retirement can also be examined from a class perspective, as an incentive that the owners and those in power use to keep people at jobs that they do not like. Instead of the moral work ethic of Puritanism, capitalism produces a "worker mentality," which rewards people for staying in a job (no matter how miserable) as a safe haven. It is a not-so-subtle way to keep people locked into unrewarding and unfulfilling jobs without thinking that anything is wrong. But the economics of the nineties have made every job vulnerable to elimination and downsizing.

In short, this deferment of pleasure until retirement represents a cultural/political brainwashing. Without preparation and without adequate money, people are supposed to magically know how to enjoy their lives once they have stopped working. The fantasy is that, as if by intuition, we will have a full social life, friendships, and activities upon retirement. Current thinking about retirement places work before play. This traditional concept of retirement is a huge scam about delaying pleasure for the future, based on the old paradigm of work and play as antagonistic. With the new paradigm of Work/Play, we can begin to create a new reality, so that retirement becomes a way of life open to everyone, a lifestyle in which pleasure and purpose are merged, ensuring more life satisfaction, and hence, better aging.

6. **Is retirement the only time when you see yourself having fun in life?**

Are you waiting until retirement to learn how to play the piano? To take tap-dancing lessons? To remodel the house? To travel to Paris? To hike the Natchez Trail?

Do you feel trapped by your work? Do you have much sense of joy or purpose in your life? At midlife, you may be becoming aware of changes you need to make in the arenas of work and play. Maybe you're working too hard, or maybe you're playing too hard, but if you aren't enjoying your life, something needs to change. Waiting for retirement only postpones the decisions you may need to make. If you wait until retirement to decide how to have fun, it may be too late.

This is a huge problem for men, especially nongay men, who often haven't developed much of a friendship network, an emotional support system, or hobbies. Usually, their wives have been the ones to manage their social life and supply the emotional component to their lives. Their work imposed a time structure, so they may never have learned to handle their own schedule. For such men, retirement can represent a sudden and shocking absence of all the structures and rewards they got from working. Since most men are conditioned to define themselves by their work, not having a job can also mean a loss of meaning and status in their lives. As a result, their health suffers from the feeling that their life has less meaning.

There is an actual syndrome called early retirement death (ERD), in which "early death overtakes men who were otherwise healthy before they retired." It is in the first year of retirement that most heart attacks take place. Cancer rates also soar, and unhealthy habits can emerge as well. If a retiree survives the first year, there is a good chance he/she will live a normal life span. More and more people are beginning to realize that retirement too often translates into inactivity and a meaningless lifestyle that is destructive to their health.

A 1998 survey for the American Association of Retired Persons (AARP) found that 80 percent of the baby boomers, ages thirty-three to fifty-two, planned "to continue working during retirement, whether for fun or out of a feeling of necessity or both . . . Today's new breed of retirees never really retires—and the choice to remain active is out of passion, more than the need to pay the bills." In the *New York Times*, an outplacement executive in Chicago observed that the work practices of the nineties has "allowed many people to achieve a balance in their lives that is so much more healthy and beneficial spiritually and emotionally and physically than just hitting the wall of a certain age and going from being a hard-working, very involved worker to not doing anything, which was just devastating to many people." A sixty-hour-a-week lawyer turned thirty-hour-a-week lawyer, John C. Wheeler of New Mexico added, "I'm more than ever convinced that the people who only relax and do not engage the mind start losing it."

So instead of retirement being heaven, it can be hell if we don't know what to do with ourselves or if we think we don't have any reason to live if we're not producing something for the good of the economy. But what about our own well-being? Our own pleasure? It's easy for gay men to discount such goals because (1) we're not paid for them and (2) we rarely feel entitled to them. But the truth is that we do deserve well-being, safety, and pleasure—throughout our entire lives, not just when we retire.

When I was fifty, I realized that I would never have enough money to retire. Since I didn't have any money saved, I realized I was going to have to work basically forever, with no retirement (at least in the traditional sense). If I were going to do that, I decided that I wanted my working life to look and feel like I was retired. For me, this meant that I would be doing what I wanted to do and truly enjoyed in terms of both work (being a therapist) and play (activism, social events, cultural events, and vacations).

Once I decided to live as if I were retired, even while I continued to work, I had to reexamine how I had set up my private practice, the rules and procedures I followed with my clients. I remembered that as a student, I had made money as an interviewer in a research study of mental health professionals. I interviewed over fifty mental health professionals across the country, asking them about their occupation, personal life, satisfaction with career choice, work habits, and so forth. Besides earning some money, the project was a way of learning about the field I was entering. I discovered a distinct group who, I thought, were the happiest with their lives. They were the ones who limited the amount of time spent working, who had an emotional life separate from their involvement with their patients, and who didn't violate their ethical or political beliefs. They also usually had some community involvement. I decided to model my life after them, to use their experience and not try to reinvent the wheel.

My relationships and activism had met most of these guidelines, but I needed to look at the amount of time I spent working. Since making money was not the main criterion of my life (I also valued my emotional life, my social events, my activism), I decided I would limit the amount of time I spent in being a therapist. So I set a limit on how many hours and how many days a week I would work. Since I limited my hours, I constantly had to make referrals, which shocked other therapists. How could I turn down new clients? Didn't I need the money? Not really. I always had enough money for what I needed, not necessarily for what I wanted, but definitely for what I needed. The important thing was that I was making enough for a lifestyle I enjoyed.

What mattered most about my lifestyle was its flexibility, which emerged only when I began to build it consciously into my profession. When I began therapy with a new client, I gave him/her the option of having an appointment at the same time each week, or we could have a floating appointment that remained flexible to his schedule. This allowed clients who had to travel for work or had sudden changes in their schedules to maintain their therapy. If a client had to cancel an appointment, he could make it up within the week at a time we were both available. About two-thirds of my clients chose the flexible schedule, and I discovered that in giving my clients a choice, I gave myself flexibility as well. It was a bonus, not a goal. I got flexibility because I gave them flexibility.

I had wanted to be flexible for my clients for several reasons. If someone called them with last-minute tickets to a concert or sports event, I wanted them to be able to call me and reschedule. Those things would add to their lives, and why should they miss them because of therapy? I didn't want them to think therapy was the center of the universe. Getting out there and living is the priority, not keeping a rigid appointment with me. Now, if the client was saying, "I just didn't feel like coming," that was different. Laziness was not acceptable.

I began taking vacations more often throughout the year and built enough flexibility into my schedule so that I could take sporadic and sometimes spontaneous vacations (and not just in August, when most therapists go away). Other therapists couldn't understand how I could take so much time off and not negatively affect my clients. But my clients could handle it because my appointment schedule was never rigid to begin with. They didn't feel abandoned if they didn't see me one week, because, usually, there were weeks in the past when they had chosen to reschedule seeing me.

Overhauling my private practice to reflect the lifestyle I wanted took some time, and I had decided that I wanted to have all this in place by the time I was fifty-five. I gave myself time to make the appropriate changes in my work patterns, and things fell into place. But I had to know what I wanted first before I could take the steps to make it happen, and the biggest change in my lifestyle—the flexibility of my Work/Play—was not something I had planned to happen.

7. How can you now live as if you were retired?

Are you satisfied with how much you work? What do you want your retirement to become? Do you want to stop deferring your retirement? Do you do what you enjoy doing, no matter if it's work or play?

You may not even have thought of retirement and what it could be like. But retirement is a concept you can apply to your current work and leisure patterns. Instead of deferring the "play" of retirement, the goal is to integrate it into the "work" of today. Remember: a lifestyle is not just for the "rich and famous." Work/Play is an approach available to everyone, and it involves thinking, making decisions, and taking charge of one's life. It is not about the accumulation of money but the accumulation of time. It also involves quality of life over quantity of life, and assessing your priorities: how much time do you want to spend working, how much money do you need for the lifestyle you want, what kinds of play do you enjoy, what is the right mix for you?

The perpetual illusion is that an abundance of money and time make the biggest difference in having a good life, but it is not true, *unless there are internal changes.* Of course, having sufficient money helps greatly, but it does not make the difference. The best example is what happens to lottery winners or inheritors of sudden wealth who spend it all and are soon back where they started. Other people may retire wealthy, but have no idea how to spend the time that they've worked all their lives for or how to enjoy themselves.

Understanding the relationship between time and money is essential in figuring out our Work/Play patterns. For both, we often use the same language: we save time and money, we spend time and money, we manage time and money. Money is always limited in the ways time is limited. They are both abstract concepts made concrete, a commodity to be traded. There's always a sense that there is never enough of either one, although we often think we can buy more time with more money. But making more money usually means having less time to enjoy the money. Money can give you more freedom in organizing your time (hiring someone to do things for you), but both are limited commodities.

What I started seeing in my clients' lives was that people who don't manage time well don't usually manage their money well either. People who are late consistently are usually the ones who have to borrow money or run up credit card bills. Living with a sense of "I don't have enough money and/or time" can lead to feelings of deprivation and dissatisfaction with life. As we are learning, not being satisfied with one's life makes aging more difficult.

Aging well depends on how we use time and money. At midlife, when we start to realize that we have a limited amount of time left (hopefully, years and years, but it's still limited), a real sense emerges that "I've got to learn to control and appreciate my time better." I've often told people that career changes happen when we realize we're going to die. Once they become aware of their own mortality, people begin to ask themselves, "If there's a limit to my time left, why am I spending my time doing something I don't like or hate or working for someone who doesn't respect me?"

My thoughts about time and money were essential to my process

of merging Work/Play and creating a lifestyle that offered the pleasures of retirement. Making a decision to have less money and more
time reflected my faith that the universe would provide whatever I
needed. When I became disabled at age fifty-six, I saw that the
disability insurance was now the conduit by which the universe would
provide for me. Once I had recovered from the hospitalizations, my
lifestyle did not look too much different from what it had before. I
had to spend more time on health care and getting plenty of sleep.
I continued consulting some clients for free, taking vacations, stayed
involved in community activism, started writing again, saw friends,
subscribed to theater and opera, and started dating again. The change
was in priorities—I spent less time with clients and activism, but
more time with social and cultural events.

Several of my friends share their dismay with me about my
lifestyle: How can I do what I do with so little money? I am flexible,
I plan ahead, I budget. I have more time than I do money, and I am
very conscious of how I spend both of them, especially when it
comes to my health. Having a private practice is a huge effort in
time and energy, and if I had tried to maintain a private practice, I
doubt my health would be as strong. In chapter 2, I introduced the
concept of choosing health, and my decision to stay on disability
was a direct result of my choosing to be healthy.

8. How would you choose to spend your time differently?

In talking about how you want to spend your time, you might
begin to identify blocked or stagnant areas that need to be changed.
Maybe you're working too much; maybe your schedule is too rigid
(a treadmill of work, volunteer commitments, gym, brunches, and so
on), with no time for yourself. This exercise gets at the heart of any
major lifestyle rethinking. By identifying where you would like to be
more flexible, you are pointing to those areas that, at a deeper level,
you know you are capable of changing. Flexibility is giving yourself
the permission to change. Flexibility is realizing you have the power
to change your life.

For some gay men, work and play become merged because both
are done by choice and involve a degree of commitment and desir-
ability. At midlife, a gay man may approach his career from a different perspective in order to do what he enjoys most, regardless of

salary or security. It's usually easier for him to make this kind of move because, by this time, he has learned basic principles about operating in the world and is able to discipline himself to work efficiently. For some men, this means having learned to focus their energies so that there is defined time for both work and play—each are done intensely and with total involvement.

Listen to your heart: What do you really want to spend your time doing? If you love your job, work it. If you love playing, think about how much you have to work to enable you to do it. If you hate your job, what would it take to change it or to learn a new skill? If you don't know what fun is, take a chance and learn. In doing this exercise, it's important to be as concrete and specific as possible. Maybe you have already daydreamed or fantasized about what you want to do with your time, but you always defer making it happen. Maybe you're waiting for retirement. Maybe you don't have any idea what to do, but you know you're not satisfied. This exercise gives you permission to be self-indulgent and express your deepest desires. It is essential that you give yourself the space to go beyond what is practical and expected.

As you examine your present lifestyle, broaden the focus from work and play to all aspects of your life so that Work/Play begins to support your overall lifestyle. Feel free to think about any and all variations on your desires for a good, satisfying lifestyle. Just as gay men at midlife begin to realize that body image is but one part of their self-image, they begin to see their Work/Play as but one component of their lifestyle. Oscar Wilde once said, "I have put my talent into my art and my genius into my life."

9. **Describe a life in which you are making a living at what you most enjoy doing.**

Running a bed and breakfast. Writing. Painting houses. Helping people. Saving lives. Teaching. Learning about new cultures and languages.

For many gay men, this is a total fantasy exercise, almost at the level of magical thinking. To spend time on this exercise and to come up with an actual visualization of this "living" requires giving yourself permission to fantasize. Imagine your own personally created heaven.

Getting to make money at what we enjoy doing is an important goal, perhaps the main one, a dream come true. But it is not possible for everyone, since not everyone can make a living as a painter or an accountant or a swimmer or a photographer or a carpenter. But there are other ways to be happy about your work that have more to do with feeling that one's time is under one's control, rather than preoccupied with making money. If one has to put time into a "job" that only pays money and does not give satisfaction, then it can be seen as a way to provide money and time to do what one wants in the other hours after work, which is a trade-off, but one that gives you a lifestyle that fulfills your needs.

During midlife, many gay men come to accept what may be a nontraditional work history and begin to redefine Work/Play into a lifestyle. Basically, we begin to remember our childhood fantasies about what we wanted to be when we grew up. A social worker I know remembers that he wanted to study horticulture as a child and become a botanist, but was told it wasn't an appropriate career. Part of my continued enthusiasm for dancing finds its roots in an early desire to become a professional dancer, but that meant not being a "Professional" with a capital P so I stopped taking my dance classes.

If you're stuck in your current position, this exercise might give you direction and inspiration to change. If you're working at a job and not interested in a career, the time you spend fantasizing about how you want to spend your time might give you a new attitude about your work. You might approach the job with a new outlook, recognizing it as a means to giving yourself more pleasures in your life. This exercise will prompt you toward priority changes and new goals.

Once you have started thinking about what you really want to do, you may run up against an economic obstacle: It doesn't pay as well as what you do now. But that may force you to prioritize time, money, and satisfaction with your life. Maybe you're willing to trade money for increased satisfaction. If you enjoy what you're doing and can live comfortably (which all depends on what you feel you need), then maybe you can make less money and still be happy. Give yourself permission to pursue this dream from a different perspective. Be creative and honest with how much time and money you really need.

Miguel was a dissatisfied lawyer at a big New York firm. He had tried his hand at litigation and did not like it—it was too adversarial.

He liked the idea of law but found the day-to-day practice of it not to his liking. He also found that being Hispanic was not in his favor for becoming a partner—he would probably remain an associate forever. He had always had an interest in show business but never gave it much thought since he felt that he had no particular talent in that area. He was fascinated with theater and liked being around people who were in the business. Over the years, he found himself gravitating toward people who were in theater or were trying to break into the field. When he grew more frustrated and unfulfilled by a traditional lawyer's career, he initially thought of leaving law and going back to college for some other career.

In discussing his dreams and fantasies, Miguel kept coming back to show business. We talked about his becoming an entertainment lawyer. Such a move would mean his having to apprentice himself for a time, while he was grounding himself in the new information he would need for that field. This also meant taking a cut in salary, but that began to seem like a small price to pay to find out if he could be happy in this field. He made the decision and started exploring those companies that handled entertainment law. When he found a company that would give him this experience, he soon found that he had made the correct decision. He is quite happy in his newfound career, and he has actually been able to bring in his own clients. Most important, he no longer feels like he wasted his time going to law school, a decision he regretted for many years.

10. What are the steps you have to take to create Work/Play in your life?

At a bookstore signing, the best-selling gay novelist E. Lynn Harris once told a story about what finally motivated him to start writing. He had always wanted to be a novelist, but kept putting it off. Despite a successful sales career in the computer industry, he wasn't happy. Once when he was telling a friend about the novels he was going to write someday, the friend said, "What are you waiting for? You are the only one standing in your way." Two years later, he had self-published his first novel, and today, his books appear on best-seller lists across the country.

This exercise brings the fantasies of Work/Play you just explored down to ground level. What would it take to make the fantasy come true? Issues of responsibility, discipline, and flexibility are paramount. What sort of roadblocks have you put up to bringing about what you have claimed to have wanted?

Educate yourself about the job/career you want. Talk to people who do what you want to be doing. Plan, budget, and manage your time and money in order to get where you want to go. Determine the risks involved, as well as your own balance sheet of assets and liabilities. Take a deep breath and take an action.

Given the changing economy of the nineties, with downsizing and mergers and global market forces at work, having a steady job is a good thing that can't be thrown away on a whim or without planning and forethought. When making a major career change, it's important not to confuse risk taking with impulsiveness. In contemplating any career move, a person needs to inform himself about the possible move, list the potential risks and rewards, and then make a conscious decision to make the change. But if a person has a horrible day at work ("I'm mad at my boss; this job sucks") and just walks out the door never to return, he is being impulsive. Like the conscious risk taker, he's also taking a leap of faith, but until he can see beyond his anger, he won't know where he's headed, much less where he'll land.

Whether it's a new job in the same field or a total career makeover, take your desires and fantasies seriously. Obviously, it is not expected that all will be resolved in this area by the end of this chapter. But the seeds have been planted about Work/Play and the responsibility (discipline, compromise, reprioritizing) that you must assume in order to bring about changes for a more rewarding and satisfying lifestyle. The most important point is for you to be thinking of your life in terms of lifestyle—a holistic approach to satisfaction with your entire life, not just your work, and not just your play.

John's Story

John's story is a good example of someone who learned to integrate his personal interests with career choices. The lifestyle he created was a form of Work/Play in that he made a living at what he most enjoyed doing. In addition, he discovered a new concept of *prosperity* that had a much broader definition than financial concerns.

John began therapy with me from a referral by a physician that I had known. He had many stomach complaints and was looking for a stomach tranquilizer. He had been in therapy off and on since he was eighteen years old. As a teenager, he had been an actor and had tried many other jobs without much satisfaction. He came to therapy very unhappy with his life, and his emotional state was producing his physical symptoms and anxiety attacks. He was in the fifth year of a relationship with a man eight years younger, who was also his business partner. Since they lived together as well, he was feeling challenged by their proximity and by their age difference. He also felt he had been manipulated by the way his lover had used John's insecurities about being alone and lonely to force him to commit prematurely. John did indeed love his lover but was not entirely comfortable with his relationship at the time our work began.

In therapy, we focused on both his physical and relationship problems—at first, work was an issue only in terms of how much time they spent together. John felt he had no space in which to explore himself as an individual. Since he was in a very symbiotic relationship and did everything with his lover, we worked on how he could take space for himself without it being a threat to the relationship. He was also afraid of his lover's own personal growth and of his own aging. "Because of my immigrant Italian upbringing, growth and change almost always represented a threat to the family, even if that family was dysfunctional and nonsupportive," he recalls. "Growth was associated with loss of love and a lose of closeness. Aging was only associated with decay, poor health, and death." The image of aging that remained most vivid for him was of his Italian aunts in long, black dresses.

"As a gay youth, I grew up with the most alarming absence of a sense of self and had no one in my home or even school environments that could direct, guide, or support me in realizing that who I was might be important. All attention was given to my artistic and scholastic achievements. Work meant self," John reflected. This lack of entitlement affected John's sense of himself, so that the future never seemed promising, but threatening and directionless. He saw aging only in terms of loss and a diminution of his attractiveness.

Over the years of therapy, John began to explore new ways of creating a home life that allowed his lover to mature and him to accept his own growth as an adult without feeling he was becoming an old man. He was also mourning the passing of his twenties where he had been involved in a passionate "first time around" love affair, when he traveled in "the fast track" and had been one of the "cuties." Though there was always a depressive side to John, there was also a bouncy, courageous, risk-taking part that got expressed in his work but not in his personal life. In reality, because of the nature of their business, there was little personal time. A real shift began in John's attitudes toward aging when we started to explore his attitudes toward work and play.

Around the time he and his lover had gotten involved, John had dreamed of doing catering work by cooking in his apartment and bringing the food to parties. He and his lover began to cater from their home for a few years, then rented space and started doing party planning with hired cooks. It was about this time that John began therapy with me. They eventually became one of the best-known, most highly respected society and corporate event planners in New York City, with parties at such venues as the Metropolitan Museum, Carnegie Hall, and the Metropolitan Opera House. They also did many benefits for the lesbian and gay community for which they did not charge anything beyond expenses. From the beginning, they had committed to be of service to the lesbian and gay community. They even wrote a party-planning book with recipes and photos.

Part of my work with John was helping him to see how to let the fun that he had in planning parties happen in his personal life. The contrast between the two was like night and day—his depressive and his buoyant side. He perceived that he had been on a treadmill for a particular definition of success without asking what it was that he personally wanted for himself. It was not so much that he had resistance to seeing a more satisfying life, he had just never thought about his life in those terms. What was essential for him to see was that he had to learn to recover the fun aspect of his work and make it reflect his entire life. By working on creating private space and not being so defined by his lover's own personal ups and downs, he began to be more spontaneous in his personal life. As he became more independent and more willing to take risks, he became happier with his lover, both sexually and emotionally. He was letting himself and his lover both grow. He stopped acting like a constricting and devoted parent and began to act more like the lover he had envisioned.

At the same time, his relationship with me became more peerlike. Our sessions were like two friends getting together and talking. A significant point came when we began to explore spiritual issues. This had always been an important area for John but he had not given it the attention it deserved because of his focus on his problems. When he began to understand that by not paying attention to this area, he was making it more difficult for himself, many of his physical symptoms (stomach problems and anxiety attacks) began to subside. As he became more comfortable with his sense of spirituality, he also began to explore some of the mystical experiences he had had. John reflects, "I found in myself a place that I always knew in my heart was my birthright—the natural order of the self in my mind is that love, compassion, peace, joy, and comfort are the spaces where we all truly reside. We lose our way from these places or they become masked or placed in disorder. Returning to these places is what therapy (our life's work) is all about."

As he turned fifty, his relationship with his lover grew even more solid and became a peer relationship that was mutually satisfying. They were able to start new business ventures and experiment with a new lifestyle. There were some fits and starts before they could develop a comfortable lifestyle that reflected this new awareness. They began to court international clients for events abroad and in the United States. They found that they loved traveling, planning parties, and living in other places. Eventually, they started focusing on only a few international clients and decided to handle only a few major parties a year. They do not see this as the only thing that they will be doing in the future—they are letting it develop and go in whatever direction seems appropriate at that time. They are clearly having fun together, doing what they enjoy, and making enough money to continue their lifestyle.

As John approaches sixty, they are growing old together without fearing the future as they had. The last Christmas card I got from them had both of them in shorts and on roller blades.

FIVE

A Circle of Strength:
Relationships with Family and Friends

One of the greatest human fears about getting older is the fear of being alone. Many of us have heard our parents or our grandparents lament the loss of their friends or spouses to illness, and the idea of not having anybody "to grow old with" reinforces a fear of aging. At midlife, as a result of facing our own mortality, we often begin to develop a conscious appreciation of our relationships, especially to our family and friends. In fact, feeling supported and sustained is a crucial component of successful aging.

Many popular self-help books for gay men focus on finding and keeping a man (*Husband Hunting Made Easy*, *How to Find True Love in a Man-Eat-Man World*), but a boyfriend often isn't the answer to feelings of loneliness or low self-worth, much less the fears brought up by aging. This fear of being alone begins early for gay men and is fueled in part by ageism and in part by homophobia: by perpetuating the image of the lonely old gay man, homophobia strikes terror in the heart of teenagers who may be questioning their sexuality. Fear of never finding happiness with "Mr. Right" can keep a gay man in the closet indefinitely, or can drive an openly gay man into relationship after relationship as a way of avoiding facing his mortality or his aging.

Being in a one-on-one relationship is not necessarily a sign of successful aging, but nurturing a spectrum of relationships can expand your resiliency by affirming your sense of belonging. It's easy to

isolate, especially at midlife, when the ageism of the gay community
can render us invisible. But taking a long look at your relationships
can reveal a source of strength: the circle of friendship and kinship
in which you belong. Many gay men can point to the love and
support from the friends they choose and family members whose
kinship they still value after the coming-out process. As you examine
this circle of friends and family, you also realize that this strength is
not always available to nongay men given their developmental path.

AT THE CENTER OF A CIRCLE OF LOVE

Richard feels as if he has found serenity. He works at a job he loves,
pursues his hobbies of cycling and two-step dancing, and enjoys a
large and diverse circle of friends. After a turbulent and self-destructive period in his twenties, Richard entered Alcoholics Anonymous
in his early thirties and began to recover from his dysfunctional
childhood and youth. With the help of a good sponsor and a supportive therapist, he was able to stop drinking, repay his debts, and begin
to figure out what he had been running from all those years. For his
tenth anniversary in AA, he threw himself a small "birthday" dinner
party for eight guests, including his sponsor, sponsees, sister, and
two best friends from college. After beginning and ending a serious
relationship in his late thirties, he is now exploring what it means to
be a single gay man at midlife. He's dating several men his own age,
but he's in no hurry to commit to anything too serious. He's enjoying
being free enough to get to know the men he's dating and to let
them get to know him before they go shopping for rings. He is
questioning whether he really wants to be in a long-term relationship
and is exploring being single as a chosen lifestyle.

Richard's journey has been shaped by a basic need: to feel connected to his own life. The motivation to belong is one expression
of this need, which can be expressed in many ways—immersion in
nature, active involvement in a community, a close relationship. Our
relationships, whether of friendship or family, romance or sex, offer
different ways of belonging. Relationships become a crucial source
of support at midlife because so much seems up for grabs. It is a
time of breaking away from past decisions and recognizing you didn't
arrive at where you are haphazardly. The awareness of the choices

you have made can empower you to reorder your priorities, in everything from work to relationships to lifestyle. The clichés of the midlife crisis—a new relationship with someone younger, pursuing a totally different career, or abandoning work altogether—illustrate the extremes of this impulse for change.

For some gay men, midlife offers an opportunity to find out what they really want—by and for themselves. "I needed to be alone and figure out who I am now that I'm an adult," Richard observed when ending his long-term relationship. "Now that I'm sober and able to identify what I need from a partner, dating is more fun. I can let myself play more and not feel so pressured to couple and settle down." Being single may be the best avenue for some, either temporarily *or permanently.* Since dating and relationships take time and effort, many gay men at midlife may decide to devote that energy to themselves, especially if they feel they've never gotten what they wanted, or even known what they wanted.

For some men, middle age makes it possible to see their history of relationships from a new perspective and finally establish a loving, mutually fulfilling relationship with another man. It can also be a time for renewing a current relationship: rekindling that original flame, including a commitment ceremony (or couples counseling!). *Midlife is the time to figure out whether your relationships "fit" your lifestyle.* How important is your autonomy? How strongly do you desire companionship? Answering questions such as these will help you to identify and prioritize your needs in a relationship before you pursue one or before you attempt to transform a current relationship. Just as each man needs to define his own sense of Work/Play, each man needs to survey his emotional world and determine whether he's headed in a direction he wants.

With the current debate in the gay community around marriage, there seems to be an increasing emphasis on long-term gay relationships (although we have few cultural examples of such gay couples). Long-term gay couples do exist, but aren't always visible or available to serve as role models (especially if they disappear into the suburbs and have little contact with "singles"). It is also important to remember that the longevity of a relationship is no indication of the maturity of the partners or of their mutual satisfaction. How many people do you know who have stayed in relationships because of the security or out of habit, laziness, or fear of change? Abusive relationships, whether verbal or physical, can last a long time, too. As when we were looking at our patterns of Work/Play, the guiding principle here is quality over quantity. Regardless of its duration, is the relationship giving you what you need? If so, how can you celebrate and enrich it? If not, can it be worked on so that it satisfies both partners? Some gay men value having *any* relationship—good or bad—over not having one, while other gay men realize that a less stressful (hence, more healthy) perspective would be to value a "good" boyfriend or "no" boyfriend, and last, if ever, a "bad" boyfriend. What's important at midlife is to start asking yourself, "What do I really want from my relationships?"

Many gay men feel they've always done what "others" wanted and didn't ask themselves what they wanted. For some older gay men, this emotional self-sacrifice may have been a way of countering the cultural disapproval for being gay. In order to win acceptance and appear as "normal" as everyone else, many gay men may have buried their own needs. But since our emotional needs cannot comfortably remain underground and unsatisfied, midlife becomes the time for many gay men to start digging deeper to figure out what they truly want from life, *their* life.

This desire to explore our needs, however, comes into conflict with a resurgence of the need to feel connected. Not since adolescence have we experienced such a heightened need for connectedness as at midlife. What's essential is that there is a significant other, not necessarily a romantic/sexual relationship. For Richard, his significant other is his circle of friends and peers, while for another gay man, it could be his lover of eight years or his new boyfriend of five months. For other gay men, it can be the gay community at large, a particular organization, or any number of social groups to which they belong. Again, this need for affiliation, for being connected, is primary; how it gets expressed is up to the individual.

This need to feel connected emerges ferociously at adolescence and midlife because those are the periods in which we most feel like outsiders. One of the reasons aging is so difficult for many gay men is because it reawakens our feelings of being an outsider—those feelings of being different, of not belonging, of being the only gay person in the world. But this time around, we begin to feel like an outsider because we're the wrong kind of gay person: middle-aged.

Given the youth fetish, body fascism, and ageism of the gay

male world, small wonder that once they turn forty (or even younger—thirty, thirty-five), many gay men feel they no longer belong in the gay community. In a sense, we *are* outsiders again. We're outside the "norm" of what our gay media projects as our "community." Having once been inside that community as young men, many of us despair at the reversal of fortune and visibility within the community that midlife can bring. Young gay men in their twenties find a gay community ready to open its arms to them, and not just figuratively. Showered in the adjectives of youth—fresh, virile, nimble, horny—they gain entry into what appears a safe haven in which to celebrate their sexuality, only to mistake sexual access for belonging.

Don't get me wrong: I believe a community can be created around sex. But if your youthful sex appeal connects you to that community, does that mean you still belong in the community when your sex appeal is no longer recognized? It's like a man who circulates in a moneyed circle but who suddenly loses his fortune in a stock market crash. Does he still belong to that community of affluence? Or is he shunned, kicked out, or rendered otherwise "invisible"?

Some men may feel their only connection to other gay men (or any sense of community) is through sex, but by limiting ourselves to only one form of belonging, based upon such an exclusive and ephemeral criteria as youth, we are setting ourselves up for rejection. If we, as middle-aged gay men, are no longer considered part of the gay community simply because of our age, how mature and developed is that community to begin with? Gay male ageism calls into question what was your membership in the community really based upon—you the person or you the cock?

If our brotherhood is to survive, we have to look at how fragmented and divisive that brotherhood can be. Whereas upon first coming out, many gay men experience a tendency to accept the gay community at face value and lose themselves in it, as they get older, there emerges another need to find themselves among all the stereotypes. In identifying for yourself where you belong as a middle-aged gay man, you will stir up deep-seated feelings of being an outsider, the same feelings your "brotherhood" is reinforcing by saying you do not belong now because you're too old.

As we try to reconcile our need to feel connected as middle-aged gay men and the ageism of our community, conflict is inevitable.

In the process of evaluation and decision-making that occurs at mid-life, many of us are exploring—perhaps for the first time—what we honestly need from another person, what we can give to another person. Such self-exploration jeopardizes our membership in the gay community because it might lead to a rejection of the community, or at the very least, aspects of the community. Letting go of the ageism and other defects of the gay male community is difficult because it's like turning your back on your best friend, who has given you security, joy, and heartache for many years.

Getting rid of all those outsider feelings is like shedding an old, hard, constricting shell you have outgrown. When a crab grows and breaks its shell, its body is totally exposed and vulnerable to attack, so the crab must be extra cautious and defensive while its new shell thickens and hardens to conform to its new shape.

Part of our fear of old age is a fear of returning to those feelings of being alone that so many of us experienced in our adolescence. But the truth is we're not alone. We have peers. Even reading this book and working the exercises doesn't have to be a solitary endeavor, but the agenda of a men's group—one that you can create yourself.

In order to understand these negative feelings and find the strength to work through them, we need to revisit earlier years of feeling different, of wanting to belong but feeling rejected, of coming out and going against the norms. Once you begin to explore those first feelings of difference, you remember and re-experience the vulnerability of being a gay child. But you will also remember the courage and strength you displayed in coming out. It's time to transfer the strategies you used to come out successfully to the process of your aging.

WHO AM I?: THE HOLOGRAM VERSUS THE REAL ME

Everybody, gay and nongay alike, grows up with a social self that they present to their family and the world. This is the self we are conditioned to believe will bring us the most affection and love. We don't really want to play football like our father did (or claims he did) in high school, but we play anyway. We may be afraid of our father and mother, but we obey their every word so that they won't get angry with us and withhold love. We keep our true feelings and thoughts secret from the outside world in order to avoid judgment, punishment, or abandonment. If the environment is hostile or violent, hiding our real feelings can be a way of surviving, of just staying alive.

Although everybody makes this decision to present a social self, nongay people aren't required to disguise their romantic and sexual desires the same way as gay people. Young gays and lesbians soon learn that it is dangerous to show the world their true desires; we learn how to self-censor so early that it feels instinctive. Everything, from our speech to our mannerisms, from our walk to our voice, gets monitored before being expressed. Research has shown that gays and lesbians remember feeling different from other kids, long before any sexual thoughts or desires became conscious. We might not even feel different from our peers, but we are called *sissy* or *fairy* at school, without even knowing what the words mean. Before we know why we are seen as different, we may feel our difference intuitively. We might get a crush on a friend in school, but our crush is on a boy, not a girl. Then we're confused because we've been told it's supposed to be on a girl. We realize that if we were honest about what we were feeling, we would be teased, called names, or humiliated. Our fear of attack or abandonment prevents us from being ourselves, and we begin to feel as if we were watching ourselves perform, from a distance, while our true self is elsewhere, hiding. I call this different self, our public or social image, our *hologram*, a 3-D image of the person we want our friends and family to know and to love.

Eventually, this hologram becomes so powerful and such second nature that the gay child feels like an outsider all the time, even to his own life. Even if he's popular, well-liked, and an excellent student, a gay child may feel like a total fraud: deep down, he fears that if his classmates or teachers or parents knew how he really felt about Danny, his best friend, all his popularity and security would vanish. So he continues to hide his feelings and behavior (from Danny as well), and feels removed from his own body, as if he were watching himself on television. Meanwhile, Danny, the nongay child, does not have to hide his feelings for Sally, their classmate, and those feelings are usually affirmed by nongay dating rituals.

Sometimes, a gay child may display nongay behavior to hide his true feelings, i.e., the exaggerated heterosexuality of a closeted gay teenager. I once served on a committee that was studying teenage pregnancy, whose members saw absolutely no relevance of gay issues to their subject. I explained to my nongay peers how homophobia can be a factor: A teenage girl might get pregnant in order to show she's had sex with a guy and therefore isn't a lesbian, while a teenage boy might have unprotected sex with a girl in order to prove his manhood by becoming a father. Since there are so few cultural images of lesbian and gay parents available to teenagers, the fact of parenthood erases any possible stigma of homosexuality. Becoming a parent protects and reinforces the closeted teenager's hologram.

Go back to your earliest memories of difference, and try to remember how you survived them. What was your hologram? The Best Little Boy in the World. The Troublemaker. The Peacemaker. The Scholar. The Athlete. Your hologram was a projection of your desire to belong, to be on the inside. But as long as we project a hologram, we remain outsiders, separated from the worlds we long to inhabit. In order to begin recognizing how the hologram operated in your life, it's important to identify the groups from which you felt excluded. Where did you want to belong?

1. Describe the different groups of people around whom you *felt* like an outsider.

Were you popular in high school? Were you always the last chosen during intramurals or sports? Did you spend hours alone in the library studying or were you invited to many classmates' parties?

There are different degrees of feeling like an outsider. You may have been class clown and popular with girls and boys alike, but did you feel like you were putting on an act the whole time? Were you valedictorian, but felt like no one was listening to your graduation speech? At your first day in a factory job, did you feel awkward, like you were the only person who didn't know what to do, or how the machines worked? In college, were you asked to pledge a fraternity? Did you get involved in student government or the campus newspaper or yearbook?

Reviewing your history for feelings of exclusion can be difficult and painful. What's important to remember is that the past is past and you can influence the present with the work you're now doing. Try to focus on how you may have felt excluded, even when the facts tell a different story. You may have been "Big Man On Campus" and popular, but you felt that it was your hologram that people were responding to, not the "real" you. The emphasis in these first few exercises is on how you *felt*, not what you thought or were told by other people. Identifying the feelings of isolation are essential to creating new feelings of connectedness and belonging.

BREAKING FREE OF THE HOLOGRAM

Although it begins as a protective device, the hologram can become an instrument of repression. The disjunction between our hologram and our "real self" can continue indefinitely, reinforcing our fear and reluctance to come out as a gay man. This "double life" is one of the most vicious legacies of homophobia because it can not only prevent others from knowing and loving us, but it can also prevent us from knowing and loving ourselves. Gay men in the military experience the hologram: on the outside, they may have an exceptional service record, but inwardly, they feel isolated and alone, terrified of being found out. Another example could be an elementary or high school teacher who's beloved by his students, but because he's closeted at work, it's difficult to accept the positive feedback he has earned. If we don't feel as if we know or appreciate ourselves, how can we feel known and appreciated by others? Once homophobia has become internalized, there is an underlying sense that what's inside (our true self) isn't worthy or good, and this shame is corrosive: it isn't tied to any particular thought or feeling, but is totally self-perpetuating. The stress of surveillance can be harmful to our health as well.

Unless a gay man comes out very early to his family and friends, he usually has a perpetual feeling of being known and loved only for his hologram, but not for his true self. When hiding becomes a way of life, the hologram becomes a permanent mask, which invariably results in a certain constriction in interpersonal relationships as well as a feeling of guardedness in the world and a constant fear of exposure—even when there's nothing to expose. These negative feelings can become so pervasive that some gay men come to distrust most of their feelings and, over time, rarely feel completely open and honest in their relationships. A constant sense of "what if" plagues their relationships: what if they knew I was gay, what if my parents knew how I felt about them, or what if my boss knew how little I care about my job.

The presentation of the hologram can become habitual, a reflex—always doing what others want from us in order to please, to be accepted, to receive love and approval. Whether it's joining the navy like your father, becoming a doctor because it's your parents' dream or a family tradition, living close to your family, voting in the same political party as your boss—these behaviors can be chosen without really knowing why you want to do them. To live the hologram, to constantly act as if you are another person—the person "they" love (whoever "they" might be: your parents, teachers, siblings, boss, boyfriend, therapist)—can produce such real pain and frustration that it can cause a breaking point in midlife.

Change is possible only if we feel entitled to change, entitled to create a life that is our own and one worth living. Entitlement is essentially a belief that you have a right to exist and to have the important elements of life: happiness, health, relationships, money, sex, laughter, fun, and so on. Entitlement, however, can also be used in a pejorative way to describe a person who operates as if the world belongs to him, as if he can do anything he wishes without consequence or responsibility. The original sense of entitlement, which gay men usually don't have, allows a person to see a path in the future for himself that is promising and bright, and to feel that good things will come his way. Hiding his true feelings for so many years can prevent any sense of entitlement from developing in a gay child, so that adolescence may become a period of just surviving, rather than a time of growth and exploration, becoming his own person. Given his hologram and society's homophobia, there's little chance for a gay man to develop any sense of entitlement *around his sexuality and emotions*. (Many gay men do develop degrees of entitlement based on class and race, as well as being male.) My experience has been that many gay men feel they have a right to *buy* the trappings of entitlement (material goods), but not to necessarily *feel* entitled.

On the other hand, since there's not a lot of cultural awareness around the issue of entitlement, people may take entitlement for granted, accepting certain assumptions as part of their existence, or "the natural order of things." It's easier for the person without this sense of entitlement to spot the person who has it. An African-American friend of mine has shared how seeing a white person's sense of entitlement can pain her, while feminists have pointed out how many men express a sense of superiority just because they're male. As gay men, we have all witnessed and experienced the entitlements of the nongay world, which makes heterosexuality the standard by which everything is judged.

In a sense, entitlement is about an expectation of treatment. If we feel entitled, we expect to be treated a certain way, a *good* way. But many of us don't have any real sense of how we should be treated. Looking through the distorted prism of the hologram, we have only the fear of how the world would treat us if we were to reveal our true selves. As a result, our place in the world seems tenuous at best, if not endangered.

Entitlement also feeds our sense of control, not only that good things will come our way, but that we can direct our life and move it toward those good things. Because of the hologram, a gay child rarely gains a sense of control over his own life. The hologram only increases the sense that he's two people: the boy the world sees and the boy he feels himself to be on the inside. This disconnection can lead to a feeling that life is happening *to* him, rather than *in response* to him. Once he feels removed from active participation in his life, a gay child begins to accept his status as a permanent outsider.

A gay man may become so focused on what he feels excluded from that he develops an identity in which he feels like an outsider everywhere, including when he is finally with other gay men. A feeling of "No matter what I do, I will never belong" becomes part and parcel of many gay men's identity. For such gay men, there's a chronic sense of comparison with others and a feeling that they are lacking something essential: I don't have the right body, the right clothes, the right job, or the right boyfriend. Coming out begins to break the grip of the hologram on our lives, but since the process of coming out can take many years, our outsider status can extend well into our development as gay adults, shaping our interactions with other gay men.

2. **Describe the different groups of gay men around whom you *felt* an outsider.**

When you came out, did you feel like a part of the gay community? Was there a gay community when you came out? Did you experience a sense of brotherhood at a gay bar? Or was your sense of inclusion stronger during gay pride events, like a rally or march? The range of gay groups is stunning, from gay bowlers to volleyball players, from S/M to scuba diving clubs, from gatherings of opera queens to two-steppers. What groups did you find most appealing, or more to the point, accepting of you? Did you identify with the images you saw in the gay media? Did you feel part of an A-list or did you dismiss that crowd?

This exercise may seem more painful than the last because it suggests that being an outsider is a continual state; perhaps it's a feeling you have experienced throughout your life. Sometimes, we are so used to feeling like an outsider that we would not be able to recognize a peer if he came up and spoke to us. Even when we join gay groups, we may keep ourselves at a distance emotionally, unable to connect with others because we're afraid of being known, of letting our guard down. Do you exhibit the same social habits, regardless of setting? Do you keep people at a distance through your "cleverness" and charm? Or do you instantly connect with everyone and become a good friend immediately? Do you participate quietly or do you become the center of attention? Recognizing the patterns of your social behavior can reveal if they are serving you well. Are you getting what you want out of your social interaction?

Certainly, there are snobs with attitude who shun everybody, so I'm not saying it's our "fault" if we feel excluded. But our own perceptions weigh heavily upon us, and we may project rejection before we actually experience it. In the chapter on body image and sexuality, I introduced Mike, who was very handsome but never seemed to connect in a bar when he was trying to meet people. One of the problems is that he never smiled, not because he was unfriendly, but because he was nervous he wasn't going to meet anybody. What was discomfort and fear got translated into attitude; when he learned to smile, he appeared more approachable and other men felt as if they could talk to him.

This pattern of hiding behind a social mask of attitude is a normal response to the way we grew up, so there's no fault or blame to be cast. We learned early that a hologram can be a protective thing. But it is also dangerous and repressive if we're trying to integrate our "true" self into our life. Once we are aware of this dynamic, it's harder to find it acceptable. By examining these difficult feelings and seeing how we maintain them through our social interaction, we plant the seeds for change, for growth out of this pain.

Sadly, coming out doesn't always make these negative feelings go away quickly. Even if we're out at work and out to our family, we may be the only gay person in the office or the only gay member of our family. No matter how "out" you may be at home, you may still experience a sense of isolation around your family of origin. After a dramatic coming-out scene (complete with mood music and tears), many families "don't want to talk about it" again, giving a gay man little opportunity to share his life with them. Telling your family you're gay gives them intellectual knowledge, but unless they actually experience the realities of your life (meeting gay friends or boyfriends, talking about gay causes and AIDS), your identity as a gay man will be largely theoretical to them and based on stereotypes. It's as if they keep forgetting you're gay.

Not surprisingly, many gay men "don't want to talk about it" with their families either. How can this be? Since the connection between being gay and feeling like an outsider has become so internalized, any feeling of belonging conflicts with our sense of being gay. For many gay men, belonging to their families, *even after coming out*, is tentative. My lover Friedrich hesitated at first to introduce me to his mother because he had never mixed the two emotional worlds: his relationships with lovers and his relationship with his mother. When we started dating, he was in his early fifties, and he was still concerned about how she would react, given her past behavior of referring to women he should pursue (even though he had come out to her years before!). When I finally did meet her, the three of us had an excellent visit, and Friedrich realized how much of his worry was a holdover from his years of not talking openly with her. For many gay men, the years of the hologram and hiding have done their damage, and it's very difficult to stop believing your family will reject you for telling the truth. What keeps many gay men from sharing their lives with their families is internalized homophobia, so that even after a gay man comes out, he can still feel the repercussions of his antigay conditioning.

Even after we come out, homophobia (both internalized and external) constantly reminds us of our outsider status and complicates, if not prevents, feelings of belonging, especially in nongay groups. I have felt this many times, especially after my painful coming-out experience as a teenager. I was sexually active by the time I was eleven, and when I was fourteen, I was arrested in a park's cruising area and sentenced for being gay, even though it was police entrapment. My coming out to my family consisted of the arrest and a trial before a judge, where I admitted to having sex with other men. No planning, no support, just drama and anguish. Except for my sister, I was an outcast and criminal. Reform school was the only option, and I was sentenced to live with my uncle, an ex-air force major. He was also a physician and horseman who volunteered to have me live with him on his ranch, where he would "make a man of me." For many years I never felt like I belonged anywhere. It was only when I turned eighteen and left home that I felt my life begin for the first time.

I've heard many gay men admit to conflicted feelings left over from childhood and adolescence, and the resulting shame confuses us even more: "I'm out at work, I have a boyfriend, I'm involved in the community, but sometimes I feel totally alone, like nobody feels the same as I do." To work through these feelings of alienation and judgment requires a shift in identity, an overhaul of our self-image from "outsider" to "insider." At midlife, our identity shifts from "what I am not a part of" to "who I am" to "what I am a part of." A first step in that transformation—and one that often comes at midlife and not before—is to acknowledge how we communicate in building our relationships.

CAN WE TALK? THE POWER TO COMMUNICATE

Our ability to include ourselves in the world around us depends upon our skills of communication, as well as a sense of our own power. If we feel like outsiders all our lives, we don't feel like we can communicate our true feelings, nor do we feel as if we have any power to change our position from outsider to insider. When we came out, we learned a new language that included us, and within a community of gay peers, we finally felt like an insider. But middle age threatens all of that by creating a new wall— ageism—around the community to which we want and need to belong.

Dismantling the styles of communication we developed as "outsiders" can take time and concentration, even with friends. A common pattern of relating among many gay men is a "triangular" conversation that can involve a lot of intimate information. Bob and Bill talk about Charles, and Charles and Bob talk about Bill, and Bill and Charles talk about Bob. But Bob and Bill don't talk to each other about their friendship, only their relationship with the third is up for examination. This form of communication (or rather, miscommunication) isn't really surprising given how men are socialized from birth not to talk about their feelings. It's the girls and the women they become who are supposed to talk, who shoulder the responsibility of communicating in a relationship. In a nongay relationship, it's the women who tell the men what they're feeling, but in a gay relationship (and not just romantic/sexual, but every kind of relationship), we have two men who often don't have a language or permission to describe what they're feeling for and about the other person.

Part of the problem is that many gay men confuse intimacy with closeness. Have you ever had a one-night stand or trick whom you poured your heart out to? Or met someone on a train or a plane and found yourself telling him intimate details that you hadn't shared with anyone? Sometimes, we can reveal our darkest secrets to a total stranger, and afterward, wonder what got into us and why we spilled our guts. Part of the dynamic is a feeling of safety. The person doesn't know you and probably won't see you again, so it feels safe to tell him all your dirt. He won't be able to repeat it or tell anyone you know (like your lover). For many gay men, intimacy is confessional, the sharing of details, but closeness is a feeling toward another person. When we're close to someone, he knows us, he knows our heart and our mind, and we have a hard time deceiving or betraying him. It's easy to mistake intimacy for closeness, and we're usually experiencing one or the other, but rarely both.

We need a new language among gay men: a way of communicating without making one another feel like outsiders, a vocabulary of inclusion, rather than exclusion. But too often we carry the sense of exclusion we first experienced in childhood on into our adult lives as gay men. Sometimes we replicate cliques that make us feel as if we belong, but only because we make others feel unwanted and not part of the group. Any sense of belonging that comes from excluding others is temporary since the terms for membership can change in the blink of an eye. Moreover, while being in the "in" crowd may provide a sense of individual power, that power is illusory because it depends upon taking the power away from somebody else.

Talking about power makes people uncomfortable. Power is one of those things that most want but few want to admit wanting. But feeling powerful over others and having internal power are very different. Power can be subtle and can exist in the most casual of social relations. In most social relations, there are two kinds of power: "aggrandized" and "inherent." Aggrandized power is the kind that gains its strength by taking power away from other people or by others giving up their own power. In our context of friendships and relationships, aggrandized power is the driving force behind cliques, the A-list, the "in" crowd, and the haves (as opposed to the have-nots). A person in pursuit of aggrandized power says, "I have power because you don't have power, and I am threatened if you feel powerful."

Inherent power comes from within, from our own sense of strength that comes from our behavior, from our treating other people as we would wish to be treated. Inherent power does not take away, but gives. Inherent power does not result from external conditions (such as other people liking you), so people with a sense of inherent power do not feel the need to bring other people down, to take away another person's good feelings about himself. Perhaps most important, inherent power cannot be taken away from you, since it comes from you. In contrast, aggrandized power carries a fear of being taken away since it was taken from someone else in the first place. There's no security in aggrandized power because it's so vulnerable and dependent upon other people's feelings of weakness.

People with inherent power want others to feel good about themselves. People with inherent power seek out others and support the empowerment of other people. In contrast, people with aggrandized power are threatened if other people feel powerful. Think about the people you encounter. Sometimes, no matter what you do, you walk away from a particular person feeling diminished, less than, less confident, unsure of yourself. It could be an aunt who always compares you to her son, or a boss who can't praise you without bringing up a detail you forgot. Just as many people struggle to accept compliments, these people don't know how to give positive feedback. Then there are people around whom you feel better being yourself, supported, full of strength. Your grandfather who taught you how to fish or hunt. A math teacher who took the time to explain a difficult theorem to you. A boss who explains how you made a mistake, but isn't insulting when correcting you. *Aggrandized power focuses on what other people don't have, while inherent power focuses on what you have.*

Aggrandized power works its way through our culture in many ways: sexism, racism, classism, and particularly for us as middle-aged gay men, ageism. The "isms" are fueled by it because they run on judgments that devalue others: which race is better, which gender is better, which class, and which age group. Gay men are not immune to the appeal of aggrandized power, which can make one feel liked, popular, safe, as if you belong—but only until the power runs out. You can feel like an insider only as long as you make someone else feel like an outsider. Given many gay men's history of feeling like outsiders, it makes complete sense that they want revenge, their time in the sun, their fifteen minutes of fame, all at the expense of other gay men.

Power is extremely relevant to successful aging, because the myth is that aging is about losing power: losing our health, our ability to function and take care of ourselves, our mental ability, our powers of seduction and sexuality. Fears of losing power only feed a desire for aggrandized power, however. As we age, we begin to look to others (usually younger people) to give us the power to feel good about ourselves. For many gay men, one of the difficult aspects of aging is the sense that they have lost something—the power they have achieved through their sexuality. But then we fall into the trap of aggrandized power: we give the young that power, the power we feel we don't have or have lost.

If you feel you have an internal sense of power, aging won't be as difficult. Successful aging is about converting our need for aggrandized power into feeling our own inherent power. This transformation takes many shifts in attitude: seeing how you are strong and have been strengthened by coming out, recognizing your achievements as a middle-aged gay man, being honest about both your strengths and your weaknesses, building upon the good feelings you have about your life, understanding the difference between inherent and aggrandized power, and finally, learning not to give your power away.

WHERE DO I BELONG?
PEERS, BLOOD FAMILY, AND CHOSEN FAMILY

To have a firm sense of a solid emotional support system is a critical source of power. To have, recognize, and identify it indicates a maturity and an omen for successful aging. One's *peers*, *blood family*, and *chosen family* are primary components of an emotional system, and at midlife, it's important to clarify your relationship to each.

The first circle in which we belong is our family of origin, which I will refer to as our *blood family*. Whereas we began to exercise some choice when we made our first friend at school, for most of our early years, we had no choice in our affiliation: we were born into a family and that was our only world.

Once we entered school and later, when we left home, we began to assemble a new family, a second circle of belonging, what I call our *chosen family* because our operating principle is choice. We decided who belonged in our new family based on peership or friendship, not biological destiny. When we first came out, we may have abandoned our blood family for a new chosen family of gay brothers, but over time, our chosen family may have come to incorporate members from our blood family, depending upon our relationship to them. Membership in a chosen family is based on the *relationship* between two people, rather than a common bloodline.

Because of many gay men's rejection by their blood families, their chosen families are paramount in giving them love, support, and direction in their lives. But our chosen families are not often recognized by the nongay world. Even the language we use fails to describe what the different members of our chosen family may mean to us. Many of us view and describe nearly all of our relationships in terms of sex: trick, boyfriend, sister (nonsexual), lover, or partner. Nongay relationships have many levels: dating, going steady, engaged, married, divorced, separated. Neither gay nor nongay people are accustomed to using those kinds of nuanced terms to describe gay relationships. Many gay men reduce all their associates into two categories: Men I've Slept With and Men I Haven't Slept With (perhaps with a subcategory of Men I Haven't Slept With Yet But Want To!).

Moreover, our romantic relationships aren't seen as valid by the nongay world (or even by us sometimes) because they don't last very long or produce offspring. In the nongay world, many "first" marriages fail as well (the divorce rate for new marriages is at 50 percent), and it may take a second or third marriage "to take" before a nongay person finds happiness. Many gay men commit too soon because the only options appear to be no sex (rendering them a "girlfriend" or "sister"), just sex (trick), or more sex (lover). Two men may move in together and set up a home, but they're really only at the going steady phase. But the language has yet to catch up to the complexity and progression of gay relationships. Only recently, with concepts like domestic partnership, coparenting, and gay marriage, have we been able to start naming our different kinds of relationships.

Even if the nongay world acknowledges our ability to have and sustain relationships, gay men are still judged as inferior for failing to produce offspring. Since gay men rarely have children, they aren't usually seen as procreative (our sex is just recreational, and so forth). But I like to think of our chosen family as our offspring, and since ex-lovers are often part of our chosen family, our sex can be considered procreative in the sense of creating and extending our chosen family.

My chosen family includes my sister, professional colleagues, and friends from all parts of my life, including from childhood and college. Ben, my late lover Jim's best friend, became my friend as well, and we remain close even after Jim's death. Ben and Jim sang in a couple of choruses together, and a small, intimate circle developed from this chorus composed of Ben and Jim and a few nongay women. We all actually traveled together, and they are part of my chosen family. We still meet regularly and have taken trips together—my sister even came on one of the trips. This chosen family would also be there in times of support, such as when Ben's lover died and later, when Jim died. Our chosen family often looks like a series of concentric and intersecting circles.

The third and final circle of belonging is our *peers*. In our discussion of role models and in many of our exercises, I've asked you to compare yourself to other gay men your age. This was to get you to be more comfortable talking about your age, but also to push you to recognize your peers by first looking at those in your age group. For many people, that's what peers are: the members of their generation, the men who've gone through (at least chronologically) the same experiences and same period of history.

When we're younger, we define our peers mainly by behavior:

we live in the same neighborhood, go to the same school or college, work in the same industry, run around with the same crowd, and sleep with the same people. To a young gay man, being a peer means doing and liking the same things. But peership is less about being the same age or wearing the same clothes than it is about sharing the same perspective on life, the same approach to living.

At midlife, peership celebrates individual differences, rather than common activities or similarities. Peers at midlife are not threatened by differences among themselves, but display an acceptance of and respect for individuality. This is very different from when we were younger, when to be different was a problem. Our feelings in the schoolyard were the same as what we felt our first time in a gay bar: We were afraid of sticking out, of being left out, of not being "chosen" (whether for a dodge ball game or being asked to dance at a disco). Consider how long it took to feel comfortable enough to ask ourselves to dance, to dance by ourselves, without a partner to make us feel comfortable.

3. **Who are the people, both gay and nongay, that you feel are peers and why?**

A nongay friend at work who started at the company the same time as you can be a peer. So can your best friend from college, who's also gay and lives close to you, your twin brother, or a workout partner at the gym.

Most people don't think of the people around them as peers; peers are something you had in high school, when you were tempted to smoke, drink, cut classes because of "peer pressure." In fact, peers are often portrayed only in negative terms by parents. Peers are also usually defined by age only: our peers are the people the same age as we are. But peers can also be identified through similar actions, behavior, or sexual orientation. I feel my co-author is my peer, and he is half my age. Peers are important because they buffer you in the world and work against whatever "outsider" feelings you may have. As gay men, such feelings run especially deep, and coming out is only part of the battle. By recognizing our peers, we lessen our "outsider" status and gain a sense of belonging and connectedness, feelings that help us along the road to successful aging.

In *The Nurture Assumption*, Judith Rich Harris turned the fields of child development and parenting upside down with her simple, but radical hypothesis: Peers matter more than family in a child's development. Her work was published in late 1998 to much controversy and acclaim, with headlines blaring "Do Parents Matter?" Once the hype and hysteria cleared, it became clear that what she was saying was that parents do matter, just not as much as we thought. The question she asked herself was, "What if children learned the things that make them who they are—that shape their characters and personalities— from their peer group?" Her conclusion is that "whatever our parents do to us is overshadowed, in the long run, by what our peers do to us."

This makes sense to me. Many gay men have a miserable childhood because of teasing and harassment at school from their peers, and some men grow up with abusive parents. But when they come out into a community of other gay men, much of that misery disappears, at least on the surface. There is always a trace of internalized homophobia, doubts of self-worth, and outsider feelings, but a new community of gay peers can effectively neutralize the negative legacies of the past, both from the blood family and childhood peers.

What I have observed about mature gay men at midlife is a striking commonality: They have taken different paths to reach a higher level of awareness and tend to be more comfortable with who they are. Part of this comfort zone is the degree to which they create a circle of peers. What's striking to me is that this level of peership is based on internal strengths and mutual support for continued growth. The masks are off and each man presents his uniqueness, which is respected.

As an adult, a gay man chooses his own family, which can contain blood family members, peers, and new and old friends, as well as role models from his everyday life. At this time, the gay man finally figures out what he needs from another person in terms of love and support, and can surround himself with people who give him what he needs. After years of rejecting his blood family as a whole, he might incorporate some of its members into his family of choice. He may not be close to his brother, but one of his cousins may have always seemed like a brother to him, and he may nurture a deeper connection with his cousin.

4. With whom in your blood family can you be totally yourself and why? Are they part of your chosen family?

Maybe you have two brothers and a sister, but have only ever felt close to your younger brother. Or you've always considered your father a friend as well as a parent. Or you and your only sister have always been close buddies, despite an age difference of five years. Maybe you haven't talked to anyone in your blood family in years. They have their lives, and you have yours, separate but equal.

The important thing is to examine your relationships with your blood family members from a perspective of comfort and honesty. Whom do you feel most comfortable around? Are you out to only one person in your blood family? Do you feel like a co-conspirator with a particular brother or cousin whenever there's a family reunion? Maybe you've never even tried to be yourself around them because of the way they've acted or some of the opinions they've expressed in the past.

Reviewing the different kinds of relationships you have with members of your blood family should clarify why you can or cannot be yourself. What are the special characteristics of the ones that "work"? What's missing from the ones that cause you the most discomfort or pain? The better you understand how you have created and maintained relationships in the past, the more aware you will become about what the relationships in your present are providing you.

5. How are you different from most members of your blood family?

Funnier? Quieter? More stylish? More bitter? Smarter? More honest? It's true. We're different. Some people think of gay people as another species, and there's probably a book to be written called *Gay People Are from Saturn, Everybody Else Is from Pluto*.

But kidding aside, we are unique and special—not just in our sexuality, but how we approach life. There are always exceptions to the generalizations, but as a community, we tend to have fun, work hard, fight hard, play hard, and survive. Whenever we encounter homophobia (it's still a nongay world, after all), it can be easy to denigrate our individual and collective achievements, but it doesn't change the facts.

Maybe there aren't many differences between you and your blood family members. You may recognize that you're similar in some significant ways while still appreciating your uniqueness. While you appreciate what your parents taught you about how to treat people with respect and you believe that family is forever, you need to be your own person as well. Maybe this is the first time you've allowed yourself to acknowledge the differences between you and them. Maybe no one in your blood family knows how you really feel about him or her or your place in the family. These exercises give you the space and time to explore these feelings, which may be painful if there's a history of confrontation or rejection from your blood family.

6. Do you feel you are a loved member of your blood family?

Are you able to feel their love or even acknowledge it? "I love you" may be a quick refrain in your blood family, but do their actions say otherwise? Is there a lot of fighting among the members of your blood family? Does your blood family even acknowledge its emotions? Do you "know" you are loved but have never "felt" the love? It's one thing to know something, but if your heart doesn't feel it, it's just not real. This disbelief can result from the way your blood family treats you or relates to you, but it can also reveal a low sense of entitlement.

The next time you visit your blood family, pay close attention to what you're feeling. A sense of dread? Some excitement? An eagerness to see some of your blood family, but not everybody? How often do you see your blood family? Once a year, for a holiday? Every month? Every week? Perhaps it's been years since you've seen them, but you have a weekly phone call from your mother. Or maybe one or both of your parents are dead, and you've lost touch with your siblings.

Typically, many gay men socialize with their blood family only under special conditions. Consider the reasons for getting together (holidays, reunion, death, graduation), and consider, too, if you're satisfied with the amount of interaction. Open up about your feelings when you see your blood family and what those times are like. Fun? Painful? Okay? Tense? The goal is to assess your relationship with them and determine whether or not you're satisfied with the current arrangement. What's important to remember is that you can change your relationship with them, whether they are alive or dead. Maybe you miss them. Maybe you're still angry with them. Maybe you don't have much feeling either way. Maybe you don't even think of them, and you doubt they think of you.

7.   How does your blood family perceive you?

This exercise may be difficult because you have to look at yourself from their perspective (or rather, what you imagine their perspective is). Go beyond statements such as "they like me" or "they hate me" or "they don't understand me." Think in a more active way about your blood family's relationship to you. Do you understand their perspective or even acknowledge that they may have a perspective different from yours? Or does this hurt too much, making it easier to see everything only in terms of yourself and your perspective? Can you accept the validity of their perspective and that they have a right to think differently? Or are you only reacting to them based on their actions and behavior in the past? Do you feel they are antagonistic to you or accepting or merely "tolerant"?

A gay man's feelings toward his blood family can be confusing, contradictory, and quite powerful, even long after he has left home. In the introduction, I spoke of the perceptual shift involved in a blood family's acceptance of its gay son, and it's worth a second look here. Many gay men expect immediate acceptance when they come out to their blood families. Yes, there will be a time of tears and awkwardness, but many gay men believe that their blood families will adjust sooner rather than later.

But the urgency many gay men feel when they come out to their blood family doesn't transfer to their parents, and as a result, many gay men don't give them the years it took us to adjust to our new identities. Many gay men have no sense of the impact of their coming out on their families. Understandably, we focus on ourselves during coming out, but once the deed is done, we need to focus on the situation from our blood family's perspective if we are to truly restore the relationship. This restoration, of course, depends upon their reaction, and I'm not urging compassion for the blood families who throw the gay son out of the house or physically abuse him. I do try, however, to get a gay man to appreciate what his coming out means to his blood family.

The second a gay man tells his parents he's gay he has instantly isolated them from their support system and given them a secret they can't share with anyone until they decide to. That decision may take years, as it did for many gay men. A gay man's coming out affects not only his relationship with his parents, but their relationship with their world, which he has permanently altered. In effect, he has created a hologram for his family. There are resources like Parents and Friends of Lesbians and Gays (PFLAG) in most communities, but it may take parents a while to get there. If a gay man looks to his own experience and measures how long it took him from that first same-sex desire until he could feel good about being gay, he will develop more empathy for what his parents are going through. When he comes out, a gay man forever changes his blood family's perception of him, and during the time it takes for them to adjust to his new image, a gay man may distance himself, lose communication, and abandon the relationships he once cherished and one day, he might need again.

8. **Talk about whom in your blood family you would turn to in an emergency.**

Maybe there's some blood family member on whom you can count. You know that if you called Uncle Jack or Cousin Sarah or your brother Tom, they would be there for you. Maybe you're superstitious and don't like to think of emergencies, so you've never thought about who you'd call. This exercise may reinforce that there's no blood family member you can rely upon, and that your chosen family is your main source of support in times of need.

Emergencies and unexpected traumas endanger our sense of order, and feelings of stability, safety, and security about the way the world operates and our place in it contribute to our ability to age successfully. If we feel connected and safe, we will be able to respond to whatever life brings us, but if we feel isolated and alone, we will react to life events with less flexibility to find resources and get our needs met. During our childhood and adolescence, our blood families provided the bulk of this emotional support, but at midlife, our reliance can shift to our chosen family, especially if our relationship to our blood family has been damaged during the coming-out process.

Take a moment to contrast your chosen family with your blood family, reviewing the exercises but substituting the former for the latter. You may find these exercises easier to tackle, since there may be a stronger, more secure feeling of your place in your chosen family (after all, you chose its members, you created it!) than within your blood family. By virtue of being of your own choosing, there's less pressure to be the son "the family" sees and more opportunity to be the man you are.

9. Talk about those people with whom you can be totally yourself.

Billy at the piano bar. Sally at work. Rod at the gym. Tony at the community college. Who are the people around whom you feel comfortable enough to let loose and enjoy yourself?

Name the people who like you for being you, around whom you don't have to pretend or put on airs. Maybe you can't be totally honest with everybody, but you can count on a couple of buddies for when you need a chat or a shoulder to lean on.

Such emotional honesty reduces our stress, as well as our "outsider" feelings, and contributes to a sense of well-being. This exercise can further deepen your awareness of your friends. Or it may spur a realization that you may not have achieved a safe place with your friends. Maybe you never feel like yourself in front of other people; maybe people frighten you, and you feel more comfortable isolating at home or at work.

Understanding your relationship patterns with friends (male, female, gay, nongay, younger, older) can strengthen whatever sense of support you have already or it can heighten your sense of the work you need to do or it can reveal your progress. Is your life full of love and support? Can it be more full?

10. Describe your uniqueness that makes you different in a positive way from other gay men your age.

You love football. Or you like to sing opera at full throttle, even though you've never had vocal training. You volunteer as a Big Brother in your town. You like to write poetry for special occasions, like a friend's birthday. You sing in a church choir. You have a garden.

You're probably not accustomed to talk about yourself in a positive way, especially when comparing yourself to other gay men. Push yourself to praise yourself. Give yourself permission to brag like a proud parent, pushing aside any false humility that keeps you from seeing your own achievements, your qualities, and your talents.

As gay men, we are told we are sick, criminal, immoral, and so forth from day one, so small wonder that we're more comfortable being negative about ourselves. Many gay men always hear an edge in a compliment and are always defensive or distrustful if another person praises them. But in looking at our lives realistically and focusing on the positive aspects, we can begin to recognize our uniqueness, even among other gay men.

Our chosen family is our own creation, and while there may be a common passion or approach to life among its members, differences are to be expected. Such is the nature of humanity, and differences are part of the fabric of an older man's life. When we are younger, we tried to avoid being different in order to avoid being stigmatized, yet ultimately by coming out, we took a bold stand against stigma and chose to declare our difference from the nongay world. As middle-aged gay men, we can now declare and celebrate our differences from other gay generations.

Our chosen family was created around a shared feeling of difference—that's why we chose its members, who met a need we felt for companionship and connectedness. Sadly, many gay men's frustration at midlife has to do partly with feeling lonely after their friends have died from AIDS. Some gay men have lost almost their entire circle of friends, and AIDS has robbed them of the support they had created and nurtured during their twenties and thirties—the support that otherwise would lessen the pain, isolation, and feelings of powerlessness triggered by their experience of aging.

But having lost a friend to death is different from never having had one in the first place. If you've had a circle of friends decimated by AIDS, it's important to realize that you have the talent to make friends and nurture a friendship. And you can make new friends— not to replace the individuals you lost, but to support you in a different time of your life. If you've never felt capable of making and keeping a friendship, midlife can be a time of looking at how you

communicate with other people and determining how you can create
support and love in your life.

11. Is there any overlap between your blood family and chosen family?

Can you imagine a conversation between your best gay friend
and your father? Or your sister and your lesbian coworker? The idea
that some of your intimate chosen family members could get to know
some of your blood family is probably novel to you—in the realm
of fiction and make-believe. Most gay men do not have or can even
envision mixing such different circles.

But given the development of gay and nongay groups like PFLAG
and GLSTEN (Gay, Lesbian, and Straight Educational Network),
such relationships are not as wild a concept as they would have
been in the past. Also, for many men, AIDS has brought their
blood family and chosen family together, sometimes painfully and
sometimes warmly. By midlife, many gay men have reconciled with
their blood families to the point where friends can be introduced
into the blood family, whose members can also be incorporated into
the chosen family.

The message is that you don't have to keep parts of your life in
isolation from one another. Keeping your emotional support system
spread out over different parts of your life—compartmentalized like
so many P.O. boxes—can be exhausting and a way of dividing your
strength. Integrating those boxes can take work, and may be awkward
and uncomfortable at first, but the payoff is a life where you no
longer have to worry about who knows all of you. The more you
can be yourself in all the worlds in which you travel, the more
integrated you will feel. The more integrated you feel (less stress,
more confidence and authority), the better your aging.

Do you keep separate sets of friends, just as some people keep
separate sets of dishes (the everyday versus the special occasion,
kosher versus nonkosher, the Ikea plates versus the Wedgwood)?

Take a moment to consider how you relate to the people in
your life. Do you have discrete groups of friends, and more one-on-
one interaction, or do you have a large circle of friends who know
one another? Maybe you welcome the different parts of your chosen
family to know one another, which makes you feel like you have

one huge family. Or perhaps your friends are unfamiliar with one another: friends from work, friends from the community center, friends from your religious community. Each group speaks to a different part of you. Maybe different people give you different things in your relationships to them.

A more isolated, separate friendship network would tend to foster fewer feelings of inclusiveness and peership. If a gay men shuttles from friend to friend, he may fall between the cracks emotionally. This separateness among his friends can allow him to isolate himself and not have contact with anybody. Isolation with the negative feelings that midlife might generate can be dangerous and lead to depression. If a gay man doesn't feel love and support, his internalized homophobia can reawaken at any time and lead to despair and feelings of powerlessness. By having an integrated chosen family, a gay man builds a better defense against the isolation that could weaken his experience of aging.

12. Do you feel you are a loved member of your chosen family?

As with the exercise for the blood family, this question focuses on the feelings and not the facts of your relationship with your chosen family. Maybe the affection you feel for and receive from your chosen family is all about action: who will be there for you when you need someone. "I love you" is difficult to say and actually feel—for both the giving and receiving ends of the friendship. You may have created a network of love even though the word *love* may not be mentioned among your friends. Similarly, you may have had a parent who never said he or she loved you "in so many words" but their actions spoke volumes. Love can be unstated but still present.

Does your chosen family always step in when you need it? Do friends ask if they can help you with a project at home? Or watch your apartment and water the plants while you're away? Do you feel comfortable calling a friend to go with you for a doctor's appointment? Do your friends listen to what you have to say? Do they understand?

Looking at your friendships will give you a better idea of patterns in your relationships. Understanding how and why you maintain your relationships will add to your growing awareness of what you have or have not created in your life. Maybe you don't feel supported or listened to by anybody. Maybe you can't feel love from anybody, except your pet. Remember: you deserve to feel loved and supported. If you don't feel that way about your life, this exercise can be a catalyst for changing your relationships or a model for you to act upon. Be honest with yourself, not immodest.

13. Talk about whom within your chosen family you would turn to in an emergency.

Have you ever been in an emergency room? It can be a frightening and confusing place, especially if you're alone. If you were in a car wreck, whom would you call to come get you? If you had to leave work because of illness, is there someone who could escort you or take you to the doctor?

Though you may have a large circle of friends, emergencies demand a certain kind of relationship, and this exercise pushes you to explore the quality of your relationships. Are there dependable people in your life? Have you been there for other people in emergencies? How well can you respond to a crisis? Maybe through dealing with AIDS, you've gained the experience to handle emergencies, and you've seen more hospitals than you ever wanted to.

Not always by choice, many gay men have developed incredible caretaking skills, as well as a high degree of self-reliance. Acknowledging those skills is another powerful building block in strengthening a gay man's sense of himself and of his preparation for aging well.

If you answered "no one" to this exercise, take another moment to start thinking about what changes you would need to make to have "emergency" friends available.

14. If you had some really good news, with whom would you first want to share it?

Your sister Carol. Your best friend Randy. Your HIV positive support group. Your sponsor. Your lover Jose. Friends can be there to guide you through the rough stuff, but it's a comfort as well to share the blessings. Do you like to share your good news and allow others to appreciate the good things in your life? Some friends can help with problems, but aren't necessarily responsive to good news. Maybe they feel needed when they help you in a crisis, but they feel envious or frustrated at your job promotion or commitment ceremony.

There are different levels of sharing, and you have probably established, whether consciously or unconsciously, a hierarchy of confidentiality among your friends. Depending upon the news, you may know exactly who would appreciate it the most. What's important is to share it with someone who will acknowledge, celebrate, and appreciate it as much as you do. We may not be able to predict another person's response or reaction to our good news, so it's best not to try to make yourself vulnerable to someone else's bitterness or judgmentalism. Don't make the good news bad by choosing the wrong listener.

Depending upon the size of your chosen family and blood family, you might have many people you can call on in an emergency or with good news. The more the better, I believe, since the higher level of support you surround yourself with, the better experience you will have with aging. To help a gay man make what sounds abstract—his "emotional support system"—concrete and visual, I ask him to do something he's probably always wanted to do: be the center of the universe.

In order to make his chosen family all the more real, I ask him to draw his world of people as a solar system with himself in the center as the Sun. The planets and "celestial bodies" represent important people in his life. The size of the planets indicate the strength of their importance to him, while their placement in relation to the sun and the size of their orbit indicates the continued importance (frequency of contacts) of that person.

This exercise can be a lot of fun, just like a science project from elementary school, but what it does is force a person to see all the elements of his world in relationship to one another and to him. It makes his world a more explicit and easily referenced one. He has a better sense of where he is, what his world looks like, and how he operates in it. To do this task adequately, he has to look at many aspects of each relationship and see its interaction with the other. The drawing forces him to see himself in the center of his world and to accept what he has created in his life.

15. Do a drawing of your social world as planetary system, with you as a sun and the important people in your life as planets (using size, orbit, and placement).

Get out your crayons and get to it. Your chosen family is your own creation, and now you get to create a solar system as well. Who's your biggest planet? Your lover? Your brother? A fellow volunteer at the community center? Maybe there's a friend from college who means a lot to you, but you don't see so often, so make him or her a comet: somebody who drops into your life every now and then, but is a powerful relationship for you. If you have a "rocky" time visiting your blood family, make them an asteroid belt. Have fun, but be honest.

When you've finished your drawing, study it, treasure it. You have created a world of love and support around you, and it's there when you need it. No matter how lonely or negative you may have felt in the past, this drawing is a visible sign you are not alone. What would this image teach a younger gay man? Do you have gay peers who are having a hard time aging? Maybe you can share this exercise and your drawing with someone close to you who can't feel the love that's around him.

Gene's Story

I wanted to tell Gene's story as an example of how someone can develop a chosen family that becomes his significant other. He has gone through many distinct periods of his life where he has had different kinds of lover/boyfriend relationships. Now in his early fifties, he is exploring the world without any particular kind of relationship in mind. He wants to develop relationships that are satisfying to him but do not meet some preordained blueprint that he has in his head.

Gene was in his early thirties when he first entered therapy as the perpetual adolescent who was now looking for direction. He was in excellent physical shape from his exercising and his work as a carpenter/cabinet maker. He spent much of his time riding his bicycle in long-distance rides with adolescents. He was quite obsessed with hanging out with these younger boys along the piers, kind of a boy in the hood. Since he was so fit physically, the teenagers and twenty-year-olds treated him as a peer. He sometimes had sexual flings with some of them. At the time, he was not particularly interested in changing his sexual attraction to younger men nor did he want to deal with issues around aging. He was most concerned about career decisions and with starting his own company, which he did, and the therapy ended after a year.

A few years later, he returned to therapy. By this time, he knew he was HIV positive, and he had a lover, a tall, thin, very youthful-looking man who was dying from AIDS. The relationship was a very loving one, but sexuality was never a dominant part of it since his lover was not his sexual fantasy. Gene had his own business at this point, but he wasn't running it very well. To really run a business he needed to be an adult, and to him, adult equaled nongay. He had a very hard time thinking of himself as approaching or being in midlife—particularly because he had an incredible body and the adult world kept telling him he was much younger. He had also given up his bike riding and was now into sailing in a very serious way. It had always been an interest, and he was becoming a definite part of the mostly nongay sailing community, in which every man his age looked ten, fifteen years older.

He and his lover had a brownstone in Brooklyn into which they put much work. The therapy during this period was focused on helping him to adjust to his lover's declining health and to treat his business as a business and not as a hobby. To do both of these things meant changing many of his attitudes about being a responsible adult and not being the adolescent. Therapy continued until after his lover's death and after he got rid of the business. A strong perceptual shift came when he gave up his business and went to work for someone else, a hard-nosed businessman who was fairly abusive to him. It was a good experience for him because it pushed him to the place where he could say, "No, this is not what I want." This had a spillover effect on other parts of his life where he began exploring new kinds of relationships in which he was not the caretaker but more the peer.

After a few years, he resumed therapy when he began to explore what he wanted to do with the rest of his life and his spiritual issues, which had always been in the background. He was now entering a relationship with a man his age, who was a writer, with whom he had more of a peer relationship. He was still sailing and now thinking about writing, which he had always wanted to do but had never done. For years he had kept a journal and explored his feelings and experiences by writing. Now he began writing in earnest about his life, including his involvement in sailing.

Through the self-reflection of his writing, he began to explore an aspect of his sexuality that had always intrigued him and had been the source of many fantasies—S/M sex. Since this was not an interest of his lover, he began to explore it outside of the relationship. He discovered sides of himself that were a surprise but not a shock. The relationship became more of a "Boston marriage" with companionship as its greatest strength. He was not exactly clear what he was searching for but he discovered that as a fifty-year-old man with a very good body and attractive face, he was much sought after as a sexual partner. He was possibly more surprised at the response people had to him as a middle-aged gay man than the kind of sex he was having.

He has also continued to explore his spirituality and accept some of the mystical experiences he had had as a younger man. He clearly is still on an exploratory path and has no idea where he will eventually be. He has continued to write and is trying to publish a collection of stories he has finished. He is still sailing and has started a gay men's sailing group. He is now getting known in the S/M community and feeling quite comfortable with this. In fact, he is being sought after by men he finds attractive for the first time in his life. For years, he had pursued younger men with mixed results, and if someone pursued him, he rarely recognized the interest or was never attracted to the man. He's become conscious that he is being turned on by what is happening in his experiences and not solely by the physical beauty of the men he is with—a distinct change from his earlier sexuality. He is quite aware that he is on a journey, but he has no idea where it will take him.

It was at his fiftieth birthday party that all this came into focus. He decided to bring together all parts of his life so he invited all the people who were important to him—his chosen family. It was Gene presenting who he was in his entirety to himself and to the world. It was a very heterogeneous crowd of people—gay, nongay, women, men, adults, children, young, middle-aged, old, singles, couples, businesspeople, sailing people, writers, and sexual partners (past and present). In some ways, it was the mixture usually more common at a memorial service, at which all parts of one's life come together, many for the first time. What was a joyous surprise for Gene was the way everyone related to one another and seemed to understand that they were part of a family. Though some had known each other before, this party began new relationships for others.

What was most important for Gene was that he entered his fiftieth year of life with a sense of wholeness about himself and a comfort with his age. For him, it's not so much about accepting his age, but accepting a new role that comes with his age. He is seeing who he is by the reflection of himself he now sees in his chosen family and not in terms of the singular lover/boyfriend/sexual partner. He is quite comfortable with this state of exploration and not defining himself in terms of "being in a relationship."

SIX

Speaking with One's Own Voice: True Self-Esteem

Working with clients over many years, I began to notice that at some point, usually in their early forties, gay men started to feel more comfortable saying what they wanted to say. We've all encountered that "feisty older man" at a party who speaks his mind freely and doesn't seem to give a damn what anyone else might think. When such people give their opinions without self-censoring, the effect can be startling to anybody who keeps silent about what he's feeling.

For many gay men, the issue is usually a reluctance to share what we're feeling, as opposed to what we're thinking. Having an opinion about politics or a community organization or the economy or a sports team or somebody else's boyfriend is relatively easy; telling someone how you're feeling is another matter altogether. The vulnerability that comes with sharing one's feelings makes many gay men (and nongay, for that matter) uncomfortable and uneasy. Many of us prefer communicating our thoughts (intellectual ideas, concepts, new perspectives on life's challenges), rather than our feelings (what I want or need, what I feel about myself, what you may feel about me, what I feel about you).

When I've encountered people who speak not only their minds, but their hearts, I've always admired their directness and strength. During my life, I have struggled to overcome my shyness and my difficulty in saying exactly what I wanted or felt, especially when it came to sex. Over the years, I have made progress, but for the majority of my life, there were always moments when I felt I couldn't express myself, when I felt as if my voice wouldn't sustain me. Today, I'm still learning how to state what I want without blame or making my lover feel in the wrong for not reading my mind. Communicating my feelings is easier with my chosen family, while some old patterns remain with my blood family. Progress is what's satisfying: being aware that the way I speak my thoughts and feelings has improved as I've gotten older.

Speaking with one's own voice requires being confident and comfortable in saying what you are thinking *and* feeling. Not just your perceptions and observations that have evolved over the years, but also your wishes, desires, dreams. What I have learned from my peers and mentors is that when I feel good about myself, the talk flows. When I feel my life is valid and worthy, I have the courage to speak with my own voice. It is a way of speaking without feeling I am talking from behind a mask, without the feeling of being both the ventriloquist *and* the dummy.

The goal is not just to speak up, but to learn how to communicate. In order to be heard, you have to learn when it's the right time to speak: when the listener is prepared to listen, which means taking into account timing, attention spans, and urgency. In chapter 5, I presented the idea of the hologram and how it affects our relationships from our childhood until our adulthood. One of the enduring legacies of the hologram is difficulty in communicating our true feelings. Emotional honesty must be learned, and for many gay men, the years spent in the closet delay, if not prevent, them from acquiring this skill in communicating.

Coming out represents a turning point not just in our sexual lives, but in our ability to communicate. Coming out means seizing a series of opportunities to be honest about our emotions: first to ourselves, then a friend, then more friends, maybe our family, coworkers, and ultimately, our entire world. The more areas of our lives in which we come out, the more comfortable we will feel about our place and role in the world. The more comfortable we feel, the more we will be able to communicate our emotions and speak with our own voice.

Our comfort level in speaking with our own voice can be measured by our ability to respond, rather than react. We earn another "merit badge" in communication when we learn the difference between reacting and responding. Too often we *react*, when we could *respond*.

When a person stands back and evaluates a situation, seeing a range of alternative feelings and actions, he can usually choose a reasoned, appropriate *response*. In contrast, a *reaction* is immediate and usually inappropriate, triggered by situations long past, but that are similar to what he feels now. Reactions are behaviors learned in the past and repeated indefinitely, until we discover how to take the time to recognize our reaction for what it is: a behavioral reaction to an emotional reflex.

For example, a friend says your boyfriend is not smart enough or nice enough for you. You get defensive, react with anger, attack his sense of judgment, or tell him he's an idiot. Actually, you're feeling hurt by what he said but you dismiss that feeling instantaneously and replace it with anger, which you use to hurt your friend. *What you feel is a reaction to his behavior.* He hasn't made you feel that way; you react that way. Understanding this dynamic may seem to go against how you understand emotions, but no one makes us feel a certain way. We choose our feelings from a range: sadness, anger, joy, rage, depression, happiness. As we get to know ourselves better, we learn to communicate better and can see that we are responsible for our emotions. Learning the difference between reacting and responding is a first step in this process.

Our goal is to get in touch with the immediate feeling in order to convey it directly and simply. Progress would be to state directly that you are feeling hurt without anger becoming an issue. If anger *is* a direct response to a situation (say, for example, you're laid off), then the anger can be expressed by stating it rather than acting with hostility or violence. Often, many feelings can exist at the same time (anger, sadness, lust) so it can admittedly be difficult to figure out and express the appropriate one(s). It's much easier just to pick the strongest emotion (regardless of how inappropriate it may be) and run with it, but that strategy doesn't foster true communication.

Speaking with one's own voice doesn't mean telling other people what's wrong with them or blaming other people for your feelings or putting people down for having their own feelings. Speaking with one's own voice means being able to say, "I feel this way (X) when you do that behavior/action (Y)." Falling back on blame or not taking responsibility for your own feelings leads to statements like "You make me so angry" or "It's all your fault I feel this way." Reactions like this reflect not only that we believe the other person is making us feel a certain way, but that we, too, can make him feel a certain way. When we react, there's usually a degree of manipulation in what we're saying. We want to make the person feel a certain way— because not taking responsibility for our own feelings runs in both directions: We believe we can control his emotions just as much as we believe he can control our emotions. But speaking with one's own voice is not about being manipulative. It's just stating directly what you feel without trying to get the other person to do anything but listen.

Once you can understand the difference between response and reaction, you will be more able to understand what you are feeling and make the appropriate response. Recognizing the difference between when you are responding and when you are reacting leads to less drama and more direct and honest communication. The first step is to learn to recognize what our feelings are so we can accurately express them. It is not as easy as it sounds since we have spent an entire life hiding and disguising our feelings beneath our hologram.

As we explored in chapter 5, the hologram can wreak incredible damage to our communication skills. A gay child/adolescent operating under the burden of his hologram hides his true feelings not only from his blood family and peers, but also himself. He hides not just his true sexual feelings, but his true feeling about everything: what he wants out of life, what he thinks of his world, how he feels about his parents, how he feels about himself. The hologram teaches the gay child to distrust his inner life. He stops believing he can communicate his inner feelings and thoughts, and he stops believing that anyone is interested in his inner life since his hologram gets all the attention, love, and support. Finally, he begins to think his inner life has no meaning since no one cares enough to see beneath the hologram. Thus, his emotions and inner thoughts become irrelevant and unimportant, even to him.

Changing this lifelong pattern of denying the value of his inner life is incredibly difficult. But when a gay man becomes aware of the hologram as the source of pain and frustration, he will begin to change. So much of the "midlife crisis" is about this pain; what it reveals is a deep, strong sense of wanting to validate yourself by

expressing your true self. This desire starts developing prior to midlife. Indeed, it's present from childhood, but typically, parents want
us to be who they want us to be. Few parents actually encourage
children to be unique and who they are. Sometimes when a gay man
challenges his parents, and especially when he comes out, they often
defend their reaction by saying, "But we just want you to be happy."
(This is a "loving" reaction from parents, as opposed to those who
reject the son and begin the blaming.) But few parents have any idea
what will make their gay son happy. Even the gay son doesn't always
know. Knowing what will make us happy requires a sense of our
inner life: what we really feel and need and think. If a gay man isn't
familiar or in touch with that inner life, looking at the home environment may shed some light.

Most kids are raised in a *nursing*, but not *nurturing* environment.
Parents can be loving but not understand the difference between
these two kinds of child rearing. A nursing environment focuses on
addressing a child's basic needs (food, clothing, shelter, social skills,
language acquisition), whereas a nurturing environment encompasses
the child's development (sense of security; appropriate, not exaggerated feelings of entitlement; encouragement of his or her uniqueness;
listening to the child's feelings and thoughts and awakening consciousness of the world and his or her place in it). Nursing parents
measure their success with the child's growth, a linear expansion of
the child (weight, height, school grades, and so on), while nurturing
parents measure their success by taking into consideration the complexity of the child's world and his developmental progress as an
individual. The goal of nursing is for the child to survive and fit in;
the goal of nurturing is for the child to blossom and be happy.

A nursing parent does not see beneath the hologram; a nurturing
parent struggles to help the child define his true self. A nursing
environment can help to create the hologram because the emphasis
is on the external, the actions and behavior of the child, not the
inner emotions and sense of self. In contrast, a nurturing environment
teaches a child to respect and honor his self. One of the long-term
dangers of the hologram is the lingering sense that "no one really
cares about *me*. It's my hologram they love." So no matter what the
person does to get love, it doesn't sink in because the "me" is never
being presented: "they don't even know me." When a nursing parent
praises the good behavior of the hologram, the gay child begins to

realize that *he* doesn't matter, just how he behaves is important, while a nurturing environment encourages a gay child to become his own person and affirms him when he asserts the beginning of a personality.

The effects of this nursing can remain even after a gay man comes out to his family. The hologram can become a way of life, a way of operating in the world that prevents us from integrating the different parts of our life into a satisfying whole, the real "me." A gay man may be out to his blood family, but they may have no genuine sense of his gayness because they never talk about it, he never brings it up, and there's no interaction between his gay life and the other areas of his life. Even as an openly gay man, he may feel "nobody knows the real me." Such feelings suggest that the hologram is alive and well.

An acquaintance of mine, Luis, was out to his sister for seven years, and she seemed comfortable with the information until he asked to bring a boyfriend home for Christmas. She had no real image of him as being gay, or of his being coupled with another man. As a result, she felt uncomfortable enough to ask him to come alone. She offered to meet the boyfriend later in the winter. Despite his mixed feelings of sadness and anger, he decided not to go home for the holidays but agreed to the later visit because he loves her and wants to work on the relationship. He realized that in the years he had been out to her, he had always been reluctant to share any details with her about his relationships, and consequently, he usually felt an outsider at her house, despite being openly gay in his own life. He is hopeful that once his sister sees him in his life, she will come around and accept all of him, not just the good sibling, but the sexuality as well. By working to integrate his sister into his world, he is casting off the hologram of the asexual little brother and developing an acceptance and appreciation of himself that results in a more authentic and integrated self-presentation to the world.

MIDLIFE: SAYING GOOD-BYE TO THE HOLOGRAM

At midlife, several factors come into play that can motivate a gay man to finally cast off the hologram and begin to express his true self. Many changes, both physical and emotional, can make midlife

seem like a "crisis" to be resolved and survived. Many gay men report
feeling when they reach forty that "life is passing them by," accompa-
nied by a feeling that so much of what they wanted to accomplish
will not happen "in my lifetime." Sometimes it's just a vague sense
of "something's not right." This sense of inadequacy feeds into a
series of questions such as "What do I really want?" and "Who am
I?" In trying to answer these questions, the desire to express our true
self can resurface, and we can begin to make decisions for ourselves,
for what will make us happy—which explains why there are so many
shifts at midlife—relationships, jobs, play, health. Why does this
happen? Why does the need to speak one's truth become such a
burning desire at midlife? What initiates this process? Many gay men
point to their changing bodies as the greatest impetus for change:
physical changes add to any emotional discomfort to bring about
change in the lifestyle. A growing awareness of our own mortality
feeds the feeling of "I'm going to die and no one will have known
the real me." *In effect, when "mortality becomes reality," many gay men decide
to make that reality the best it can be.*

For openly gay men at midlife, the hologram of heterosexuality
they maintained during their adolescence may no longer be operating, but the hologram of being what others want, of being a
projection of other people's expectations can remain extremely powerful. The "other people" may have shifted from a gay man's blood
family to his chosen family and gay peers, but since there are still
"other people" for whom he is living, answering the questions of
"What do I want?" and "Who am I?" is all the more difficult. At
midlife, a person has reached a point where he is moved to say, "I've
done it for them, now what about me?"

Since by midlife we have probably achieved a lot of things we
thought would make us happy, any dissatisfaction during this period
of our life is particularly harsh, exaggerated, and confusing. Even
with a steady job, a lover, a circle of friends, and a sexual life, we
can still be left with basic questions of "What do I want?" and "Who
am I?" These questions are not different from the ones we encountered in our twenties and thirties, but then we thought we knew
what the answers were—a boyfriend, a high-paying job, a house,
whatever dreams of happiness our economic class may inspire.

It takes time to accumulate experiences, to build more of a foundation for the self. Since gay men's development follows a different

path from that of nongay men, this foundation may not emerge until the forties or fifties, depending upon when the gay man came out, established a lifestyle, and adopted a gay identity. These "life" experiences provide a better base from which to operate and to answer the questions of "What do I want?" and "Who am I?" Revisiting the concept of our four ages, our Heart Age is more reflective of who we really are than our Clock Age. An aspiring writer, upon graduation from college, may immediately write his first novel without having ever been more than a student all his life. Such novels are rarely compelling or full of flesh-and-blood significance. Many writing teachers will encourage a student to live a little first before writing the Great American Novel. Unlike a writer in his twenties, a gay man coming into his own in his forties and fifties has a story to tell, has lived enough to express something at stake in the telling of his story: his own value.

In our discussion of work and play, I suggested that the pressure to know what we want early in life forces us to make career decisions in our teens, long before we may really know what we want to do or can separate our blood family's wishes from our own. How many of us would have more satisfying work experiences if we had been allowed to work after high school, perhaps at several jobs, before choosing a field or profession or occupation?

The same dynamic of forced decision making operates with our aging. You won't know what it's like until you get there, but by midlife, you will probably have a clearer sense of who you truly are than you did when you were twenty or thirty or even thirty-five. Midlife is the time for saying and feeling who you are and not letting other people define you. Under the hologram's influence, we may not have any sense of what others really see in us or the basis of their perceptions. Not trusting our chosen family when they express love for us, we continue to ask ourselves: Who is it they really care for? Even if "they" say the same thing about me that I would, saying it myself makes all the difference. It's coming from my mouth—my experience of myself.

Given many gay men's history of hiding their inner self from the world and the way of operating and communicating that it generates, it is imperative for men approaching middle age to appreciate who they are. Appreciating yourself means taking stock of the paths you have taken, and for once, focusing on the positive experiences too, not only on the negative ones, and looking at what you have, not just what you lack. Appreciating yourself is about knowing your objective reality, not accepting your subjective perceptions. Midlife is the time to be objective about one's history, so as to speak assertively from within and about oneself. Seeing yourself as a failure, despite a string of successes, is not being objective. Being objective means seeing your history without judgment or without rigidity (e.g. "I don't have this," "I don't have that"). Appreciating your accomplishments leads to a sense of stability and security that can counter the "crisis" anxiety of midlife. You will feel safer and more secure with a worldview based on self-respect. Self-validation provides self-security, and a secure sense of self is the best foundation for aging well.

THE PATH TO SELF-VALIDATION

Success in learning to speak with one's own voice is based in part on the degree to which internal validation occurs. During our childhood, adolescence, and even into our adulthood, the hologram has served as the primary recipient of external validation, while the inner self suffered from neglect. To age successfully requires a shift from external sources of validation to an internal sense of value, self-worth, and satisfaction with life. This shift is especially crucial at midlife, when our "externals" begin to lose their value because of ageism. At the core of this shift is our self-esteem, but before I introduce a new concept of self-esteem, it's important to revisit the connections between a gay man's hologram and his body—his two primary means of feeling validated, both of which change at midlife. To learn to speak with our own voice, we need to overcome our cultural conditioning as men to ignore both our inner life and our body. Again, understanding the mind-body connection between our physical body and our inner life will lead to hearing and speaking with your own voice.

As men, we are more defined by action, so we don't associate the male body with emotional communication. Revisiting our discussion from the body and health chapters, the gay male body is more about display and currency than accomplishing a goal as in sports and war. Conditioned from an early age to regard the mind and the body as polar opposites (brain versus brawn), we usually develop an identity around one of these poles: the nerdy scholar or the popular athlete, the successful lawyer or the construction worker. Most men feel more comfortable in one or the other, but usually not in both of these arenas. In addition, class differences can push us in one direction or the other, with working-class men seen as more physical, nonverbal, immediate (hot and sexual), and upper class men seen as more intellectual, verbal, and distant (and cold, sexually). The way class operates in America, the more economic security you come from, the more education you presumably will receive, the less you have to exert your physical body to earn your living. The mind becomes a form of currency the body once represented. For gay men, this currency metaphor seems especially apt. Younger gay men often feel that their body is their only currency, leading them to minimize the mind and emphasize the body, while as we age, we realize that both can become sources of power.

At the same time, we are conditioned to accept the equation of homosexuality with effeminacy, both in the body (called a sissy, picked last for teams) as well as the mind (don't cry like a girl, take it like a man). No matter how butch a gay man may become, the nongay culture maintains the stereotype that he wants to be a woman, because only a woman can desire another man. These cultural assumptions undermine any attempt by a gay man to exert authority or power, and as a result, we often stop speaking with our own voice—we don't believe it to be a man's voice. An example of this would be the military leadership's inability to accept gay men as leaders, despite the overwhelming evidence of courage and leadership ability displayed by gay men (and lesbians) in the armed forces. Many in the military may accept the idea that a gay man can fight, can defend, and may die for his country, but few are willing to follow a gay man into battle (or so the generals tell us). This resistance to accepting gay men as leaders and authority figures is not limited to the military but extends to all areas of our culture. When I was appointed director of a day hospital in Brooklyn, many of the hospital's staff said I wouldn't be a good authority figure, despite my record of confronting management on staff issues in the workplace. I was well-liked by the staff, and they knew I could mediate well, but they couldn't accept me transferring those skills to a leadership position over the day hospital.

When confronted by such homophobia, we gay men face a painful dilemma: be true to ourselves and experience social rejection, or not be true to ourselves and experience self-rejection. In short, we're compromised either way—if we're true to ourselves, we're outcasts, but if we conform to a particular hologram and become who "they" want us to be, we deny who we are. Simply put, homophobia is bad for your health. Every time we deny who we are it represents a mini-suicide, psychologically and physiologically. We are saying we don't know who we are and we don't want to know (or want anybody else to know for that matter). It may seem hyperbolic to say we are killing ourselves with denial, but the pressure of deception produces constant stress, which can weaken our immune system and invite all kinds of other mental and physical problems. Not speaking with your own voice forces your emotional issues (how you think and feel) to emerge on the physical level, with rashes, stress, gastric problems, or nervous tics.

If we decide to be true to ourselves, then we have to integrate the two parts of ourselves: mind with body. By linking who we want to be with who we are, we can eliminate the hologram and begin to express ourselves. The first step is being open about our sexuality; staying closeted only maintains the hologram. Our coming out as gay men is a Declaration of Independence from the tyranny of the hologram. By declaring and asserting your right to be open and loving with another man, you have refused to feed the social image of heterosexuality you once adopted to survive.

But the work doesn't stop there—we soon learn that being openly gay isn't the answer to everything. We might still have lousy jobs or lackluster relationships (though now, at least, with men, instead of faking it with women). The hologram may still be operating, even if we may be less conscious of it once we have come out sexually as gay men. There's still a trace of it—dictating who we are, what we do with our lives, how we interact with other people.

Eliminating the hologram requires discovering your true self and esteeming it—a two-part process that is more likely to happen at midlife, when our motivation has shifted from wanting to be who "they" wanted us to be, to expressing "who I am" in all areas of our lives. True integration starts with a need to validate the self and to honor the self you have created. The goal is honesty: What you see is what you get. When there's no sense of disconnectedness between how you think of yourself and how you express yourself, you have begun to dismantle the hologram. When you begin to realize you have no control over what others think of you, the opinion of yourself that most matters becomes your own.

If this journey to self-validation sounds familiar, it's because it mirrors the process of coming out. To eliminate the hologram fully requires a second coming out: as middle-aged. That small, still voice that once whispered, "I'm gay," returns at midlife as you begin to assume a new identity: "I am gay. I am middle-aged. I am good. I have a life worth living." The creation of your midlife self will be easier because of the creation of your gay self.

SELF-ESTEEM AND "OTHER-ESTEEM"

To speak authentically with your own voice requires learning how to treat yourself and understanding the self you have created. In a word, it requires self-esteem. Self-esteem is usually understood to mean what you think of yourself, and is most often described as either high (positive feelings, strong sense of self) or low (negative feelings, poor sense of self). It seems like in the nineties, self-esteem finally "arrived" as the hot-button issue whenever social issues are raised. The laundry list of ailments related to low self-esteem is staggering: drug addiction, eating disorders, alcoholism, divorce, street violence, gangs, teenage pregnancy, HIV infection, high crime, child abuse, domestic violence, and so forth. But it's much easier to point out the effects of low self-esteem than to change its causes.

Many, many books have been written about the effects and legacy of low self-esteem, but very little seems to deal effectively with raising self-esteem. Despite the helpful advice found in many of these books, people still feel bad about themselves. We look for easy answers because it is human nature to seek simple methods over complex ones. It's easier to follow a diet with ten no-nos, than the complicated diet known as "The Zone" that practically depends on a calculator to determine what, how much, and when a person can eat.

I think one reason so many self-help books fail to help is that we don't change our frame of reference for self-acceptance. We can start our day with affirmations, we can wear bright clothes, keep our hair trimmed, and our bodies lean, but if our frame of reference is still *how other people see us*—if we are relying on other people's opinions to make us feel complete and good about ourselves—then we will soon lose our path of change amid the undergrowth and brush of other people's opinions about us.

Self-esteem builds upon the daily acts that we perform *to esteem ourselves*—not what we do daily so that others will esteem us. It doesn't matter how much we love ourselves if the foundation of our self-esteem is what others think about us.

I'd like to introduce a new conception of self-esteem as *the respecting of your own created identity*. It's more than just self-validation. I think many gay men don't feel validated and worthy precisely because they have had to invent themselves. We *have* to create ourselves, often from scratch, with very few models (and those are usually just negative stereotypes), yet we often don't acknowledge the degree to which this is true. But I'd wager that *one of our greatest gay gifts is our self-invention*. Given so little cultural support and encouragement, gay men are free to become whatever they want, *assuming* they can cast off the expectations of others.

For many gay men, the process of self-invention reaches its fullest flower at midlife: we are in a position to reap the benefits of years of honesty, planning, and adventure, although many of us may not be able to recognize the strengths and achievements we have mustered so far. What becomes clear at midlife is that *the created self keeps being created*. A gay man at midlife faces new roles and responsibilities, new passions and challenges, just as he did when he came out.

What I'm after is not only understanding how you perceive yourself operating in the world, but with *whose validation*. By midlife, a gay man has accumulated enough life experience to know himself. By examining his life's journey from birth to midlife, he can achieve a more solid sense of self from which to act for the rest of his life. When he learns to appreciate the full context of his life experiences, a gay man assumes major components of self-esteem: appreciation, authority, and authenticity. He begins to feel his own sense of power and worth, and it is from these positive feelings that his true voice emerges.

So why do so many gay men have problems expressing their emotions and speaking with their own voice? Sometimes it's hard to think positively of yourself when you don't even feel full ownership of your self-image. Perhaps you haven't given yourself permission to esteem yourself. Since self-esteem is about bestowing esteem upon *your* self, we often diminish ourselves by basing our self-concept on the opinions of others.

Much of what we do to increase our self-esteem is really what I call "other-esteem," since it is the esteem of others that we really care about. Dieting, makeovers, new cars and homes, or keeping up with the Joneses are all ways to get people to pay attention to us and reward us with their approval or envy. How much of all that is about us and about what we want?

A gay man may say, "It *is* about what I want: a boyfriend. If I don't have the right body or the right clothes, I'll never get noticed and I'll be single and bitter and old." When I ask him why a boyfriend is so important, he'll say that having a boyfriend makes him feel attractive, accepted, "normal." But then I remind him that no one makes us feel a particular way. While our feelings are reactions to other people's behaviors, *the pursuit of other-esteem is a reaction to our own feelings of inadequacy*. But no matter how desperately we crave it, other-esteem is a losing battle, a no-win situation, since we have no control over what other people will think of us.

Our concern for other-esteem can appear in the most common, daily activities. Once when I was eating lunch in a park, I noticed other pieces of trash and litter along the path as I was taking my trash to a garbage can. I stopped to pick some pieces up, and by the time I reached the trash can, my hands were full of other's people's litter. For a brief moment, I thought, *I must look like a weirdo picking up all this garbage*, but in the next instant I thought even more strongly, *Tough shit! If more people did this, the park would be clean!*

Of course, I thought reflexively for a moment about how I looked, about what other people might think of me, but my newer reflex won out: I knew what I was doing was good, and somebody else's opinion wouldn't change that. If I stop to think about what other people are thinking about me, I am giving up the power to express myself. I am handing my self-esteem over to somebody else and diminishing my own sense of power.

There's an old joke about this concern for what others think of us: "If you really knew how rarely other people thought of you, you wouldn't spend so much time worrying about what other people think of you."

A gay man will never know his own power if he continues to rely upon others' perceptions, since he will remain vulnerable to manipulation and control. Remember the discussion of power we had in chapter 5 about our relationships? Other-esteem is a tool of aggrandized power, while self-esteem is an expression of inherent power. Others can control us as long as other-esteem is operating, yet gay men find casting off the iron grip of other-esteem is extremely difficult, given our cultural conditioning. From childhood, we have measured our value by external, usually nongay, opinions (parents, siblings, teachers), which have determined our behavior by sanctioning it or disapproving of it. Over the course of our lives, these voices, the opinions of others, have become the "shoulds," an automatic way to judge the self.

Sadly, this process does not automatically stop when we come out. The gay male community has its own set of shoulds that we inherit upon coming out, and we know them well, especially the ones involving ageism and appearance. Coming out doesn't totally eliminate our mode of operating under other-esteem, but shifts the "other" from the nongay world to our gay peers.

Coming out as a gay man is an incredible act of self-esteem, throwing off so much negative, homophobic other-esteem. But when we begin to accept the negative opinions of our own community (gay life ends at forty, no one wants you), we fall back into the trap of other-esteem. When we do not acknowledge who we are—attractive, middle-aged gay men strengthened by our life experiences—when we let others or wait for others to validate us (with a flirt, a cruise, a sexual overture), we are diminishing our own power.

Nobody else can give you self-esteem. You can't start esteeming yourself until you get rid of other-esteeming. It's about valuing yourself—not creating "new" value but recognizing the worth that's already there. It's about seeing and validating all aspects of yourself, including your age. You did it before when you came out as a gay man, *despite your fears of rejection*, because you knew you were worth more than the lies of homophobia. You can do it again by coming out as a middle-aged man, because you realize you're worth more than the lies of ageism.

When I was thirty-five, I attended a conference at Columbia University of an activist organization called the Gay Academic Union. For the space of about six hours, I experienced a total recognition of all parts of my life: I was an intellectual meeting with my peers; I was a panelist in one session; I was a professional doing my networking; I was a sexual being flirting with new men whom I found sexually attractive; and I was an activist organizing with those who shared my politics. As I was leaving the building, I realized it was a powerful first for me: I didn't experience any feelings of "less than" or "other than" or "different from." After years of college and being a professional and coming out as openly gay, I was just being who I was, and it felt great! I wondered if that was what nongay people felt all of their lives. I realized at that moment that I wanted to devote my life to making this happen to other gay men and lesbians as early in life as possible, instead of seeing them wait until they were in their thirties or forties or even much later.

What felt good at the conference were the feelings of wholeness and the integration of all the different parts of my life. But it's hard to enjoy those positive feelings if you aren't prepared to feel good about yourself. A lot of people don't feel good about themselves and can't seem to shake it. Many go into counseling with this unhappiness as their main complaint. Locked in circular thinking, they waste a lot of time in the therapist's office by staying too focused on wanting to feel good by *talking* about wanting to change, but not taking any action. Talking, talking, talking. Yes, mutual dialogue and self-reflection are part of the process, but they are not the only components of therapy. Talking is the best first step, but we can't feel good until we do good. That is, until we adopt behavior that we feel good about. And we won't adopt behavior we feel good about until we shift from a mode of other-esteem. All the therapy in the world won't work until this shift occurs and the client begins to take actions for himself, rather than for all those others. This phenomenon is well-known to those recovering from addiction: sobriety won't happen unless the addict is doing it for himself. You may enter a rehab because of your lover or chosen family, but you won't stay sober unless it's for you.

You can't learn everything from therapy, so I often gave clients "homework assignments" as a way of getting them to focus on their issues outside of my office, to spend time thinking and acting on their lives more than once a week. If a client felt stuck and rigid, I'd ask him to do something out of the ordinary each day, breaking his usual routine. It could be small (take a different route to work) or large (place a personal ad), but there would be no value judgments. The emphasis was on taking an action. If a client felt deprived or unloved, I'd tell him to buy himself something that he wanted, not toothpaste, but a gift for himself. Other times, I'd ask a client to read a particular essay or text, or practice learning to smile at strangers, or to write a letter to someone he had been avoiding (which he may or may not end up sending). Similarly, I hope you will find some help in what you're reading here, but this book is only a part of the answer. The other part is taking what you have read and learned and putting it to use—doing, working, living, shifting your perspectives.

Many people come into therapy with a particular agenda ("I hate my job"; "I am depressed"; "I can't stand my parents"; "I don't like myself"; "I'm bored with my relationship"; "I'm unhappy"), so there is a sense of where change is needed. But often, a person will want to feel better before making any changes in his behavior. "I hate my job, but I want to wait until I'm not depressed in order to job-hunt." "I want to do couples counseling with my lover, but I want to feel stronger first." "When I retire, I'll have time to write my novel." This resistance to change has many sources, from fear of making things worse to the cultural myth of waiting for the right moment to pursue a dream (as we found back in our discussion on retirement). But by delaying action, people remain stuck, unhappy, and frustrated. Many times I'd suggest a client stop therapy if I felt he was treading water and our process had become stagnant. I'd ask him to stop coming, go out and live his life, and then after six months, we'd talk about whether therapy would be fruitful for him or not. If a single client kept wanting to find a lover but he never went out on a second date, I'd tell him he wasn't going to meet a man because our relationship was too much of a substitute. Just as when I was setting up my private practice and gave my clients a flexible schedule, I always stressed that there was more to life than therapy. Changing a lifelong passivity or stubborn patterns of behavior can take time, and the first step is often a perceptual shift around the behavior.

During my early twenties, I cruised public restrooms a lot, and I spent a lot of time condemning myself for this behavior. I was in analysis three times a week, but I felt stalled and unable to make progress on this or any issue. My analyst had a traditional approach: He was totally silent, while I was supposed to free associate for the entire session. But without any direction to our work, I had no sense of progress. One day, when I was cruising johns, I began to imagine heaven as a place where I could cruise all day, every day in a john.

This image of heaven thrilled me and appalled me at the same time. I was disgusted with myself for having that thought. At the time, I was in graduate school and working in a clinical psychology program. My supervisor was a British lady, very prim and proper, but totally comforting and intellectually stimulating. One day, I found myself sharing my frustration with my analysis, my cruising behavior, and my distress over my "ideal" image of heaven, with her. She thought a moment before responding. I was extremely scared and anxious, not knowing what she was going to say. Finally, she replied, "I'm so glad you have a place where you feel safe and comfortable and good about yourself." Her nonjudgmentalness and her ability to have a positive feeling about my behavior shocked and amazed me. In the next few minutes I spent talking with her, I was able to make more progress than in the previous year with my analyst. I very quickly stopped analysis with him and began to work with this woman.

Instead of talking about wanting to change as I had with my previous analyst, I was able to change my behavior, or at the very least, change my perspective about this behavior and what it was doing (or not doing) for me, under the guidance of my new therapist. Her initial response jarred my perception—and told me there were other ways of looking at myself and at this behavior. I was still operating in other-esteem and wondering what others would think of me if they knew of my behavior, but her response had started a process of change: a shift in my negative perception and condemnation of myself. (The change wasn't about switching therapists, but that did help!)

Years later, I applied this kind of perceptual shift to my own clients. In the late seventies, I encountered a client who claimed to be "addicted" to the Mineshaft, an infamous backroom bar in New York (now defunct). This man loved going there every night and having wild sex with new people, but he would later beat himself up over the behavior and feel bad about himself. He told me he wanted to stop going there, and he wanted me to tell him how to stop going. I replied by saying I was not going to do that since it was clear to me there was something positive for him in going there, and until we knew what that good thing was, I was not going to suggest he stop going.

It turned out that it was the only place he could express what he wanted in terms of sex. In his words, he could "sleaze" and have fun there and nowhere else. We worked together until he understood going there could be a choice, something he chose to do that had a very positive aspect. Then we worked some more to see how he could transfer the feelings he enjoyed there to another arena, namely his own bedroom. He saw that he never condemned himself while he was at the Mineshaft. He had a great time there; it was only afterward that he judged himself and began to beat himself up for going there. It wasn't what he did there that he condemned; what made him feel bad about himself was that he went to the Mineshaft to do it. Once he realized that he could have the Mineshaft experience at home, we focused on how he could ask for and receive what he wanted sexually from someone he was intimately involved with. He eventually no longer had the compulsion to go there. The Mineshaft became one of many alternative sexual experiences he could choose from. His goal became to go there when that was the exact experience he wanted (anonymous and with many partners). It wasn't the Mineshaft itself that concerned me, but the fact that a sexual behavior had a compulsive aspect in which he felt no choice. (Ultimately, he recommended several of his friends to my practice with the very same complaint, and to them, I became known as the "Mineshaft" therapist!)

The danger of the compulsion was not about the place or a particular act, but the feeling that he had no choice about his sexual behavior. My central assumption is that a person always has choices about his life. Although I may cushion it a bit, depending upon the circumstances, my message is pretty clear: Don't sit on your ass and bemoan your life. "Once I get my act together, I'll . . ." or how about "I'd get my life together if only I knew where to start." One of the biggest ways to get your life together is to act, to do. "Only by doing" could be my mantra. This may seem to conflict with a more Eastern approach of being present for your life and staying in the moment. Again, as men, we are overconditioned to act with the body, not the mind. But I'm saying *action can be of the mind*: a shift in perception *is* doing, acting. Once there's been a perceptual shift, a behavioral shift is more likely to follow and be easier to make.

What's also critical here is a sense of the time frame. Being in the present is an ideal mode of operating in the world, but when you're stuck in quicksand, you need to get out of it. Too many people assume not changing is easier than changing. I find that many people hold on to a difficult, negative perspective ("I'm too old to go dancing," for example) more tenaciously than taking a simple action (getting enough rest and maybe not dancing all night). Action is not meaningful unless the change in attitude is also present. It's a circular dynamic in which each reinforces and strengthens the other.

Moreover, growth and movement into newer areas, such as life planning and spirituality, aren't possible until a firmer sense of "who I am" has been achieved. Speaking with your own voice is the most concrete manifestation of a firm sense of self: It communicates that you value your own opinion and the person expressing that opinion.

It took me a long time to value my own voice. In 1974, I was involved in the movement to have the American Psychological Association (APA) make a statement depathologizing homosexuality. This was after the American Psychiatric Association depathologized homosexuality and dropped it from its *Diagnostic and Statistical Manual of Mental Disorders* (DSM). As one of the founders of the Association of Gay Psychologists and as a known activist, I was the first openly gay psychologist to speak before the APA's Council of Representatives, the rule-making body of the APA, which was meeting in Washington, D.C., at the annual APA conference.

Though my voice shook a little, I was worried more about what I was wearing than what I said. I presented our argument calmly, collectedly, and all the work my colleagues and I had done paid off when the council voted to reclassify homosexuality as a healthy orientation.

The very next day, I was back at my job as the director of a day hospital. It was not going to be a good day—I had to speak with an employee, a social worker, who was doing a bad job, and whom I needed to put on probation. I experienced more anxiety, fear, and a greater inability to be direct with this person than in speaking before hundreds of my fellow professionals at the APA's Council of Representatives.

What was the difference? One involved speaking for a public cause and the other expressing myself in a one-on-one confrontation. I had no problem asking the APA to depathologize homosexuality because I believed in the cause; it was valid and worthy. But to ask someone in a one-to-one encounter to change a behavior because *I* thought it was important was another matter. I think I didn't really believe that my opinion and sense of authority mattered very much,

whereas before the APA I was backed up by the weight and reputa-
tions of many colleagues, gay and nongay alike. Clearly, when it
came to my own life, I wasn't giving my own voice the same amount
of weight and authority.

Overcoming our self-censoring may the most difficult task of all
since our voice needs to be heard in all areas of our lives: Work/
Play, blood family, chosen family, and within our community at large.
Many gay men learn to speak their minds directly at midlife because,
quite simply, they finally realize that what they have to say has value.

1. **Who are the people that you know who speak their mind?**

Your best friend Carlos. Your lover Eli. Your mother. All of these
people tell it like it is. Their honesty can seem brutal sometimes,
not because of how they speak their thoughts, but because you're not
accustomed to hearing people respond directly. This exercise is not
about focusing on those people who spout off or who are into a
reactive mode all the time, but the people who take the time to figure
out what they're going to say before their reactions overtake them.

People who speak their minds can come across many ways:
strong, articulate, clear, smart. But if they are reacting, rather than
responding, they may seem hostile, judgmental, or holier than thou.

What are the characteristics of the people you know who speak
their minds? Can you identify any similarities between them and you?
Maybe you share the same opinions, but you prefer to keep quiet
about them. Maybe you feel less sure that you'll be heard. Maybe
you're worried about other people's reaction to what you have to
say. In our discussion of role models in chapter 3, I suggested that
the strongest and most effective role models are those people around
you who offer living, breathing examples of how to take charge of
their lives. A role model doesn't have to be a superstar or celebrity
to have an impact on your life.

For example, if you admire the way a co-worker interacts with
the boss, consider how you can emulate his or her pattern of communication. What makes that person more effective? Is he direct when
he asks a question? Does he raise points during a meeting? Is he
casual or joking around the boss? Try to identify what makes his
communication with the boss so effective, and then examine your
own interaction with the boss. Is it a matter of shyness? Have you

always been reluctant to speak aloud, even if what you have to say isn't controversial? Perhaps it's a matter of respect or a sense of propriety left over from childhood, when many of us heard "don't speak unless spoken to."

2. At what age do you feel it is appropriate to speak your mind?

Sixteen: when we can drive. Eighteen: when we can vote. Twenty-one: when we can drink. Thirty: when we stop being "young." Forty: the crest of the "hill." Sixty-five: when we retire. Seventy-five: grandpa! Ageism creates assumptions and myths around both ends of the age spectrum, so that many people associate speaking freely with two camps: children too young to know better and old people who don't give a damn what people think. The rest of us fall somewhere in the middle between stating directly what we mean and being hypervigilant about not offending or making a negative impression.

Most people grow up hearing that only "old" people are allowed to speak without being spoken to. Too many overly expressive children are told to shut up by overworked and exhausted parents. As a result, many people, gay and nongay alike, develop mental blocks in speaking their minds. Age can't be the determining factor since both young and old speak more freely than those of us in the middle. It must be characteristic of the person. So what qualities do children and old people share? A sense of freedom. Less restrained emotions. No self-consciousness. A joyful embrace of life (but with different sources: the newness of experience versus the self-knowledge gained from many life experiences).

3. In what ways do you now feel that you are old enough and have had enough life experience to speak your mind?

Have you begun to acknowledge all that you've experienced? Coming out. Being gay. AIDS. Creating a self from scratch. Relationships. The death of a parent or lover. Settling into a home. Your experience has given you things to say, and you can acknowledge them without judging yourself. The facts speak for themselves, and you can learn to speak for yourself as well. You now know the difference between speaking your mind (responding) and just spouting off (reacting). Think about the times when you give yourself the permission to speak up and when you self-censor.

4. **Think about those times and situations when you are feeling strong and find yourself able to speak your mind.**

When you share confidences with your best friend over brunch. When you ask for a raise that you and your boss know you deserve. When you are protesting an anti-gay film. When you invite your parents to come to your home for the holidays. When you ask some-one new out on a date. When you talk to your pet.

This exercise may be extremely difficult since most people don't feel or rarely feel as if they can speak their minds. Maybe you've never felt strong when you were speaking, especially if you were being honest and heartfelt. Be as specific as possible. The important point is to start making connections among your physical body, emotions, and behavior. Feeling strong is both an internal emotion and a specific, recognizable physical feeling in the body. It feels good to speak your mind: you can feel a rush of positive energy as you speak.

Under what circumstances do you feel strong—how much of it is external and dependent upon what others do and how much is entirely up to you? If someone is a friend, is it more difficult to speak your mind? What if the listener has authority over you in some way? Or is it a matter of preparation and faith that what you have to say is important and worth hearing? The more you can identify how you participate in situations in which you feel free enough to speak your mind, the more you will realize that it's within your control to bring about those situations more often and extend those feelings of strength in all areas of your life.

5. **What are the kinds of situations where you censor what you want to say?**

When you enter a room full of strangers. When you attend a professional gathering. When you go home for a family reunion. When you go to a cocktail party where a friend has promised to introduce you to some new men. When you make a presentation at work. Asking a friend for help. Initiating sex with your lover. Getting volunteers motivated for a project. Asking your physician about a new HIV treatment.

This is a situation-specific exercise that tries to pinpoint exactly when you withhold or withdraw. The more specific you can be, the better able you will be to make changes in your behavior. Of course, it's not always appropriate to speak freely. Speaking with your own voice does not mean disregarding tact and timing. If your boss criticizes you in front of other people, hold your response until you can collect your thoughts. Reacting inappropriately in such a situation could have serious consequences. Speaking with your own voice recognizes that there are situations where it is realistic and responsible to censor—*in order to make an appropriate response at the right time,* when the listener can actually hear what you have to say. By noting these situations, you will become more aware of when you censor and when you do not have to. You are learning to become more conscious of how you communicate.

6. What prevents you from saying exactly what you think and/ or feel?

Be as concrete and honest as possible. When you stop yourself from saying exactly what you think and/or feel, what is your thought process? What is influencing your decision to censor what you want to say? Are the blocks external: awkward situations, bad timing, no opportunity, nobody's listening? Or are the blocks more internal: other people's feelings, embarrassment, ignorance, fear, wanting to please other people?

The more you can identify the internal blocks, the more you can think about making changes. External blocks can be difficult to overcome, but as with most changes, an internal, perceptual shift usually points the way toward dismantling an external block. Speaking with one's own voice means getting rid of all those other voices (parents, teachers, government, religion) that block us from validating our own emotions and thoughts. Speaking one's mind is essential to successful aging—the acknowledgment that what you have to say has value is a major component of esteeming yourself. Letting those other voices speak for you keeps you locked in other-esteem.

If you still don't feel free enough to speak your mind, push yourself to realize any avenues for change. Maybe you need to speak up, literally, when you're in a group. Maybe you need to stop worrying so much about other people's possible reactions to what you might say (their feelings are their responsibility). Only you know what your internal blocks are, so only you can remove them. Did a parent once shut you up by calling you stupid? Did a teacher ridicule you in front of class one day?

See if you can find commonalities between situations in which you feel inclined to withhold what is inside. Only you control what is inside you, just like the seed holds the tree within it. When you let go of the husk of fear and rigidity, you will begin to grow to love the sound of your own voice. You will be in control of when and where you can and cannot speak your mind.

The voices of fear and resistance: "But what about other people? Or awkward situations? Maybe it's not all about me?"

Of course there are aggressive, overbearing people who soak up all the attention in a room and never let anyone get a word in edgewise. When confronted by such people, try to stay aware of how you may be restricting yourself and/or when you feel you have to watch what you say. It's important to distinguish between situation-specific times for guardedness and a general state of communication in which you never get to say what you mean to say. Your discomfort can be a clue about what makes you clam up and what personal characteristics keep you closed off. In short, what are the external stimuli that set off internal patterns of not speaking your mind? Is it when there's an authority figure involved, your boss or parent? Or if you're fine speaking professionally, do you have trouble sometimes setting personal boundaries with a friend? Or do you have a hard time expressing an attraction to somebody new because you're completely convinced he won't find you attractive, so why bother?

One of the most difficult blocks to overcome in speaking with your own voice is a fear that no one is there to listen, or there is no one with whom you can be yourself and speak from your heart. If you have these feelings, the world can seem a painful and limited place. If you can think of one person who listens to you, the sense of isolation will decrease. It may be someone you don't consider very significant to your life—a co-worker, a familiar face at the community center, a cousin whom you've always been able to talk to. It's important to recognize when you are capable of speaking your own mind and having someone hear you.

It's easy to feel like life is all or nothing—either you're loved and supported or you're lonely and desolate. Resist this bipolar frame of mind: it's dangerous and unhealthy. You will find that if you can eliminate words like *always* and *never* from your vocabulary, the world will seem less rigid and lonely. The more flexible you can become, the stronger you will feel because you can acknowledge your ability to adapt and incorporate change into your life. This internal sense of strength will loosen up your vocal cords, and you will be able to speak your feelings and thoughts more freely. This openness will not only make you appear stronger, but will make you feel stronger. Speaking with your own voice is both an emotional and physical experience; when you stop censoring yourself, your body will begin to feel looser, lighter, with less tension from holding back and the stress of watching what you're saying.

Censoring yourself is all about your comfort level with the situation, the listener, and your voice. By comparing situations when you feel a need to self-censor and situations when you have no problem saying what you think, you'll become totally conscious of this aspect of communication. By focusing on how much you can control some of these elements, you'll begin to realize your responsibility in communicating what you think and feel. By identifying the situations where you self-censor, you'll establish a baseline of behavior from which you can measure your progress. If you know you get more nervous around authority figures, practice seeing them for who they really are: people with more responsibility, but not more worth than you. If you get all tongue-tied when asking somebody out on a date, consider meeting people in a way that makes your intention clear: answering a personal ad, using a dating service. There might be new behaviors to adopt in learning to speak with your own voice, but the attitudes are equally important.

7. **Picture yourself being able to speak your mind anywhere and with everyone.**

What if everything you had to say was not only listened to, but anticipated? Just like the ads a few years ago: When E. F. Hutton speaks, people listen.

Imagine a fantasy world in which you could always say exactly what you felt. What would you say? What opinions could you finally express? What have you always wanted to say to your parents? Your lover? Your friends? Your boss? The President and Congress?

8. What steps do you have to take to make this a reality?

What steps do you need to take to open up and stop holding all those feelings in? Other people's feelings—their responsibility! Your fears—your responsibility! The point is to become conscious of all the factors influencing how you communicate with others. Power. Emotions. Fear. Envy. Anger. Blame. Not wanting to sound like a snob or whiny or privileged. What you share with other people is totally within your control; how you communicate is a visible and audible expression of your inherent power. Censorship can be a choice appropriate to the situation, but not an all-inclusive way of behaving everywhere and with everyone. If you never speak, you'll never be heard, and all those thoughts and feelings will eat away at your insides. I'm concerned not just about how you censor emotions like anger and sadness, but even joy and satisfaction. We have a voice for a reason, and expressing our own voice is a gift not just to ourselves, but to the world around us.

9. Do you physically feel the difference in your body when you are censoring yourself and when you are speaking your mind?

Much of our work with these exercises throughout the book have focused on identifying our feelings and thoughts about hot-button issues like sex, family, and work—and it's difficult for many gay men to get in touch with their true feelings. Many of us are so accustomed to hiding what we're feeling, even from ourselves, that it's hard to break through our emotional resistance and denial—even when (and perhaps especially so) the feelings are joyful.

An essential tool for helping a person to know what he is feeling is to associate a physical feeling with certain emotions. What does feeling "good" feel like in the body? What happens to your body when you're angry? Sad? By associating your physical feelings with certain emotions, you may be able to sense your feelings by recognizing a familiar physical feeling. This is important as our body does not lie to us—we can hide or deny our emotions but the body cannot lie. It may be the most direct source we have to help us in those cloudy moments.

Since as men we are typically conditioned to ignore what our body tells us, it can be hard to look to our bodies to tell us what we're feeling. One system of belief that can help is the 4,000-year-old Hindu idea of *chakras*—the seven energy centers in the body that serve as a "coordinating network of our mind-body system" as Anodea Judith puts it in her book, *Wheels of Life* (an excellent "user's guide" to the chakra system). A chakra—usually visualized as a vortex of energy—can be "measured as patterns of electromagnetic activity, centered around the major nerve ganglia." Judith observes, "Butterflies in the stomach, frogs in our throat, pounding in our heart, and the experience of orgasm are all manifestations of the presence of chakras in our body."

For the purposes of our work, I'll keep this overview brief. *Chakra* is a Sanskrit word meaning "wheel" or "disk," and Judith suggests, "The body is a vehicle of consciousness. Chakras are the wheels of life that carry this vehicle about—through its trials, tribulations, and transformations." A "healthy" chakra system is one in which energy is smoothly flowing. The seven chakras form a pathway of energy from the core of the body up along the spinal column and into our mind. Each chakra can be seen as a "spinning wheel of energy." The chakras have many names; there are also colors, meditations, and exercises associated with each one. The lower chakras are more focused on survival (sex, work), the middle chakras on communication (voice, throat), and the higher chakras on spirituality (peace, understanding). Traditional Hindu belief values the higher chakras over the lower ones, but modern practitioners like Judith believe that all the chakras are important and work best when integrated as a whole into a person's consciousness.

The seven chakras are the following: Root (base of the spine), Lower Belly, Solar Plexus, Heart, Throat, Brow, and Crown. This list may sound familiar, in that the system begins in the body and moves "upward" to the mind and spirit, much like the journey I have mapped out in this book. We began our journey with the body and sex, moved into Work/Play and friendships, and have now arrived at the Throat—where we are becoming conscious of our true "voice." By realizing when we are censoring ourselves and when we are speaking freely and comfortably, we are exercising our Throat chakra—you can feel the difference, bodily and emotionally, when the energy is flowing and not constricted.

What are your physical sensations when you're fearful or anxious? Tightness in the throat, sweaty palms, a racing heartbeat, and so on? And what are the sensations in your body when you are peaceful and calm? A sense of flowing or fluidity? Are these the same or similar to the emotions you experience when you are self-censoring or speaking your mind? You may have never connected these sensations with what your mind is going through, but our emotions and our body are interconnected. They are in dialogue with each other, regardless of whether we are conscious enough to listen.

10. **Does it feel like you are speaking from two different parts of your body in the two different situations in the previous exercise?**

Your body can clue you in if you're self-censoring. The goal is to actually recognize when you are censoring yourself by where in your body your feeling is coming from. If you feel a constriction in your chest, chances are you're having to withhold something as you speak. If you feel a rush of energy, then you are probably speaking your mind and feeling good, strong, upbeat. The more conscious and aware you are of when you are censoring, the more control you will have over whether you choose to do it or not. Often the physical feelings can help you recognize and identify your emotions and put you more in control. Don't ignore what your body might be telling you, even when you are faced with an uncomfortable situation when the way you automatically handle it may just not feel right. Your body is your friend, not your enemy. The more you can pay attention to your body's messages, the more you can help yourself all the time, not just when you feel the need to censor yourself.

11. **Imagine that when you speak your voice is coming only from that part of your body that you associate with speaking your mind.**

This exercise utilizes the tool of *anchoring*: when a physical place or action in the body is anchored, or connected, with a certain emotion. The physical feeling becomes a way to bring about the emotion. The next time you feel confident and strong, remember what your body feels like at the time. Then when you are confronted with a situation in which you feel powerless, you can summon emotional strength by focusing on making your body feel powerful. For example, think about being totally comfortable talking with a close friend and how it feels, your physical stance, your inner feelings of safety and security. Then when you are in an uncomfortable situation, perhaps with your boss or another authority figure, you can act as if you are talking with your close friend by remembering how it felt physically and putting yourself there. This "as if" quality works on a physical as well as emotional level. In a sense, this exercise is like a posthypnotic suggestion. With practice, you can call upon the physical feeling to put you in a comfortable mood and mode. The positive feedback you'll receive from others will reinforce that feeling of comfort and satisfaction.

The poet warrior Audre Lorde offers great inspiration in the discovery and nurturing of your own voice. In "The Cancer Journals," she documented her experience of breast cancer and the healing possibilities of language and the powerful act of speaking our experience. At one point, as she describes the "transformation of silence into language and action," she addresses the reader directly: "What are the words you do not yet have? What do you need to say? What are the tyrannies you swallow day by day and attempt to make your own, until you will sicken and die of them, still in your silence?"

Give yourself permission to be and speak as strongly as possible. Go ahead. Tell your story. Transform the silence.

Ron's Story

I chose to tell Ron's story because he is such a perfect example of someone who has lived much of his life entirely for other people. For many years, he did what he felt was expected of him and was not even aware of what it was that he wanted. He just found himself in situations where he was very unhappy and angry but did not know what to do to change the situation. As he was so well indoctrinated in being "the good Catholic boy," it was hard for him to consider that he had dreams and wishes different from what was expected of

him. He was to do good and take care of other people; this was
reflected in both his personal life and his career choice—social work.

In 1969, the same year of Stonewall and the birth of gay liberation, Ron married a woman in the hope that he "could become
straight." He was the father of two sons by the time he was twenty-
three, and for eight years, he maintained the deception of his true
desires and provided for his family. Despite his tremendous guilt and
unhappiness, it was only with tremendous personal conflict that Ron
could leave an unhappy personal situation. In order to leave a situation, he had first to recognize that he was unhappy and act upon
that awareness. He usually handled these situations by doing more
of what he had already done—by becoming the caretaker and good
boy, no matter how much this infuriated the person he was with.
He became silent, retreated emotionally, and wondered why his good
behavior was not appreciated. When he finally accepted his being
gay, he left his wife and started to live a gay lifestyle, but he brought
this pattern into his gay relationships.

Ron began therapy with me when he was involved in his first
serious gay relationship with a younger, quite histrionic man who
was extremely manipulative and possessive. It was a very unhappy
relationship in which Ron withdrew because no matter what he did,
it did not seem to be adequate for his lover. Ron was very unrealistic
in his perceptions about his lover and what he could do to make
their life together better. At the same time, he was a very high-level
administrator in the Connecticut state mental health system. He also
had a close relationship with his Italian, Catholic family, especially
his brother who was a priest.

Our therapy became focused mainly on ending his relationship
with his lover. It was clear that they were totally incompatible and
neither wanted to hold on to the relationship enough to change
his behavior. A source of conflict within the relationship was Ron's
responsibility for his sons. The lover treated the children contemptu-
ously, and fights between Ron and his lover poisoned the atmosphere
of the household. Ron eventually left his lover when he realized that
he could no longer remain with this lover and provide a place for
his sons to visit. He took the big step and moved out, living alone
for the first time. Still, his primary responsibility was to his sons but
not to his own happiness.

He resumed therapy a few years later when he and a new lover began having problems. His new lover was very similar to his first lover in that he was also very manipulative and extremely demanding. He was constantly complaining how Ron was not satisfying him by removing himself from genuine interaction with him. Though Ron loved him, it seemed that his lover never felt loved by Ron, especially since Ron wanted to be alone at times. He could not understand why Ron did not want to be with him all the time even though he had separate friends and spent time away from Ron. Ron's response to his lover's complaints and contradictions was to withdraw and become passive-aggressive, which only exacerbated the problems. His withdrawal and noncommunication just made his lover more guilt throwing and demanding. Like Ron, his lover was also HIV positive but in much worse health. In time, his lover used his illness to manipulate and demand more of Ron, who took care of him until the end. Ron resisted the urge to walk out many times because of his "caretaker" mentality. No matter how he felt toward the person, he could not see himself as the kind of person who could ever leave a person who was physically sick.

In the three years he lived alone after his lover's death, Ron finally began to work on "his issues" rather than focusing on the problems he had at home. It was difficult for him to understand initially what his issues were since he had no real sense that he had a right to his feelings and to what he wanted just for himself— his whole life had been determined by what other people wanted and demanded.

Now in his late forties, he was in charge of all youth programs for a significant part of the state and could have stayed as long as he liked. He was still very supportive of his sons who lived with his ex-wife, a surgeon. As his health became a bit worse, he started thinking about what he really wanted to do with his life that would give him pleasure. As someone who had lived a life of responsibility, he decided to take an early retirement. He lived in Key West, Fire Island, and New York City, and was clearly not getting seriously involved with anyone. He was slowly learning to say exactly what he wanted to the men he was dating. This took time as he initially would just leave a situation without saying why he was discontented or unsatisfied. He slowly became more comfortable saying what he wanted or did not want and did not consider the other person's expectations of what he would say. It was not that he was becoming inconsiderate or unfeeling; he now saw that he had a right to say what he wanted and how he felt. Previously, his Catholic, conservative background prevented him from pursuing an interracial relationship, but when he began to live for himself, he discovered his interest in black men. Two years ago, he began a relationship with a black man his age who was settled, clearly an adult, and very much in love with him, too. Though he had an apartment in South Beach, he has since moved to California to live with his lover.

It seems that Ron needed a period of doing exactly what he wanted and not answering to anyone else. This gave him time to look at his life and what he really wanted and not to let the circumstances around him dictate what he "should" do. For the first time in his life he was able to break the patterns of the past. Without hurting anyone else, he finally experienced his own life and an appreciation of who and what he was. He finally reached a place where he did not feel he needed to be with a lover and would only consider it if the person was someone with whom he felt compatible and comfortable. When he met his present lover, he was ready for an adult, committed relationship in which he would not run away. They have had a commitment ceremony in which his two sons gave him away. In his early fifties and now in good health, he feels genuinely happy for the first time in his life.

PART THREE

Soul

SEVEN

A Personal Value System

When I ask gay men about their values, I get a lot of blank stares and comments like "Are you talking about that family values stuff?" or "I haven't given it much thought" or "I don't really judge others." Whenever the word *values* is mentioned, a stream of associations begins in many gay men's minds: "values" leads to thoughts of "family" or to thoughts of "religion," both of which almost always lead to negative judgments.

It may be scary talking about values because of its popular association with morality and negative judgments. Many gay men avoid the subject because of the close association of values with religion and with those who want to outlaw or pathologize homosexuality. In fact, our most vocal antagonists are using "family values" and "traditional American values" to persecute gay people. Such phrases suggest that gay people have no values and/or represent a threat to people who do. I think we lack effectiveness in challenging such "value" campaigns because we're avoiding the real issue: What *are* our "values," both individually and as a people?

Perhaps this silence about our values is a legacy of our internalized homophobia, but by being reactive, rather than proactive, we have let anti-gay forces set the terms of the debate. I believe, as do several of our leaders like Harry Hay, Ginny Apuzzo, and Urvashi Vaid, that we *do* have values (Vaid calls them morals), that we *are* a spiritual people, and that we *do* promote an ethics of behavior modeled after principles we hold to be, as our American founders decreed, "self-evident."

In her book on the lesbian and gay movement, *Virtual Equality*, Urvashi Vaid observes a connection between our status as outsiders and our values: "Queer moral vision—our view of what is right and what is wrong—necessarily arises from our particular experience of injustice. . . . Our experience of marginalization is central to our capacity to be moral as individuals and as a political movement." Coming out gay in a nongay world, she observes, we have created an entire community and ethical system to honor principles such as honesty, self-knowledge, and pleasure.

I want to be as specific as possible when talking about values, precisely because there's so much confusion and anxiety around these words and their meanings. Around the topic of homosexuality, a lot of "value" words get thrown around: morals, ethics, values, family values, Christian values, American values, right and wrong, unnatural, the Ten Commandments, the Bible, the Koran, and so on. Granted, most of these terms are Judeo-Christian, while clearly other religions such as Hinduism or Islam have teachings and language about homosexuality. But since, for the most part, America is portrayed by the media as Christian, the public debate is usually framed in Judeo-Christian language. In addition, certain phrases like "family values" are repeated and used by many different groups of people, all of whom are assuming they know what it means. But I suspect that when I use the term, I have a different meaning in mind than when anti-gay fundamentalists use the same term.

In many areas of this book, I've called for a new vocabulary among gay men, and I've encouraged us to learn a new language appropriate to our culture and a new way to communicate with one another. Our personal value system is no exception and it requires a new vocabulary.

Values are principles, neither good nor bad, by which we live: honesty, joy, pleasure, fame, power, service, notoriety, justice, greed, perfection, humility. Or if those are too abstract, consider: "Judge not, lest ye be judged" or "Might makes Right" or "The Personal is Political" or "Make Love, Not War" or "Love your neighbor as yourself" or "My country, right or wrong" or "Wherever you go, there you are" or the Golden Rule. Values are not strict commandments of behavior, but ideas that you honor in all that you do. They are what motivate you, even if you are unaware of them. The goal is to become aware of them so you can better understand the direction of your life.

Ethics are the rules that guide one's daily actions and determine a pattern of behavior that results from holding a particular set of values. For example, if you value perfection, then you most likely will hold your behavior up to a strict code. Or if you value pleasure, you will most likely build a life in which play and sensuality are a priority. If you value power, then you will pursue the different paths to power. If you value honesty above all other principles, then you will treat people in a certain way and will treat yourself a certain way. *Coming out is an ethical act; honesty is the value.*

Ethics are easily confused with *morals,* which are often freighted with judgmentalism and bipolar thinking. Good versus bad. The "shoulds" that haunt and torment us. Like ethics, morals are grounded in behavior, but there's a sense of righteousness about morals, a sense that if we don't follow them, we cross a line from morality to immorality and become vulnerable to another person's condemnation (or praise). Morals are a tool of aggrandized power, while ethics are an expression of inherent power.

Every person has *a value system,* a set of principles that motivate, determine, and govern their behavior. But each person decides for himself what those values are, consciously and over the course of his life—that's the *personal* part of the personal value system. There are a lot of values to choose from, and their sources are many and varied; some are overt and some are implied (and very often at conflict with one another): the world's religions, different forms of government, economic models, philosophical systems, as well as our interaction with other people. For much of our early lives, we aren't really aware of the values we are absorbing from our environment. But we develop an internal sense of what's important and what's not important from observing the values expressed and upheld by our blood family, peers, school, community, and nation. These values have an external source (not of our own creation), but may become so internalized that we don't feel them operating in our lives. But we all have values, even if we can't identify them. I would say, "To have values is human, to be conscious of them is divine."

WHAT ARE MY VALUES? A MIDLIFE ASSESSMENT

Many gay men react to talk about values by *not* wanting to talk about values, by denying that values apply to us or that we've even considered what our values might be. But we do have values that we live by, every one of us, and part of the opportunity at midlife is to discover and affirm (or change) what those values are. Once we have identified our values, we can develop priorities and begin to make the changes necessary to reach our goals.

This discussion of values is relevant to midlife, because the anxieties and changes necessitated by aging offer an extraordinary catalyst to becoming conscious of your personal value system. At midlife, change is in the air, and part of all the change is recognizing what brought you to where you are at midlife. We need to understand all our motivations, all of our parts, both good and bad, positive and negative. As the principles that have driven our actions, our values are the true expression of our motivation. Once we can identify what's shaping and influencing our behavior, opinions, relationships, and so forth, we can better understand ourselves, and more important, begin to direct ourselves to what we really want in our lives. Examining our personal value system can enable better aging, because we finally realize what we've been working toward all these years. Once we are consciously aware of the connection between our values and our behavior, we have a clearer picture of how to get what we want.

Many gay men find it difficult to describe their values; it's hard for most people. We may not ponder about why we do what we do, or what we're struggling toward. Sometimes our ears are filled with static from those other voices we hear: the "shoulds," the values that others (blood family, peers, community) are expressing in their behavior toward us. In the previous chapter on finding one's own voice, I emphasized the movement away from external validation (other-esteem) and toward more internal affirmation (a true self-esteem). After learning to speak with your own voice, you're more able to say "who I am" and articulate "this is what I believe in." But this is not as easy as it sounds.

This chapter continues that journey to the interior of what you hold to be "you," the self you esteem, the self you value as worthy. As you progress to the core of your identity, you begin to develop a sense of what feels "right" for you. But I'm not talking about "right" and "wrong," not in any moral or judgmental sense. What I'm after might be better described as feeling "correct." It's about a sense of appropriateness, a feeling of wholeness about what's true and integral to the person you want to be—not who your mother, your father, your lover, your friends, or your community wants you to be.

But what feels "right" is more than "what I am most comfortable with." If you're disagreeing with someone, you might react, "But I know I'm right. It feels right." Be mindful when you're reacting and when you're responding. If you're feeling threatened or challenged in your values, you may react defensively. Instead of accurately reflecting what you believe, this reaction might be a reflex, a way of protecting your values and possibly justifying whatever behavior is at stake. But do you feel "right" in your bones? When you stop reacting and actually respond to the criticism, are you speaking out of a feeling of honesty? Is what you're saying making you comfortable and relaxed—do you believe yourself?

By exploring this sense of what feels "correct" internally, you can begin to identify your value system. What you'll soon discover is that we each have at least two value systems: our ideal and our lived. Our *ideal* value system is the one that motivates us, that we hold out as our ideal principles and behavior, while our *lived* value system is the one that we actually manage to accomplish. As with much of life, many of us have an idea of perfection toward which we continually strive. Then there's the reality we live. For most of our lives, we struggle to achieve this ideal lifestyle: a circle of friends, job, home, relationship, and finally, the kind of person we want to be known to be. Then there's the reality of the friends we have, the apartment, the credit card debt, our very human boyfriend, our actual job, and our mixed self-image.

Between the ideal and the lived, we spend our days (and nights!). When there's a large disparity between the ideal and lived values, a person is more tense, defensive, and liable to self-judgment. When we fail to live up to our ideal, we beat ourselves up and create negative feelings about ourselves. But how do we distinguish between what our gut is telling us and our denial? The less conscious we are about our lived values, the more we set ourselves up for failure, more negative feelings, and less mental health. In some schools of psychology, the discrepancy between our ideal values and our lived values is one measure of mental health. Consequently, perfectionism (a rigid attachment to the ideal) is probably one of the worst attributes with regard to mental health (and by extension, physical health).

One crucial arena in which many gay men have struggled with this discrepancy between their ideal and lived value systems is safer sex. Especially in the early days of HIV and AIDS, there was no consensus around what sexual behavior was "safe" or "unsafe" or "risky." For example, different studies have concluded that oral sex without ejaculation and without a condom is high risk behavior, while other studies have revealed less risk in that activity. Unless he is operating in complete denial of the possibility of HIV infection, every gay man has had to deal with the issue of safer sex and make decisions about it. Which research have you followed? Which risks have you been willing to take? What is your dividing line between unsafe and safer? Are you deferring certain kinds of sexual pleasure until more definitive research is available? Are you taking chances? As with most values, no behavior is written in stone. We may change our beliefs and our actions from day to day, depending upon new information or circumstances. Our value system, like our sexuality, operates fluidly.

To borrow the language of safer sex education, we "negotiate" our behavior each time we act. Similarly, we negotiate our value system when faced with contradictions or new information that may influence our decision making and our belief system. Perhaps one of the most difficult things to accept about being human is that we don't always live up to our ideals. On those days, we don't like being caught between the ideal and the lived, we don't like being fallible, we don't like being imperfect.

Perfectionism is the epitome of other-esteem. We want to be perfect in order for others to esteem us. The time and energy we spend pursuing perfection and other-esteem can never provide us with true self-esteem. Only by shutting out the other voices—of our parents, our religious doctrines, our friends, our community—can we find our own true voice. When we begin to articulate the values we live by, that voice becomes stronger and clearer, which further emboldens our sense of self-worth and our value system. This process is most definitely a spiral: Finding and speaking with your own voice frees you to identify and express your value system, and recognizing the values underlying your behavior will strengthen your ability to say what you mean and mean what you say. Such understanding of your motivations, your values, and your goals enables you to take action, where before you may have felt hesitant and afraid. Such self-knowledge gives you a vision of your life, and as Vaid has observed, "Vision is sharpest in its practice, grounded by a moral framework."

THE ROOTS OF BELIEF: YOUR FAMILY'S VALUES

As with most of a gay man's life, his value system represents his own self-creation. His ethical principles are a product of his life experiences, and his "lived" values make manifest his understanding of the world. His raw materials are the best parts of the different value systems to which he has been exposed. At an earlier age, there was the total adoption of the parental and/or peer value system (for example, Protestantism), which may have later given way to the total rejection of these values and formation of a different value system (for example, Buddhism).

Midlife is the time for integrating whatever is valuable from our roots into our present system of belief. By midlife, most of us have reached a state of independence from the value systems of our blood family, and part of building a chosen family is about discovering people who share your value system, whatever it may be. Just as our individual actions speak volumes about our values, our chosen family expresses our value system as well. We learn this relationship between a group and its values early on, in our original blood family. An understanding of family systems remains crucial to how we absorb, create, and reinforce our value system.

1. **How would you describe the value system of your blood family or significant family members?**

Were you raised Irish Catholic or Orthodox Jewish? Agnostic or atheist? Muslim or Korean Christian? Southern Baptist or Yankee Episcopalian? Whereas many families may pass on the value systems of their religions, there are also political and philosophical systems to consider. Were your parents Democrats or Republicans or Marxists? Free-thinkers or existentialists? Beats or hippies? What sort of culture were you raised in? Rural or urban or suburban? Mixed or homogenous? Was the family integrated into the community or were you considered outsiders?

Try looking at your blood family as a system that organizes itself to achieve a common goal: to define and perpetuate itself. Each member of the family has a role (the Mediator, the Scapegoat, the Problem Child, and so on) that contributes to that goal. In addition, each family has a "theme" —an operating principle that governs the behavior of the family as a whole. These themes are not necessarily negative or positive (and usually some of each), but they operate to define the price of membership in the family: What did you have to do to be a member of the family?

Imagine your blood family as the cast of a TV show. Did your family resemble *Leave it to Beaver* or *Roseanne*? Did your family try to portray the "perfect" family, with no tension, everybody on good behavior, calm and serene? Or was your family more "real," dealing with life's difficulties and blessings as they arose, with strength, affection, and humor, even when there were arguments? Did your family have a code of conduct that prohibited any show of emotion? Or were they expressive and affectionate? Was your family explosive, fighting all the time, loud and violent? When strangers entered the household (a neighbor, a relative from far away, or a teacher), did all that negative behavior stop and a patina of calm and "normalcy" come out of nowhere?

When working through these exercises, try to get *beneath* the behavior to the actual values that were expressed by the behavior. How did your blood family operate, and therefore, what values were presented as important, as goals? I'm not asking whether your family went to church, or if they were neighborly, but how the members of your family communicated with one another. How were conflicts resolved? Was making money a primary goal? Were people who made a lot of money held up as examples for the children to follow? Who were the role models for the family? Was "get ahead at all costs" the message you heard most often? Where and how were the boundaries between family and nonfamily drawn? Were there references to your mother's side? Your father's side? How important were the connections by "blood"? Did you have a nuclear family or an extended one?

Looking back at your blood family may be painful, but it's extremely useful to consider the value system in which you were raised.

Examining your blood family can reveal any discrepancies between the "ideal" and the "lived" family, between the family image projected to the outside world and the actual family in which you were raised. No doubt, our parents' behavior was based on some underlying principles, even without their knowledge. Were there a lot of rules in your house or was it more like "anything goes"? Was the letter of the law followed or the spirit of the law? Did you eat meals together or did everybody do their own thing? Were manners and respect for others taught, or was there a lot of yelling and fighting? Did you get along with everybody, did you fight with your siblings, or were you always angering your mother or making your father proud?

Again, it's important not to equate values with morality. I'm asking for the operating principle, what was rewarded and what was rejected in the household. Actions speak louder than words—and the lived speaks louder than the ideal. In reviewing your life history, you may uncover "clues" to your family's theme, such as strange behavior, or events that seemed to disrupt whatever calm existed. For example, in an alcoholic family, denial is a strong theme. Such a family might portray itself as "perfect," with no fights, no arguments, never raising voices. Or a family might consider it "no holds barred," with nothing withheld, everything expressed, no boundaries. Another family might be "family first"—it's us against the world—with people outside the family not to be trusted.

It's absolutely essential to recover a sense of the family system in which you were raised because it might offer a key to understanding your current life. The way conflicts, emotions, or problems were handled in our family is a major influence in how we define ourselves and what we consider "good" or "appropriate." Try to come away from this exercise understanding the values of your family. Although you may have said goodbye to that way of life a long time ago, its influences may still be affecting your present. By going back and thinking about how you were raised, what you were taught to value—money, formality, denial, creativity, discipline, emotional censorship, honest self-expression—the better able you will be to identify what influences have remained. You can't understand your present life until you have a serious, vivid sense of what values were operating in the past and may still be operating. This self-reflection gives shape to the reality we learned growing up. At midlife, we can create a new reality and begin to see the past as one kind of reality, as well as part of our new reality.

By this point in your life, reexamining your childhood will also bring to the fore any differences you experienced as a gay child. Acknowledging that you developed very differently from a nongay child can create a greater appreciation of who you are now. As discussed in other chapters, a gay child rarely grows up with a sense of appropriate entitlement. Part of that missing sense of worthiness stems from realizing at an early age that difference is not valued by most families. Any feelings of difference (or outsider feelings) arising from being a gay child can feed a growing sense of alienation from his blood family and a sense that he is not valued as an individual because he is different. As a result, a gay child may learn to operate in survival mode, and childhood becomes a situation of just getting by with the least amount of damage.

The failure to value difference (and by extension, a gay child) may or may not be conscious in a family system. Depending upon the degree of deception between the gay child's hologram and the actual child, a family system may or may not have any idea that one of its members cannot maintain his membership. If difference is not valued by the family system (and we can tell depending upon the way the family reacts to anybody who's seen as different, be it a neighbor or relative or community figure), a gay child will look for acceptance and validation from his peers outside the family system. Often, this need for acceptance is so strong that a gay child will long just to be accepted by anyone, regardless of his or her values or beliefs. Many nongay children use their peers as a way of validating their family system, but many gay children reach out to their peers to escape from a family system that does not value them.

2. **When you were growing up, did you have friends who had value systems similar to yours?**

While our parents and family provided a host of influences on our sense of values, our peers also contributed to that process, especially once we entered school. While there are a range of possible schools (public, private, parochial, Quaker, Catholic), most of us probably had only one option. Depending upon the school, you may have been exposed to a particular class or religious group that may or may not have been your own. Your experience fitting in or being an outsider would have influenced the values you were absorbing. If you were working class, but attended a private school on scholarship, you may have received mixed messages about money, achievement, success, and family. If you were raised Jewish but attended a predominately Christian school, you most likely would have experienced some confusion about your place in the world or a heightened sense of your minority status.

As you look back to your early peers, try to discern any values you may have shared or the areas in which you differed. What kind of friends did you make? Kids with similar interests like baseball or music? Or those with the same religion? Or maybe those who lived on your street and rode the same bus? Those early friendships are crucial in our socialization process and for what we come to know as our values. Did you pick friends who agreed with you on everything or did you like a variety of friends, with different opinions? Did your friends all look alike and come from the same background, or did you like getting to know somebody different? An important distinction to consider is whether you chose peers by virtue of their values or whether you took on the values of your peers. Usually, our first peers are forced upon us, either by geography (neighborhood, same school) or class, so it's no surprise we take on their values and they take on ours. Did peers not really enter into your world? Maybe you came from a huge extended family that made the whole idea of peers irrelevant.

The desire to belong, as I discussed earlier, is a powerful motivation, and membership in a family, a circle of peers, or a community can provide a deep sense of belonging, protection, and nurturing. As you consider the price of membership to belong in these different circles, try to remember both the positive and negative aspects of the experience, as well as the positive and negative values that you absorbed.

Just as individuals pay a price of membership to belong in a family system, a family system pays a price to belong or not belong to a larger community. Just as family members observe and absorb their values from the parental figures, a family observes and absorbs its values from the culture that surrounds it. By recalling the world in which your family system operated, you can begin to identify more of the values that affect your personal value system.

3. How would you describe the value system of your neighborhood, or community and/or church, while you were growing up?

What was your neighborhood like? Did you know your neighbors? Did people know everybody's business? Was it a close-knit community or did each family mind its own business? Was there a lot of interaction between families, maybe just on big holidays like Halloween or the 4th of July? Were you allowed to go out after dark? Did you go to church or synagogue or mosque nearby? Did your family socialize more there than in the neighborhood? Did both your parents work and leave the family to the care of a neighbor or a community program? Or were you a latch-key child?

As you describe the parameters of your community, think about what was valued: the social contract between neighbors? Public education? Civic pride? Competitive materialism? Collective activities? Just as families may subscribe to an "ideal" set of values and live another set, communities can declare a commitment to a principle (quality education) but then fail to live up to that commitment (through poor funding of public schools, for example). By examining the values by which your community lived, you can begin to see the source of your attitudes toward politics and social issues.

As we mature, we enter new communities that may challenge or affirm our personal value system. Perhaps the most powerful influence upon our values as adults is our decision to come out. Coming out puts the price of our membership at risk in all our previous groups: blood-family, peers, community. But surviving the coming out process strengthens our sense of integrity and wholeness by closing the gap between our ideal and our lived values.

COMING OUT: A NEW VALUE SYSTEM

Upon coming out, many gay men find new peers and a new "family" of like-minded gay brothers. The etiquette and social rituals of the gay male world represent a new value system that can ease the effects of earlier value systems that may not have validated us. The work of gay intellectuals, the strategies of gay activists, the images of gay media, and the opinions of regular gay men on the street combine to create a new value system for the gay man just emerging from the closet.

While we may adopt new values as gay men, being out doesn't necessarily remove those early influences or destroy the roots of those earlier value systems. A common fallacy in dealing with family members when you come out is to say, "I'm the same person you've always known, I'm just being honest about my sexuality now." But that statement really denies the true significance of both the hologram and the act of coming out.

Most likely, before coming out, you haven't shown your blood family or your nongay peers or your community all of yourself. They've seen the hologram—and perhaps they've been perceptive enough to have seen the real you beneath the hologram, but such awareness is rare. You may feel like the same person after coming out, but you're not because you're changing your relationship with all those various groups. You are no longer the same person because you are providing new information about your life. Each person has to get to know you all over again. You may still worry about their response, but there is an incredible lightness that comes after coming out: the burden of maintaining the hologram has been lifted.

Many gay men think of coming out as only making a sexual adjustment, but coming out represents a major change in one's value system. In effect, you declare, "the principle of being honest about who I am is more important than whether you like me or accept me." Yet coming out is rarely recognized as an ethical act that expresses a value. Urvashi Vaid suggests that "being out of the closet may best be described as a moral act because it moves us closer toward truth and away from falsehood, toward virtue, away from hypocrisy."

A friend of mine told me about coming out to his family. He was then in his late twenties, Jewish, from New Jersey, and he called his parents and asked them out to dinner at a local restaurant. He went to see his family, and before they left for the dinner, he told them he was a gay man. His mother and father became hysterical—crying, arguing, and yelling. After about an hour, they dried their eyes and went to dinner. At the restaurant, his father surprised him and his mother by ordering a bottle of champagne. When the waiter returned and filled their champagne flutes, his father raised his glass, saying "to honesty" and toasted the family. His father was still upset and tearful, but he could see beyond his own pain and disappointment to acknowledge the son's decision. In that dramatic gesture, his father was celebrating the value of honesty. The father and son were agreeing on the same value system (at least for that night).

TODAY'S VALUES: ORGANIC AND EVOLVING

Now that you have examined the value systems (family, peers, community) in which you were raised and in which you came out, let's look at the present. What do you believe in now? What affects your day-to-day decisions, the way your family and community did when you were growing up? Can you detect how those early influences are still operating or have you really broken away from them? Is there continuity between your early value systems and your current thinking?

As much as we may try to distance ourselves from the values of our blood family and our roots, we may surprise ourselves when we realize that we are very much our parents' children or very much a Southern Baptist or Orthodox Jew. Remember how long it took you to overcome the shame about being gay and the self-loathing that this society instilled in you? Then it's little wonder that we find ourselves still affected by our early teachings about values and ethics, what's "right" and what's "wrong." Even after we're grown and can look back to see whatever discrepancies existed between the ideal and lived values of our family system, we may find it difficult to let go of those values.

We can physically leave our native communities but psychically stay. Leaving home often involves an attitude that says: This is where I was, there's another world out there and I want it to influence me. At this point in your life, where do your present values stand in relation to the ones of your roots? Where have shifts occurred and what difference do those shifts make?

4.   How are your present values similar and/or different from those of your blood family?

At any family gathering, there are always topics to be avoided: politics (Daddy's a Republican, Mama's a Democrat); health (Aunt Shirley's cancer, AIDS); religion (Cousin Bob married a Jewish woman); sexuality (Uncle Jack is bringing his new "friend"); race (Sister Joanne is dating a Chinese man).

For many people, the family is like a minefield, with certain subjects sure to explode and destroy the family's fragile balance. "When I go home, everything's fine until my mother brings up my work. She thinks being a singer is a waste of time. She wanted me to be a doctor and she's never going to let me forget it." Or "All my siblings are married, and a few have children. Still, my parents ask me when am I going to settle down and find a man. It doesn't seem to matter that I have a good career. They're always reminding me of their friends who have gay sons and why don't I give them a call?" Clearly, these parents value being in a relationship!

Part of what drives this tension is the different sets of values that members of the family have adopted for themselves. Upon returning to their blood family, many gay men experience the problem of regressing to former roles: the good little boy, the quiet young one, the rebellious teenager, the mediator between Mom and Dad. When you return to former behavior, you're falling back on the known paths through the minefield of the family system, especially if the family values members who don't make waves or disturb the peace. We learn to navigate this minefield so early that we may not be conscious of what we're doing, but the roles and behavior emerge suddenly when we visit our blood family.

Sometimes, returning home is "moral limbo," when you'll do anything to get through the weekend. Faced with bigotry or hostility, many gay men won't confront the family member who's responsible. Or if a gay man isn't out to his blood family, returning home can be a brief return to the closet and, psychologically, a "minisuicide" in which he denies his gay self. If a gay man suppresses his values in the face of conflict with his blood family, he is saying that maintaining the family's façade is more important than his own sense of worth. Either path—his denial of differences between him and his blood family or his active challenging of those differences, which leads to stress and conflict—can be detrimental to his mental, as well as physical, health.

Any alienation from our blood family reinforces our "outsider" feelings as gay men. Often we don't feel we belong in our blood family's world, where there might be a different value system operating, so we avoid reunions or trips home because we don't want to have another fight about why we're gay or why we vote Republican or why we work in a nonprofit organization or why we're not in a relationship.

It can be reminiscent of the first time we returned home after any first, extended stay away from the family (maybe it's a summer with Grandma or a trip with Outward Bound or a first semester at college). Exposed to new ideas or new people or a new environment, we come home flush with excitement about what we're discovering about the world, and we run smack up against our family's underlying expectations and values. We have stepped out of our rigid and structured role in the family system, which is committed to maintaining the status quo.

Rather than totally cutting ourselves off from the family or totally surrendering to it, many of us struggle in between: taking the best of what our family offers and being open to new ideas. Creating your own set of values is not a neat, linear process, but a rocky trip of exposure to new values, some of which you may end up accepting. There's no formula for creating your set of values, because there are too many elements and variables at play. What's important is to validate your journey toward a set of values you can live by. That journey doesn't stop when you reach college or when you come out or when you turn forty or when you retire. Values are organic: a living, breathing set of principles that shape and determine your daily life.

Moreover, your personal value system keeps evolving and becoming more your own over the course of a lifetime. It's important to recognize how and why you've changed your values. Each new relationship—friend, family member, lover, boss—offers an opportunity to assess your values. One of the many slogans of Twelve-Step recovery programs is "Take what you like and leave the rest." No one can live your life but you, and no one has to live up to your values but you.

One of the myths of aging is that people abandon their "radical" youth and adopt more conservative values as they get older. Actually, Bernice Neugarten, a pioneer of gerontology, completed a study in the fifties that suggested the opposite: that as people age, they intensify. Her research found that people who were radical got more radical, people who were conservative got more conservative. A person's actions may differ over the course of a lifetime as he becomes more pragmatic and less confrontational, but the underlying motivations, goals, and values remain the same. I would add that perhaps only a life-changing event, especially one as powerful as coming out, could shift our values so dramatically.

Once we begin to distance ourselves from our childhood home (not just geographically, but psychologically), we are eager to find other influences: a teacher at school, a coach, a celebrity or public figure. What these role models provide is a sense of what you value, what you want your life to represent or accomplish. Revisiting our discussion about role models from chapter 3, remember that role models represent an ideal toward which our lives can move. We still have to live our own lives, but role models and the value systems they communicate can steer us in the right direction.

When many of us came out, we looked to the gay community's standards and rituals to define our behavior and our identity. Many of us found a difference between what we heard in the media, both gay and nongay, and our own experiences. Again, we found a difference between the ideal and the lived. Anecdotes among gay peers help to establish a system of values that shapes our lives. Most likely, we have joined different groups of peers over the course of our lifetime that have affected our values at various ages. Involvement with our peers creates a system of values that generates a set of ethics. Our ethics can range from etiquette (how to handle a first date) to philosophical questions about the nature of being gay (do we have a purpose as gay people?).

Can you identify ways your values have changed from when you were younger? Maybe you put up with some types of behavior—both in yourself and in others—when you were younger that you don't find acceptable now. If there are children in your life, maybe you find yourself more concerned with the future, the legacy of the present, than before. In the last twenty years, the gay community has come to recognize its own diversity, and you may find yourself more comfortable mixing with different types of gay people than the kind of boys you hung out with when you first came out. Or do you find yourself more rigid, with a "circling the wagons" mentality of keeping close to people with similar ideas and experiences? When we're young, life is often lived very much in black and white, good and bad, but as you age, the full spectrum of life and the complexity of its rainbow hues emerge.

5. **How are your values different from those of other gay men
    your age?**

Consider the cultural references that define your generation of
gay men and all that you have experienced, fought for, and survived.
Vietnam. Watts. Stonewall. The first gay pride parades. Watergate.
The founding of lesbian and gay community centers and organizations. Studio 54. Anita Bryant. Harvey Milk. Ronald Reagan. AIDS.
The Marches on Washington in 1979, 1987, and 1992. The Gay
Games. Jesse Helms. Don't Ask, Don't Tell. Ellen.
    Were you a child of the fifties and sixties? Where were you in
the seventies? Did you serve in Vietnam or were you part of the
antiwar movement or both? Where were you the year of Stonewall?
Did you move to one of the big cities in the seventies? Did you
participate in starting up the first gay organization in your community? Or did you find a boyfriend and settle down? Start your own
business? Were you the first openly gay man to live in your
neighborhood?
    Those common life experiences have helped create a sense of
values for our community. You may or may not share those values
with your gay peers. Do you feel out of synch with gay men your
age or do you feel connected to your generation? Do you share
political beliefs or community involvement with your gay peers?
Some gay men at midlife may feel the annual pride celebrations are
for the newly out or the younger generation, rather than for them,
while other middle age gay men may feel that the pride marches are
like our national holiday, a time for all of us to celebrate ourselves
and our diversified community.

6. **How are your values different from those held by younger
    gay men?**

Like any generation, we might shrug off the younger generation
with wonder and dismay. What are these kids doing with all these
piercings and tattoos? Maybe you thought punk died in the seventies.
And all that time at the gym and that awful house music—how can
they stand it? What about our fabulous seventies disco music? Or do
you identify with how they create their gay selves? Maybe you've

had a tattoo since you were in the navy or you've always kept up-to-date on the latest club or dance remix.

Or do you think the younger generation is too "out"? Maybe you've never felt discriminated against and don't understand their need to be so open and vocal about who they sleep with. Or maybe you have been discriminated against and harassed all your life, so you see the closet as a form of protection. You're out to a small number of friends and family, but not the world. Did you feel a wave of fear and nausea when the word *queer* was resurrected in the nineties? Many gay men have painful associations with that word and others (*faggot* and *sissy*), despite attempts by younger generations to reclaim them as words of empowerment.

Our relationship to younger gay men is complicated by our community's ageism, which leads to exclusion and confusion, if not outright cruelty. But looking at our own lives, do we have the same values we had when we first came out? Do we think the same as when we were twenty-five? It's absolutely natural that we will have different values from our gay peers and our gay little brothers—we are a community that spans many generations.

What matters is that each gay man feels he has a set of values that reflect who he is, his needs, and his uniqueness. There's a tremendous discussion about gay marriage in our community, and while older gay men may not want the institution for themselves, they can respect the desire to *have* that option and they will fight for the right to choose that arrangement. While we may not embrace the choices others make, we can respect their right to choose.

When I was seventeen, many of my gay and lesbian friends felt we had to make a decision either to live a gay lifestyle or to marry as a heterosexual in order to have children and raise a family. We knew we couldn't have both. A teenager coming out today doesn't face this same decision. Younger gay men have more options, but they don't know everything. Having faced and feared rejection by younger men, many gay men give up trying to cross the cultural and generational divides in our community. Do you have any sense of who the younger generation is or what they want? Do you see younger people as children who need to be trained? Or do you see them as inheritors of the dream, capable of taking our community into a new direction? Can we not both teach and learn from one another? When neither side of the gay generation gap takes the time to find out about the other, both generations lose.

7. How are your values different from those held by nongay men your age?

Consider your nongay peers. What do they believe in? Is there common ground between gay and nongay members of the same generation? Do you see more similarities in values with peers of the same age (both gay and nongay) than with younger gay men? Perhaps this exercise is difficult because you don't see nongay men as peers or perhaps you still feel "less than" when compared to your nongay peers. Most likely, you may share some values with nongay peers if you have similar economic, educational or political backgrounds. On the other hand, your relationships, sexuality, and experience with AIDS will mostly likely create different values from those of your nongay peers.

Instead of comparing yourself negatively with your nongay peers, try to affirm the life experiences that have shaped your values. As gay men, we can find common ground with nongay men, yet we also travel across a landscape unique to our development.

8. Have there been experiences that significantly influenced your values?

Given the fluidity of gay male culture and the impact of AIDS, many gay men have witnessed and survived life-changing experiences that affected their value systems. Deaths, illnesses, crimes, and political victories and setbacks have most likely influenced their worldview and their role in their community. They may not have realized these events were affecting their value systems because the shift may have been gradual or may not have appeared relevant to their values. But a value system is a growing, organic belief system that is not set in stone. Values do give rise to concrete behavior and a system of ethics, but even these manifestations of a value system are open to evolution and reinterpretation.

When I was in graduate school, I served for a time as an extern to the Municipal Court in Chicago. I was responsible for helping my supervisor evaluate people who were arrested, and once when we were sitting in on juvenile court, I witnessed firsthand how justice is not always served in this country. The first defendant was around fifteen years old, short, blond, slightly stocky, with a Polish name and background. He was charged with assault for the third time. When the judge asked the boy for an explanation, the local Catholic priest pleaded leniency for the boy, whose father had disappeared and whose schoolwork indicated no great scholar. The judge released the boy with a severe warning and in custody of the priest.

The next defendant was a young black high school senior, who had been accepted to college for the following fall. He had never been arrested or had any blemishes on his record. He was charged as an accomplice to auto theft. A friend of his had asked him to go for a ride in a new car. When the police stopped the two teenagers, the driver confessed to having stolen the car and also admitted that the defendant didn't know the car was stolen. The judge sentenced the defendant to a year in reform school, thereby ruining the start of his college career and possibly his entire life. As the boy was absorbing the sentence, the judge added, "That'll teach you to keep better friends." From where I was sitting, I saw the defense lawyer wink at the judge as he spoke this last remark.

I was disgusted by the stark contrast between the two cases, and the lawyer's wink signaled to me that the whole justice system was corrupt. A white kid was walking away and a black kid was being thrown away. I also had an insight between me and the black youth. I could pass, he couldn't. I could hide being gay—the difference that made me vulnerable to discrimination—but as a black citizen, he was forever visible and subject to prejudice. I realized how the two of us were connected, that oppression has many disguises. Witnessing those two verdicts was a life-changing event that continued to shape my value system years after the fact. Intellectually, I had supported equality and civil rights, but that experience gave me an emotional understanding of the issue.

At midlife, your lifestyle is in a state of flux, as significant changes in career, relationships, and your priorities become not only possible but also probable. This level of change is made possible since your perspective and values have broadened and deepened with experience. While you may be very conscious of making these lifestyle changes, you're probably less conscious of how your values are driving this transformation. You might think changing your life will betray your upbringing and the value system in which you were raised. But as I discussed in chapter 6, the midlife crisis isn't about creating a radically new persona, but about discovering the person you've always wanted to become. We don't become the people we want to become until we stop becoming what other people want us to become.

For a gay man, this transformation begins when he comes out and goes against the cultural and familial conditioning to be nongay. At midlife, the transformation deepens as he faces another decision— will he become the stereotype of a middle-aged gay man: invisible, sexless, powerless, bitter, tired, and lonely? Making the decision to assert his power and to break the myths of middle age, a gay man draws upon and affirms the value system that has brought him thus far. This awakening into the strength of his value system and lifestyle anchor him more firmly in the present with more clarity and appreciation of what he has accomplished.

A gay man at midlife stops using the external world as his main reference point and focuses on what is correct for him and his developing vision of the future. This transformation begins when he starts to act more from internal values rather than from trying to please others. Growing up gay in a nongay world, many gay men found that pleasing others was the surest means of being accepted (or the closest thing to it). This mode of operating is everywhere in our culture, from how activists lobby for legislation ("we promise not to talk about sex") to how we reenter and protect our blood-family systems (not sharing details of our gay lifestyle).

But living to please others demands a tremendous amount of energy, time, commitment, intuition, and ultimately, self-sacrifice. At midlife, many gay men begin to realize that it's not worth it; pleasing others is no guarantee of personal satisfaction or security, which is what prompted their people-pleasing behavior in the first place.

9. Is trying to please others still a primary value for you?

Pleasing others is a difficult value to let go of. It translates into saying, "I'm a good person. I devote myself to others." But what about devotion to yourself? This exercise gives you permission to explore whatever discomfort or frustration or anger you may experience by putting too much effort into pleasing others. This may be the first time you've considered a connection between how much you work to please others and how your value system operates in your life. To stop pleasing others puts at risk all the positive feedback you get when you please other people: "You're so good to me." "I don't know what I'd do without you." "You always make me feel special." But are you good to yourself? Are you there for yourself? Do you recognize that you're special?

My emphasis on not living to please others may sound selfish. "Great, that's all we need: more narcissistic gay men." But I am making a distinction between someone who is *selfish* and someone who is *self-focused*. Selfish is expecting other people to satisfy you; self-focused is realizing only you can satisfy yourself. Selfish is expecting other people to meet your needs; self-focused is knowing only you can meet your needs. Selfish is relying upon other-esteem to make you feel good; self-focused is learning how to esteem yourself.

Identifying the ways in which you can decrease the amount of energy you spend trying to please others can be difficult because feelings of guilt and betrayal will immediately surface. "How could I stop doing this or that?" Let other people take care of themselves; you take care of yourself. If it's volunteer work or activism, set limits on your time; do your part because you believe in the work, not because you want people to like you and think you're a good person.

The less time you spend trying to please other people, the more opportunities you have to take a hard look at what pleases you and how you can attain it without guilt. Do you value what people think about you over your own self-image? The specific changes you undertake in order to transfer energy into pleasing yourself will help close the gap between your "lived" and "ideal" value systems. By making your "ideal" more "lived," you can become more realistic about what your personal value system is and how you can live accordingly.

10. Describe the five most important values by which you live.

This is an opportunity to prioritize all that you believe in and live by. Financial security. Honesty. Family. Joy. Pleasure. Fame. Power. Peace. Service. Notoriety. Justice. Celebrity. Greed. Perfection. Humility. What are the five pillars of your value system? You probably have more than five, but try to focus on these top ones you are most conscious of.

In effect, I'm asking you to establish a hierarchy of values in order for you to examine your life and see if you're living up to your values. Are you pursuing your "ideal" values or are you living according to a different set of values? There is no judgment here. There is only your satisfaction with yourself to consider. If you feel constantly bombarded with negative feelings that you're not doing enough, heeding the "shoulds," or not living up to your ideal, then maybe it's time to reconsider for whom are you living—because you're not living for yourself, that's for sure.

11. How do these five values influence the way you lead your life?

If you value honesty, you'll probably be out in most arenas of your life. If you value family stability, you'll probably act to maintain a harmonious status quo. If you value hard work, you'll be devoted to your career or volunteer efforts. If you value the "common good," you will find an abundance of opportunities to improve your community. But what happens when these values conflict with one another, or your life holds contradictions?

The purpose of all these exercises is not to feel guilty about any contradictions you uncover. Rather, it is to help you to identify and accept your personal value system. Contradiction can point the way toward conflict or compromise. If you value honesty, yet you are asked by your boss to be dishonest, you might come to realize that you need to change jobs. If you value social justice, but realize your local community does not support affirmative action, you may decide to help secure passage of that kind of legislation. Whichever value is at stake, you may see that you would rather change your behavior to match your principles, since the principles are paramount to you. It is important to accept a less idealized set of principles that you can live with and still retain your ethical system, rather than live a life of guilt, self-recrimination, and contradiction.

I had an experience in my early thirties that totally transformed my value system. In 1968, I was working as a staff psychologist at Lincoln Hospital in the South Bronx, a predominantly Hispanic and African-American neighborhood. It was my first full-time job, and I was working in a community mental health program. I had also become involved with Psychologists for Social Action (PSA), an activist association of professional psychologists who were committed to social justice, which in those days meant the civil rights and antiwar movements.

When I began work, there was an incipient fight brewing about huge discrepancies in salaries between the psychiatrists and the paraprofessionals (people from the community working in the program). Since I was new on the job, I watched from the sidelines at first, but then I joined a committee of workers who were trying to negotiate with the administration on the pay issue as well as other working conditions. The tension escalated until the workers decided to stage a sit-in to take over the administration building across the street. The action was planned for a Friday, and I was called Thursday night and told that there were probably going to be arrests the next day. My coworkers wanted to be sure I was going to be there, and they told me, "We need you." As one of the few white professionals supporting the action, they told me, my presence would "validate" the action.

When I hung up the phone, my night of agony began. I firmly believed in the cause and the justice of the worker's case, yet it was my first job. I was only thirty-two, and I feared being arrested would stop my career before it had even started. I had come out to only two of my coworkers as a gay man, and now I would be branded a radical—two "blemishes" I wasn't sure my career could survive. I wrestled with the decision to get arrested and kept rationalizing my noninvolvement. But then I found myself asking the familiar words of the Talmud: "If not now, when?" I realized I would always have a reason to justify not getting involved. I was known and trusted by Hispanics because I spoke Spanish and made an attempt to learn and understand their culture, while African-Americans also trusted me because of opinions I had expressed over civil rights issues. Also, unlike most of the staff, I was the first white professional who had taken many walks into the community, seeing where and how people lived, so people in the neighborhood knew me. I wasn't just a professional at the hospital. I barely slept that night, but I knew there was no way I couldn't participate the next morning. Maybe it was the spirit of the times, maybe it was the values I had learned from mentors like Bernice Neugarten and my first lover, Joe, but I was ready to put my career on the line for what I believed.

When I went in the next morning, I was the only white professional staffer there, ready for this confrontation. The main ringleader approached me and asked me not to get arrested. It would be better if I were available to raise bail money for the people who were arrested. I witnessed the action, then helped to organize support and money to release the twenty-two people who were detained by the police. The sit-in was successful and prompted an eventual six-week strike by many of the staff (white, black, Puerto Rican) that led to negotiations among the hospital, the university, and the city, as well as federal officials.

Despite the way things played out, I had been ready for the worst and came out of the experience better prepared to act on my beliefs. I had acted with integrity and would continue to do so. The important thing to remember is that my decision wasn't without fear. I was terrified, but I felt I couldn't live with myself if I didn't do it. My visibility during the action and subsequent negotiations did close some doors, but it opened others. I continued my involvement with PSA and ultimately became its national coordinator in 1970. I left PSA in 1973 to focus my activism on gay issues, then spent most of the seventies working on lesbian and gay mental health organizing, and in the eighties I began working with AIDS activism and later with the International Lesbian and Gay Association (ILGA), finally pursuing my dream of global action.

It may seem like oversimplifying to point toward that one decision to get arrested as a turning point in my life, but it really was. In making that decision, I examined my lived values versus my ideal values. I realized I needed to take that action in order to live up to my own standards, independent of what others (including my superiors) thought of me. For me, it was about integrity and sense of purpose, and I have never regretted my decision.

From our larger political organizations to our sexual practices, many gay men are examining their belief systems and deciding what will they stand for, where their energies (both time and money) will go. Your life always reflects your values, but what's important for your mental health is that you express your values, whether they are concerned with gay marriage or adoption reform or "don't ask, don't tell" or literacy or breast cancer or hunger or poverty issues. Participation in the Bigger Picture contributes to your mental health because you are connecting with people with similar values and you are giving your life a meaning.

12. **What is the picture you have of a gay man your age who has a well-developed and livable value system? What do you have to do to be more like him?**

Look around and see how your peers are expressing their values. Do you see contradictions between their "stated" values and how they live their lives? It may remind you of how your blood family talked one way, but acted another. It may be difficult to find a peer who has integrated his value system into his ethical behavior—it's not an easy process for anybody. The goal is to find a person who lives according to his values: who says what he values and lives by what he values.

By this time, having identified contradictions and conflicts between your own behavior and your own value system, you are more realistic about what you can and cannot expect of yourself. Let this gay peer serve as a guide for integrating the ideal and lived values by which you operate. Maybe the steps you need to take to be more like him are small, maybe they're big, but manageable when broken into baby steps. Anchored in the present, after having reviewed the values that have operated in your life, you are now able to understand how your own value system helps to create the life you want to live.

Frank's Story

Frank was a friend and had never been in therapy with me. I chose to tell his story because he seems to have made one of the most solid recoveries from a grieving and mourning period I have ever witnessed. I feel that his strength in this area came from his personal value system, which was shaped, in large part, by his blood family. Though Frank did not consciously see what he had learned from his parents' value system until we talked about it, it became quite clear to him that he had learned some very basic principles of living that have held him in very good stead.

Frank was born in France in 1940 into an educated, upper middle-class Jewish Romanian family. His father was thirty-nine and his mother thirty-one, and there was also a four-and-a-half-year-older brother. His mother's upper-class background and his father's success as an engineer developing international patents allowed them to create a new life for themselves in France, where they had arrived in 1932 having fled Romania because of anti-Semitism. They rebuilt their wealth and fled just as Nazis were entering their town, leaving relatives and all wealth behind. They arrived in the United States with their clothes and a diamond ring. They slowly built up a business of laying pipelines and became financially secure again.

Frank tried to be what his father was and what he wanted Frank to be—an engineer. He went to engineering school just to please his father, but hated it. Eventually, he went to business school with the idea that it would help him run his father's business. Frank ignored his own desires and abilities—he just had to be an engineer. He saw his father as a sexual man who traveled a lot, and Frank had reason to believe his father had mistresses. In contrast, he saw his mother as an asexual person who did not complain at all. She handled the losses and moves without despairing or losing hope. She went from having wealth and servants to cleaning her own home and living frugally. Both his parents adjusted to the reality of their lives together; both gave Frank a philosophy of living life on its own terms—making the best of it and moving on.

I believe that because of his family's long history of leaving everything behind and starting over, Frank learned that he was able to recover from loss and get on with his life. This was not just in terms of leaving possessions and a comfortable lifestyle, it meant leaving relatives and friends and having to move to a foreign country. Dealing with his lover Jean Louis's illness and death was the first major life event in which he had to put these values to the test. (He also used these values when his brother died and left a family with many debts. He stepped in and took responsibility for them so that they could get their feet on the ground and would not suffer for the mistakes that his brother had made.)

Frank was thirty-three when he met Jean-Louis, who was twenty-five and a butcher in France. They were together for almost twenty-three years until Jean-Louis's death in 1995. Frank felt he handled the death well because he saw it as a fact, not negative or positive. He feels he survived the test of the death through the pain—he learned from it and from being there for Jean-Louis. Frank recalls, "I had money but I was not tested. Coming out was one test and taking care of Jean-Louis was another. I was a mensch. I proved that I could do it. I was there. I adjusted my life to his—it was my primary focus. This was the first time I proved to be a man."

Until his lover's death, Frank saw himself as a weak person. When Jean-Louis told him, "Thank you for staying with me," Frank realized that he had done something special. He knew of lovers who had abandoned their partners but he had stayed and loved from the beginning of Jean-Louis's illness. For many gay men, caring for a loved one until death has become a communal initiation rite. The experience inspires many men to embrace their lives more fully, while others remain in grief. "There were times I wished he would die and knew that I had a life beyond. I could feel that there's more beyond. I discovered that the most interesting men that I have met were also men whose lovers [had] died. The second lesson after his death was that I could live alone and enjoy my life."

In talking about his ability to recover from his lover's death and start a new life without denying his feelings, Frank talked about his long period of coming out and recalled how he had gone into therapy to be "straight." He felt that the struggle of coming out over such a long period is what contributed to his philosophy and gave him strength. "The angst of coming out and fighting against things in yourself and not permitting yourself to be yourself—this is another test. What I got was osmosis from my parents. My parents were not a part of the Jewish tradition. For my father, life continued through the lives of his children—duplication is the role of the child. I knew after Jean-Louis's death, I knew that my life would be different for my having done something. I did join grieving groups after his death but I reached a point where I got nothing out of it—too many were going over the same thing and were not moving."

In terms of Jean-Louis's death, it was not that he was callous or unfeeling—Jean-Louis was the first man Frank had truly fallen in love with—but he had a realistic understanding that Jean-Louis was gone. He was sad, mourned, and felt intense pain but did not go into a depression. His sadness didn't permanently stop him from continuing his life in a positive way. The joie de vivre that he had before his lover's death continued, though he initially had doubts that he could have these feelings after Jean-Louis's death. He had started a relationship after the death that slowly developed into a love affair over a number of years. Though it eventually ended, Frank is grateful for that relationship as he had feared he could never love again and this relationship proved that he could. Though he would have liked it to have continued (the other man was not ready for a commitment), he was very thankful for the relationship since it gave him hope and feelings of love. (At the time of this writing, this man has now reentered his life and feels he is ready to be in a relationship with Frank.)

Frank remains committed to his life, which is stronger because of his experiences of coming out, caretaking, and grief. "I am a good role model because I can accept aging better. I enjoy life. I am willing to accept change—I can deal with it well. I do not want to be stagnant—I want an interesting life with no dull people. I want people who are alive. I want an exciting life."

EIGHT

Self-Control:
Taking Charge and Life Planning

Control gets a bum rap these days. Everybody wants it, few have it. "Control freak" is a derogatory term usually reserved for bosses or boyfriends. To be called "controlling" is a sign that we have usually crossed some kind of boundary and tried to do what no one can: control another human being.

But there's a huge distinction between being in control and being controlling. Being in control is about controlling yourself, while being controlling is about trying to control others. I have found that if you have the former, there's no need for the latter.

Central to the issue of control is our notion of power, specifically whether or not we understand the differences between inherent power (self-control) and aggrandized power (trying to control others). I introduced these concepts of power in the context of relationships, but on a deeper level, power is related to whether or not we feel we have control of our lives. If we feel strong and autonomous, if we feel as if we hold some power in our lives, we are experiencing inherent power, so control may be less of an issue. But if we feel powerless or that our power is threatened, we crave control and may exaggerate our need for it. In extreme situations, wielding power over another person becomes a substitute for any sense of personal power. Bullies, spouse beaters, abusive parents, and the like may destroy the lives of those around them through violent behavior because they lack a sense of inherent power. They know only one form of power—the kind that comes from hurting and trying to control other people.

I define *control* as *taking charge of the self*. Taking charge means taking responsibility for one's choices. Taking charge is about responding, rather than reacting, to the choices one has made in the past. Taking charge means knowing that more choices are to be made in the future. Taking charge is what midlife is all about.

AM I REALLY LOSING CONTROL?

Midlife can be a time of beginning to feel a loss of control or a heightened sense of powerlessness when the physical body begins to age. Suddenly, we may recognize we have no control over the passage of time and may fear losing total control of our own body. Most people can accept that there are some things that are out of their control, but when your own body starts to change before your very eyes, the fear and anxiety it provokes can trigger an increased sense of powerlessness. Many gay men feel betrayed by their aging bodies. Those feelings can wipe out all other feelings of power since so many of us are defined by our bodies.

Robert is a fifty-two-year old marketing professional. He has been active in the Atlanta social scene for more than twenty years, yet he has lost his sense of the power he once had to attract other men. He's handsome, with short, brown hair, stunning blue eyes, a great smile, and a wonderful sense of humor. Yet after he turned fifty, he felt as if he couldn't attract anybody he was attracted to. He feels he has no power over his aging body, and that other men see him only in terms of his age. He thinks he's invisible. As a result, he has given up trying to maintain his body: he's stopped exercising, smokes and drinks to excess after years of moderation, and feels powerless over the state of his body. While he continues to feel his professional and social power, at his many social engagements and in his work responsibilities, he no longer feels like a sexual being.

Robert's perceived loss of power is cyclical and self-perpetuating: once he started to feel powerless, he started to give up his power to make decisions and drifted, without a sense of direction or more important, a sense that he has the power or ability to direct the course of his own life. He hasn't really lost power, but he has lost the ability to *empower* himself. *Empowerment is the recognition and affirmation of your inherent power.* Empowerment is the key to understanding why control and aging well are interconnected.

Successful aging has to do with feeling good about oneself, about one's achievements, and about one's sense of inherent power. The more confidence we have in ourselves, the more we have a sense that we can change direction in our lives, that we can go after what we want, and that we can take charge. This circular reinforcement increases our sense of autonomy and strength. Finally, the more we feel our own strength, the more satisfied we are with our lives, and the more satisfied we are with our present situation, the more comfortable we are around aging. When we feel powerful, we stop seeing our aging in terms of loss because we stop feeling as if we are losing control over our lives. We begin to realize that power not only means "to be able," but also "able to be."

I also believe there is a connection between empowerment and entitlement. In discussing the hologram and the experiences of a gay child, I noted that few gay men survive their childhood with much of a sense of entitlement. For many gay men, entitlement is a feeling that comes after they leave home, come out, and begin to affirm themselves as gay men. The coming-out process offers a blueprint for affirmation: when you start to feel powerful as a result of coming out, there's a natural flow to feeling a sense of positive entitlement. Coming out as a gay man empowers you to feel entitled to good things in your life and mirrors the entitlement many nongay children develop as they mature. Our coming out does for us what the typical socialization does for nongay children. For a gay man, this new feeling of entitlement is based on who he is and what he does as a person (internal power), not what he receives by virtue of his gender, sexual orientation, skin color, parent's money, where he was born, or social connections (aggrandized power).

For many of us, coming out was a clear and conscious choice, after much self-doubt and inner struggle. As we came out as gay men, we reconditioned ourselves to feel good about our sexuality. Each individual follows his own path to self-acceptance, and learning to respect that path, wherever it may lead, is essential for mature development. For gay men, the first step is usually an attraction to other males, then sex, assuming the label of "homosexual," and finally creating a gay identity. Although each individual's path is different, *all paths involve decision making.* Each coming out follows an individual pattern of choices.

Aging well requires the same degree of consciousness about our choices in life, both past and present. Previously, we may have been unaware of some of our choices, but now, at midlife, something—an encounter with ageism, a fear of losing our attractiveness, an awareness of mortality—or some precipitating event propels us into consciousness, and we begin to take notice of our decisions. Of course, the catalyst is different for each person: turning forty, being laid off, the birth of a child, the death of a best friend or lover or parent, can all trigger a sense that "I'm becoming one of 'them' and getting closer to death." For me, it was the moment I began to see my age in the number of years left, rather than the years behind me. In short, aging is a crisis that can make us acutely conscious of how we are leading our lives.

One of the aspects of my work has been to assist other gay men to take conscious charge of their lives. My experience has been that few gay men really felt as if they were in total control of their lives. So many of us feel that we are victims or outsiders of one kind or another, either from the environment in which we were raised or from the homophobic culture that surrounds us. (Perhaps this feeling may be different or less intense for gay men coming of age in the nineties when our community is more visible and tolerated in at least a few urban areas.) Feelings of alienation have burdened many gay men since childhood, and as a reaction, many of us have just gone with the flow and accepted that little we do or decide will drastically affect what happens to us.

When I was in my late teens and living in Chicago, my lover had a good friend who had the misfortune of always picking up guys who beat him up. At the time, I didn't really understand why this happened to him so much. Now I see that he was attracting or was attracted to a certain kind of person. He felt like a victim most of the time, and he never seemed to make a connection between the choices he made about his sexual partners and the aftermath of violence.

Obviously, this reluctance to look for cause and effect isn't limited solely to gay men. We live in a society that can be overwhelming to an individual, in which economic and political forces can weaken anybody's sense of personal power. But what's important for gay men to understand is that they have already revealed a tremendous amount of personal power by the very act of coming out. Holding onto an observer-victim perspective, however, prevents many gay men from appreciating the courage and heroism that can be involved in coming out.

When I point out the incredible significance of coming out and the courage needed to do it, many gay men dismiss it as just an event in their past, nothing special, once extraordinary but no big deal anymore. When I ask them to tell me their coming-out story, many gay men remember the anxiety and terror they felt beforehand, but they forget or play down the planning and many months (usually years) of thought that went into the decision to come out. I push them to recognize the strength it took to go against the current, as well as the honesty to challenge the mainstream. When I call coming out a courageous act, many gay men look at me strangely. They point to their fear and trembling and deny they acted with courage. I remind them that courage is action in the presence of fears. To put your family's love and affection, or your job security at risk requires a tremendous amount of courage. Brushing your teeth—an act without fear—is hardly a courageous act, but coming out most definitely is.

By focusing on coming out, I try to help each man understand his history in a new way by examining the decisions he has made, not just about his sexuality, but about his entire life's journey. The goal is to understand we have been making decisions all along, in which coming out was just one. I use coming out as a metaphor for our entire lives: like coming out, life takes courage, planning, support, much thought, risk-taking, etc. To begin to see our lives as a series of decisions made from a variety of available choices requires a new paradigm. This new perspective involves questioning and perhaps rethinking the ways we understand our own sense of power and control, as well as the consequences of our decisions. To bring about this shift in perspective, I ask gay men to go back even further, prior to their coming out, and really get down to basics in recognizing the pattern of their decision making and the choices they've made.

THE TAPESTRY OF OUR LIVES

For many people, "life" exists as a series of unrelated events that happened to them and are linked only by linear time. Understanding how your decisions have shaped your life happens only when you stop looking at your life as a series of unconnected, linear events. I was born, I went to school, I went to college, I came out, I moved to Los Angeles, I got a job, and so forth. By taking a closer, more thoughtful look at significant events from your past, you can begin to realize that a part of you was making decisions the whole time— or not making decisions. (A decision does not necessarily involve an action; passivity *is* a decision, even if it's unconscious.)

Before you can change the pattern, you have to recognize what it is. It's useful to invoke the metaphor of "the tapestry of life." The beauty of a tapestry is created by the weaving of thousands of strands of thread: many are unique in color, texture, and length. Up close, you can see each thread, distinct and separate; from a distance of five feet, that same thread blends into the larger pattern. The pattern grows and shifts depending upon your perspective; the same tapestry can reveal many different patterns, depending upon your point of view.

Now consider the events of your life as the individual threads of a tapestry. You may have considered your life events to be unconnected to one another except by time (how is going to college in Chicago related to growing up in Texas; how is joining a book reading group related to going to law school; how is serving in the army related to being the youngest in a large family, and so on). But viewing them from a distance enables you to see an emerging pattern. You begin to realize that the events of your life have been influenced by the choices you made at points along the way. Becoming conscious about your life means appreciating how a decision made when you were fifteen affected a later decision when you were twenty and a third decision when you were thirty-five. Identifying the connections becomes a means of recognizing the continuity of your life, in short, the "pattern" of your life's weaving.

As you move away from focusing on each individual event to recognizing the overall pattern of your life, your past choices and actions will come into focus. You may not have fully known why you left college at nineteen, but later, you might realize that you weren't getting what you needed from that environment. Perhaps going to work gave you the support and discipline you were seeking. Look for the ways that a particular event or choice (each of them a thread, to stay with our metaphor) can play a role in different parts of your life.

Recognizing this overall pattern of choices, decisions, and consequences is essential to understanding your personal history as a dynamic flow over which you clearly exercised more control than you may have been aware of at the time. This tapestry approach redefines a static past with many repetitions (such as relationships with similar problems) into a dynamic history that leads to the present. Acknowledging the steps you have taken, the threads you have woven into your tapestry, you have a better sense of how you've been making choices—not as a passive observer of your life but as its creator and director.

The more you can see these threads (events) as the result of past choices, the more courage it will give you to make choices in the present. By acknowledging your part in the weaving (how certain threads reflect the painful choices you made in the past), you gain a sense of control that allows you to continue to weave the tapestry of your life. You can make similar or different choices (either correcting or repeating behavior) that will produce the same or alternative pattern of events. Perhaps you can begin to recognize the potential of the present to make different choices. At midlife, you are still weaving, but like many of us, you probably want to go buy some new thread for the loom.

Identifying your life's tapestry is a way of building a foundation for dealing with the future as well. For many gay men, the future we fear is really just the projected past. When looking at our past, we have trouble seeing beyond the negative events and the negative behaviors we may have learned in our (possibly dysfunctional) background. Focused on the past, many gay men just see the future as more unhappiness, and our concern for the future may be just a fear that our past will repeat itself.

I like using the tapestry metaphor because it's nonjudgmental (and, to quote Sally Bowles in *Cabaret*, "I think it's pretty!"). Our threads aren't inherently good or bad, and together they weave a particular life's tapestry that is neither inherently good or bad. It is our tapestry and nobody else's. With this new perspective on his past decision making, a gay man can recognize his strengths and weaknesses and how he has been guiding himself in his life. This recognition that he has been guiding himself is the essence of empowerment. Becoming conscious of your self-control affirms your inherent power.

During our lives, there are decisions that we felt we just *had* to make (coming out, getting a job in a particular field, living in a certain city). When we look back, especially at midlife, we can begin to discover why those decisions felt "right" (not as in right and wrong, but in the sense of alignment with our personal value system). Acknowledging our ability to have made choices in the past affirms and strengthens our ability to make choices in the present, regardless of whether they are the same or different or new and improved. At the very least, they will be more conscious choices.

When I decided to move out of the home and life I had created with Joe, my first lover, I knew I needed that particular experience in order to grow. I was going to be a student at the University of Chicago, and by moving closer to campus and living alone, I could be more integrated in the total academic experience and be exposed to all aspects of life at the university. For a time, while making this decision, I had the feeling of being in midair, over a chasm, 10,000 feet above a valley. I didn't know where I would land since the ground on the other side was completely covered in fog. I just knew that I had to jump. In midair, looking down yet moving across the chasm, I found one source of courage: knowing that I had had to make the leap in order to grow. Even though I was terrified and filled with anxiety, I moved out on my own.

Life is filled with moments like this: when we know we need to act, but are unsure of the consequences. Few decisions make the difference between life and death, though we may feel and think otherwise at the time. Only upon reflection and after reviewing our past can we see the decisions we made for what they truly were. Ten years after coming out you may not remember the note of strength and vulnerability in your voice when you told your parents you were gay, but the years do not diminish the courage in that act. At midlife, facing your past and renewing your present begins by identifying such moments and events that changed your life's journey.

1. What are the five significant events that have altered your life?

There are probably more than five events that have affected your life, but stay focused on a few critical ones, rather being overwhelmed by too many. Also, you are the one to define "significant." For some men, it's the first time they felt an attraction to another man. Or their first kiss. The first time they had to hide their gay feelings from their family. The first time they had sex. Or maybe it's when they went to college or showed up at their first job. The first time on their own in a new city. The first time away from their family. The day they were called "faggot" at school. The first time a friend was diagnosed HIV positive or the first time they had a blackout from drinking. The first time they brought a boyfriend home to meet the family. Or the first time they walked into a gay bar. Their first breakup. Their first realization that they were not alone in the world. The first time they encountered death.

I'm curious about significant events that contributed to a paradigm shift in your understanding of the world—the events that made you change direction or make new priorities in your life. What events brought you new information that changed your world perspective? These events may not be thunderbolts from the sky, but small, ordinary events that led to shifts in perspective, which eventually led to a paradigm shift. Consider internal changes as well as changes in behavior. Emotional "breakthroughs" can happen on a day in which nothing unusual has happened, yet your perspective on a relationship or a career decision may have suddenly shifted.

We've all had moments that changed our lives. We may see these as events over which we had control or we may consider them lucky breaks, moments of chaos, or just plain bad luck.

2. Talk about the "good" and "bad" luck that you have had.

Do you ever win at Bingo? Do you live in a state with a lottery and spend your $2 regularly, hoping the same numbers you pick every week will hit the jackpot? Some people say they never win anything, but that doesn't keep them from trying. In a culture so obsessed with winning and losing like ours, we are inclined to court Lady Luck in all that we do: lucky numbers, lucky clothes, lucky days of the week, lucky songs, and so on. Other people remind me

of a weekly skit on *Hee Haw*, a country music variety show popular
in the seventies and eighties, in which four sad-faced hillbillies would
sing, "If it weren't for bad luck, I'd have no luck at all."

Do you feel lucky? Or do you feel you attract bad luck? Although
winning the LOTTO or a long-shot horse race or the Publishers
Clearinghouse Sweepstakes is only a dream for most of us, we tend
to translate daily events into good and bad luck: catching the right
bus, being caught without an umbrella in a downpour, meeting a
future business partner at a cocktail party, always ending up in the
slowest line at the bank or the grocery store, or finding a $10 bill
on the street. Even life-changing events can be seen in terms of luck,
both good and bad: meeting Mr. Right "across a crowded room,"
being a teenager when your father dies, getting approval of a mortgage, contracting the HIV virus, and so on.

Count up the number of times in the past week when you've
felt like the beneficiary of good luck or the victim of bad luck. Don't
leave anything out, whether it's a raffle at your local bar or a gay
bashing in your own neighborhood or getting a job from an ad in
the paper. The point is to flesh out those events that felt like they
just happened to you, the "innocent bystander."

3. **What could you have done to change the outcome of these
    events?**

*Change the outcome of good luck? How can I change my bad luck? Luck
is luck, it just happens.* Before you think I've gone off the deep end, I'll
say flat out that I don't believe luck exists. Actually, I believe it
operates as another myth (like retirement) to keep people working
hard and deferring their happiness. For example, the dream of winning the lottery keeps many people from questioning the social contract in this country that perpetuates inequalities in opportunity,
education, and income. The poorest people keep the lottery running,
and luck becomes a poor man's substitute for hope.

But more relevant to our discussion, the concept of good and
bad luck reinforces a person's observer-victim perspective. Bad luck
absolves a person from recognizing his role in the event, while good
luck equally absolves him from appreciating the actions he's taken to
achieve what "luck" has brought him. Maybe you're thinking, *I'll
concede not winning the lottery or the raffle, but what about the bad stuff? What*

about when my best friend died? What about when I got laid off? What about when my lover of seven years cheated on me? I don't think these events are about luck; they are about life.

I'd like to reframe "luck," whether "good" or "bad," as events that present many alternative responses, one of which we choose. I'm not denying chance, the random events that happen in life, some of them unfortunate and some of them fortunate. In assigning meaning ("good" or "bad") to these chance events, we've chosen to handle them in a certain way. Too often we use "good" and "bad" luck as a way of accepting a situation or of denying our responsibility in a situation. Rather than saying it's good luck, appreciate your good fortune or your ability to take advantage of an opportunity. Rather than saying it's bad luck, look at the decisions you may have made that contributed to the outcome.

When I discuss this approach toward luck with clients, I initially hear a lot of anger and blame. *How was I responsible for my friend's death? Or How dare you suggest I made my lover break our monogamous agreement?* My motivation behind this exercise is to eliminate "luck" from our vocabulary of responses to what life presents us with. It's important to recognize "It was a lucky break" or "I've got the worst luck" as reactions that try to explain reality without having to take the time to gain a clearer perspective on the situation. It's clear to me that "luck" can be used to hide both a pattern of strengths (good luck) and bad choices (bad luck). When we use luck to explain our reality, we're relying on feelings of powerlessness, passivity, and ultimately, no control over our lives.

By reframing the events we have called "luck," we can trace what led up to it and recognize our role in the situation, if any. This exercise is not meant to produce guilt, but to help you achieve a realistic appraisal of your history. This approach to personal history is from a *proactive* perspective: try to determine whether there is anything you may have done that would have resulted in a different outcome. In retrospect, you may see that you could have done something differently. Maybe there was an alternative decision to be made—if none, the goal is to see the situation as a lesson to be learned. There's always something to be learned from an event, even one with negative consequences.

But again, what about the bad stuff? Called faggot all during high school. Being fired for being gay. Kicked out of your home by parents or landlord. Police entrapment in a public restroom or park. A black eye from your boyfriend. The death of a parent or best friend or life partner. By reframing "bad luck," I am not denying that terrible things happen as part of life's events, but what I am after is for us to recognize situations that are within our control and situations that really are beyond our control.

Many gay men throw up their hands at the "cards life has dealt" them. A dysfunctional childhood. A limited amount of talent or skills. A desire for men. Much of this victim attitude is a direct result of internalized homophobia, and it takes a tremendous amount of energy to break through this feeling of always being a victim, of always being controlled by others. This is not to say that there are no forces of homophobia and stigmatization operating in our culture. As gay men, we take on and absorb whatever external homophobia we encounter until it's internalized as our own. But in becoming conscious of our victim attitude, we can begin to draw some lines, recognizing the outside forces as well as the effects of our own internalized homophobia.

So what do we control? Our actions and our responses. What do we not control: other people's actions, responses, and reactions; other people's emotions and perspectives; and the consequences of our actions on other people's feelings. Understanding the limits of our control over other people is one of the main stumbling blocks of therapy, and as I discussed in chapter 6 on finding your own voice, it's this simple: *We don't make people feel a certain way. We do something, and they choose to feel a certain way, and vice versa. Our feelings are our own.*

What keeps many gay men from accepting this responsibility for their feelings are two emotions that have been brandished against our community from the beginning: guilt and blame.

GETTING BEYOND GUILT AND BLAME

This country is obsessed with guilt and its evil twin, the confession. Whether it's a confessional to a priest or rabbi or therapist or best friend or talk show host, we love to tell our secrets, feel guilty, and move on to forgiveness. We're good at dishing out guilt as well, with unfortunate Jewish mothers becoming the stereotype of the nagging, guilt-producing parent.

But guilt, like luck, is a reaction to avoid responding. Called a "useless" or "empty" emotion by many therapists, guilt nevertheless exerts a powerful hold on many gay men. Guilt not only cuts off communication (with the conversation ending, "I feel so guilty"), but also breeds passivity in the guilt ridden. The more we can confess and feel guilty, the less urgency we feel to stop our behavior. The guilt we feel becomes the atonement, the price we pay for actions that harm other people, as well as ourselves.

Actually, as with any emotion, there are two forms of guilt: dishonest and honest. Honest guilt means accepting responsibility and not doing "it" again (whatever we've done that produces guilt). Dishonest guilt is guilt for guilt's sake—with the person pointing to his guilt for how badly he feels, but not badly enough not to do "it" again.

Guilt is an appropriate response only the first time a mistake is made. When the mistake or action is pointed out to us, we now know what to do, the lesson is learned, and the appropriate response is to make amends, if possible, but not to hold on to the mistake and beat ourselves up over and over again. The second time we make the same mistake, it's a choice, made with knowledge of the consequences, and guilt isn't an appropriate response. But so many of us fall back on our guilt again and again, not learning our lesson, and holding on to past behaviors, and that's when the real mistakes begin.

In addition, there's blame, to fill in when we don't want to take responsibility for our actions and decisions. Like guilt, blame is usually a reaction, an emotional blanket that will cover whatever role a person plays in a situation. Blame is not always a negative emotion: it can identify who's responsible, who contributed what toward an outcome of a situation. But pointing fingers can take the focus off the person doing the blaming and relieve them from the burden of communication. "I don't want to talk about it; it's all your fault." A pattern of blaming other people for all our problems can prevent us from ever learning how to respond to life; as a result, we can live a life of reactions. Blame rarely stops with identifying who did what to us. We can begin to hold other people responsible for later events that happen to us: "It all started with so-and-so . . ."

4. **Who are the people you have blamed for some of the negative aspects of your past and present life?**

Your mother for calling you sick. Your father for ignoring you. The kids at school for tormenting you. The anti-gay supervisor at work. The professor who failed you in the required course for your major, which meant you had to go to summer school and not graduate with your class. The boyfriend who left you. The boyfriend who gave you herpes. The boss who screamed at you until you quit.

Really go into all the areas of your life where you feel victimized. Give yourself permission to blame. This is not a part of ourselves we like to show. We prefer to appear like adults who take responsibility for life and what happens, but we may harbor long-standing resentments and feelings of victimization that will not go away until we acknowledge them.

It's okay to blame, or at least to acknowledge that you've blamed people in the past for negative events in your life. There's no denying the reality that many gay people have been mistreated, abused, and persecuted. In addition, there are the "bad" things that happen to everybody: illness, poverty, unemployment, depression, addiction, or death.

But blame gets us only so far. Blame allows us to pinpoint responsibility on an action, but it doesn't qualify as a response to that action. In most cases, blame is a reaction, not a response. From our previous discussion on reaction and response (chapter 6), we know that reactions are emotional, not thought out, intense, and more like instantaneous emotional reflexes, whereas a response is chosen, appropriate, emotionally honest, and fully thought through.

So how do we tell when blame is not a good thing? When it identifies only the other person's responsibility and keeps the focus only on what the other person did. When blame begins to deny the possibility of our responsibility, we are operating under a self-delusion of innocence. More important, blame can maintain the victimization stance in life by holding other people responsible for our behavior. Another person can cause an event that pains and hurts us, and it's tempting to blame him for what we're feeling. But that would deny our responsibility for our own feelings. Blaming others for our feelings of powerlessness or victimization can prevent us from ever achieving a sense of inherent power. To carry blame around like a security blanket is another dynamic that cripples us and prevents us from realizing how much control we possess over the outcomes of our lives.

This perspective on control and taking charge of our emotions (and by extension, our actions and our lives) is one of life's greatest tools. I cannot stress enough how crucial it is for a person to see that even when there was no choice in the *outcome* of a situation, he did have a choice in *how he responded* to the situation.

To help communicate this concept, I'd like to define responsibility as "response-ability," the ability to respond, rather than react. The more we are able to respond—and not react—to our tapestry as it is woven, the more we can acknowledge our role in the weaving. Once we stop reacting to the events in our lives—the raw threads of our tapestry—and begin responding to our present, we can stop blaming others for our present.

One of the difficulties of aging is when we feel unhappy with the present, especially any feeling of the have-nots: we haven't accomplished much, we haven't gotten what we wanted out of life, we don't have much time left. We may blame our displeasure or unease with the present on our parents, our past, bad teachers, stupid bosses, a cruel stranger, and rotten luck.

Reframing your past as a dynamic flow enables you to see where you have taken charge of your life (as well as where you have not). Taking charge doesn't mean knowing all the answers. You may have a sense of the quality of the life you want, but not necessarily what it looks like. We need to visualize what we want without being specific about the form it takes. Revisiting my history of Work/Play, I didn't know how my dream of working for the United Nations would ever play out. After coming out, I gave up faith in it because I knew I couldn't be openly gay at the UN. Years later, the dream came true (helping a community take care of its mental health) but the details did not (I worked within my own community of gay and lesbian peers as opposed to a Third World country). Ultimately, the work I did with ILGA and the UN resulted in the lesbian and gay employees at the United Nations starting their own group. As it turned out, the reality was much better than the dream.

Aging heightens any dissatisfaction people may be feeling, but by focusing on what they don't have or "should" have, many gay men ignore the worth of what they do have. This next exercise may

seem similar to the first one in this chapter, but the focus is much
more intense. Instead of listing events that "just happened" to alter
your life, I want you to explore your own role in creating your
present life: What events in your past have you decided are responsible for bringing you to today?

5. **What are the significant decisions you have made that have
    drastically changed your life?**

This exercise is loaded with words like *significant* and *drastically*,
but the focus here is on the proactive decisions you have made,
however large or small. These are the self-starting actions that you
undertook to make a difference in your life. The most obvious one
is coming out, but these decisions can be as varied as exercising
twice a week, being more honest with your family, setting limits on
your work hours, developing better work habits, smiling more, accepting compliments and not dismissing them, and so on. But you
don't need many of these decisions to effect drastic changes in your
life. Remember: complicated doesn't necessarily translate into effectiveness. Sometimes, a series of decisions becomes too complicated
and just creates busyness. If you're running yourself ragged with too
much "self-improvement," you'll have no idea what would really make
you feel good about yourself, and most likely, you'll just become
exhausted and frustrated.

What's important is the before and after consequences of the
decision, no matter its size (and small decisions may have to ripple
out to have "significant" repercussions). A decision can seem minor
or simple, but it may reflect an underlying complexity to the situation. As I expressed in the chapter on values, one of the most complex principles by which to live—the Golden Rule—is very simply
stated: Love your neighbor as your self. How we love ourselves, how
we love our neighbors, how those two relationships can mirror each
other are all complex to work out. For example, what if you decide
to be more open and honest with your blood family? Such a decision
would mean letting them know that you have a social and emotional
life, in addition to the professional news you share with them. You
might decide to go home for a holiday only if your family's invitation
includes your boyfriend, whom they've never met. Your willingness
to make such a decision may motivate your family to rethink how

they may take your presence for granted at times. In turn, that re-thinking may lead to a dialogue in which the relationship is repaired or improved, or at the very least, changed by your simple decision to be more honest.

Perhaps what's most significant about these decisions is that they reflect a willingness to take responsibility for your own happiness. For a variety of reasons, we're not always convinced that we deserve happiness. But being happy with one's life is one of the best ways to age well. So doing something only for yourself each day is not only a way to honor yourself, but a way to age well. It's saying you are important enough to treat yourself well, and that you are entitled to good things and to please yourself and to be happy. Once you start doing the little things, the resulting positive feelings build to a solid sense of autonomy, inherent power, and control of one's happiness.

You may still find yourself getting angry again and wanting to blame someone else for a decision or event that changed your life. Some of the biggest life events are out of our control, and we can only survive the fallout.

6. **Explain the distinction between an event over which you had no control and the control you had over the way you responded to the situation.**

Your parents divorce. A friend dies. A business collapses and you lose your job. A lover decides he needs to be alone so he leaves you.

There are always parts of life over which we have no control, no matter the particulars of a given situation. But we can always control our response to an inevitable outcome. Most people do not make this distinction. Many gay men justify their inaction or negativity by referring to the "no control" part of this statement and do not acknowledge the parts over which they had control. It takes a mature ego to see this distinction and live by it.

What about those of us who believe we have no control over anything, it's all in the hands of God or Allah or a Higher Power or the universe? There's an Arabic proverb that says, "Pray to Allah and tie your camel to a post." Spiritual belief is not incompatible with taking charge of your life, and few religious systems depict its members as totally powerless or without free will.

Faced with a situation over which we have no control, it's much easier to react rather than respond. We can react with the most immediate emotions we're conscious of (anger, tears, distress) and spend a lot of time acting out these emotions and not really responding to the situation at hand. We react: "See, I'm a victim, always have been, always will be." In contrast, we could respond with "This hurts in the moment, but I can survive. I always have, I always will." We can be victimized, but we don't have to stay or feel like a victim forever.

I learned this lesson firsthand when I was gay bashed one Halloween. I was walking with my friend Marty on Hudson Street in Greenwich Village after the Halloween parade. It was very crowded, and I saw a bunch of young teenagers coming toward us and acting belligerently. I moved out of their way, and when I turned back to continue talking to Marty, I realized he was on the ground. When he hadn't moved out of their way, they had called him faggot, and two of them jumped him. I rushed over to pull them off of him, and when I turned around, I realized that there was a third. He was about sixteen or seventeen and had a broomstick raised over his head. It was all in slow motion for me—I remember thinking I do not want to hurt him nor do I want to be hurt. I was looking into his eyes, which were filled with hate yet seemed hollow; I felt as if I could look right through him down into his feet. When he brought the broomstick down, I put up my arm. I do not know if it broke on my arm or on my head but there was a loud cracking sound, and the stick broke. The jagged edge split open my scalp and started a gash at the top of my nose, down the side of my cheek to the lip. After I fell down, the boys disappeared into the crowd, and though there were hundreds of people around, no one stopped them. Marty and I managed to make it to a hospital, where it took fifty-five stiches to close up my face wound. I had a broken nose, two black eyes and two permanent scars.

Afterwards, I was filled with anger and knew that it was not good for my healing. When I went to report the incident, the police did not want to call it a fag bashing. But I persevered and convinced them to let me look at all the mug shots of teenage assaulters. All the photographs were of black, Hispanic, or Appalachian-looking teens. The three who had attacked me and Marty were all white— the one who hit me was shorter and stockier than me and was probably from the Irish projects of the east side. Anyway, I knew I had to come to some resolution with my anger. I remembered that young man's eyes and how empty they seemed. I kept thinking that prison or detention would not help him change if they ever found him. I finally thought that if he were found, I would ask that his sentence be that he come to see me for two years in therapy. I believed that we would spend the first year dealing with our mutual anger at each other, and the second year we could actually get down to helping him make a change. Once I imagined this sentence, the anger disappeared and I felt resolved. I began to realize that I really did not have to hold on to my anger or experience any more emotional pain from this incident. I had received such an outpouring of love and concern from my friends that as time passed, the actual incident seemed more like a pimple than a scar. He was the hurting and lonely person. While painful in the moment, this fagbashing ultimately had only positives for me. I actually became the NGLTF poster boy for the antiviolence campaign years later with the pictures I had taken right after the bashing. More importantly, I learned how to experience and let go of my anger at being victimized, but I didn't remain a victim.

Revisit the events you listed in exercises 1 and 5, the ones you saw as "just happening" to you, as well as the "significant" ones you decided. Remember your feelings afterward? Try to accept that you can take as much credit for the positive feelings as for the negative feelings. Instead of hearing only, "It's all my fault" or "He's the one to blame," imagine saying, "I am responsible for how I'm feeling right now." Or "I'm angry and I recognize my right to feel this way." Or "I feel rejected and I feel lousy and I feel like getting even."

Examining these feelings will bring about a different understanding of these events. The more a gay man can develop a sense of responsibility for his actions, reactions, and responses, the more he can begin to see his past in terms of alternatives, a perspective that has implications for the present and the future.

7. **In what ways has nonaction or passivity been the way to handle difficult situations?**

Maybe you haven't had much feeling at all when confronted with difficult situations. Maybe you just wanted to hide from the

situation and from the world. Or maybe you regressed into a childhood role of pleasing others to get by, or not making waves. Nonaction or passivity can be safe, for a time; but the long-term effect is
terminal powerlessness. Passivity is always a choice, regardless of
whether you're conscious of it being so. A friend once quipped, "I'm
very proactive in my denial," about the hard time he was having in
therapy. He knew what he had to do, but clearly, he was holding
on to passivity as much as he could. But we react with passivity; we
respond with proaction, that is, positive action.

8. **In looking back over significant events in your life, what kinds
    of patterns do you see?**

This is actually a two-part exercise: looking at the pattern of
significant events as well as the pattern of your reactions/responses.
Do you see commonalities in the type of events? Do they have
similar outcomes or do they deal with similar issues? Or do you see
a randomness where all kind of things just happen to you? Maybe
all of your relationships have ended over the same issue, or maybe
you have always had long-term relationships, or maybe you have had
a series of intense, passionate relationships. Do you handle all events
the same way or do you react to some and respond to others? Maybe
you can communicate well in relationships, but job pressures make
you anxious and tongue-tied.

By having a better *understanding* of your past, you can make a
more realistic *evaluation* of your past. Understanding is different from
evaluating. Understanding your past means acknowledging the
strengths and courage you have displayed over the course of your
lifetime, especially in the decision to come out. Evaluating your past
means being honest about the amount of control you've had and
how your past decisions have affected the present. Understanding is
the recognition that your life is a tapestry; evaluating is the recognition that you are the weaver.

9. **Can you see the future as manifesting these patterns?**

In my previous discussion of the future, I remarked on how many
gay men dread the future because of a fear that it will merely repeat
the past. In reviewing your life in the course of these exercises,

patterns of events and the control you have displayed in those events are beginning to come clear. If you've identified patterns of passivity and reactive behavior, you may now be more alert about not letting the pattern repeat itself. If you have discovered positive patterns of proactivity and "response-ability," you may now see how strong you are, how well you can handle what life brings you, and how much control you've really had.

Seeing your patterns of behavior and control in a new light will probably reduce your anxiety over the future. You may be able to see your hidden reserves of strength and feel more able to handle the future. Whatever degree of strength and control you can identify in your past will reinforce attempts in the present (and future) to take charge of your life. While you may have trouble identifying many events for which you could plan and exert control, there is one that many gay men have in common: coming out.

10. **Spend some time thinking about all the strengths it took to come out and all the risks you took in that process.**

When many teenagers and young men realize they're gay, their world will never be the same. From the moment of awareness until coming out can be a torturous period of self-doubt, terror, self-loathing, and just plain stress. The road to coming out is a difficult one that requires much planning and thinking and preparation, and that journey puts at risk all of the traditional sources of support (family, friends, peers, church, school, community). Coming out makes the theoretical possibility of "gayness" suddenly real for many people, and a gay man can never assume how someone will react to his coming out. But most of us escape the closet by drawing upon our strength and courage.

As gay men, we rarely feel justified in patting ourselves on the back, but coming out is an ideal opportunity to do so. By midlife, we have become aware that our identity as gay men makes us unique and special, and that knowledge emboldens us to come out in all areas of our lives: home, work, church, community. Once we can reframe coming out as a lifetime dynamic of affirming ourselves, we can better see our coming out as a courageous flow of events of which we are the master. It is critical that we appreciate what it took to come out and how much we risked losing. Yet the majority of gay men speak of the gains of coming out: less stress and fewer lies, more freedom and self-esteem. The more we understand what was at stake in coming out, the better able we will be to handle the aging process, since midlife represents another coming out.

11. Think about becoming a middle-aged gay man as another coming out.

Aging—like being gay—is one of those events over which we have no control, but *how* we age—just as how we come out as a gay man—is completely under our control. Like discovering our homosexuality, aging is another "crisis" that we have the ability to resolve successfully and happily. This time, however, the energy and planning and courage we displayed in overcoming homophobia (both the nongay culture's as well as what we had internalized) will be put to use in rejecting the ageism, both of the culture at large, and especially gay male culture. In both instances, we are rejecting one culture's values and adopting those of another. In coming out, we rejected deception and self-loathing; in successful aging, we are rejecting the gay male culture that prizes youth and adopting another gay male culture based upon another definition of attractiveness.

Understanding the connections between aging and coming out will eventually decrease your anxiety around getting older. The knowledge that you survived coming out and went on to create a lifestyle for yourself, as well as the hindsight that coming out was the best thing you could do for yourself, will put aging in a new perspective. Just as when you were planning and taking charge of your coming out, you now have the opportunity to take charge of your aging.

FORGIVENESS: THE UNEXPECTED GIFT OF MIDLIFE

As gay men review their life history and begin to accept their own participation in its outcome, a surprising discovery has been the emergence of forgiveness toward parents and others. For most gay men, forgiveness at midlife was not a goal. They didn't set out to forgive anybody, but what happens is that the more they begin to appreciate their life—liking who and where they are at midlife—the more they can recognize the influence of their blood family without anger or blame. Once we can understand that we did indeed have some control over where our lives have ended up, we can see our parents as primary influences who contributed but did not single-handedly determine our lives. As many of us become more appreciative of who we are now, we also express more gratitude for those early influences. We stop blaming our parents for what is negative in our lives. Parents become other adults who were doing their imperfect best.

Forgiveness may be best described as an absence of blame—it doesn't mean turning the other cheek or being a martyr. Forgiveness is not saying, "I forget what happened," but realizing that what someone did can no longer hurt us. I am not talking about extreme cases of physical violence or incest or emotional abuse. But I am concerned about the usual problems with parents: the arguments, disappointments, and the silences.

For years after I left home, I harbored anger and resentment at my mother for the way she raised me. When I was fifteen, my probation officer (assigned to me after my arrest at fourteen) once told me that my mother was the most bizarre and strange person he'd ever seen outside a hospital. All I knew is she seemed unable to take care of me and my sister, so after hearing this, I relaxed some and no longer expected her to take care of me. I had already assumed more control for my own well-being by learning to cook and clean at an early age. She was also physically withholding. As a child, I used to joke that the fastest time in the world was the moment between when I reached out to hug my mother and she would pull away. In a way, my own mother taught me what *not* to be. Once I learned how to get rid of my own passivity and powerlessness, I could look beyond her poor treatment of me to see the incredible pain and unhappiness of her world.

This kind of forgiveness may seem unlikely at this point in your life. There may be painful memories that you have yet to deal with, but it is likely to happen. I wasn't expecting it, but for me, forgiveness of my mother emerged as a consequence of my realization that I was responsible for my own history. Forgiveness was a by-product compared to the greater shift in understanding my history and the control I had exerted at various times.

Many of my clients have spontaneously talked about this happening after they began to see their past as a dynamic unfolding—as opposed to a discrete, static sequence of events. Perhaps we can forgive others only when all the pieces are in place: awareness of the past, conscious choices in the present, and forgiveness of ourselves when things did not work out according to our plan.

12. What would you have to do to forgive your family for the negative aspects of your life?

Many gay men hold their blood family responsible for much of their unhappiness. "If only they hadn't treated me that way" or "If only they had taken the time to listen." Sadly, their decisions are in the past and cannot be changed. But the present is ours to change. When you start to take responsibility for your own decision making, even some of the negative influences can help move you into a positive direction.

But what about their irritating behavior? See it as a need for attention, maybe even love. *But their comments can be so vicious.* Don't focus on the words, but the person's pain behind what he or she is saying. Blame has already served its purpose, and you may be ready to stop using blame as a way of not taking responsibility for your life. By looking over your past, you will realize how much influence you have had in creating your life, as well as the amount of time you have been "on your own." As you begin to feel more and more like an adult, the familial blame will recede as you distance yourself from the child you were. When you can accept that you have done the very best you could, it will become easier to see your family members as doing the best they could at the time. The more contented you are with your present life and the more you feel in control of your future, the less you will feel the need to blame. In a sense, you are the adult now and capable of forgiving your parents as if they were children (even though you are still the child of your parents).

13. What positive aspects of your life can you thank your family for?

Only after you begin to move toward forgiveness can you acknowledge the positive gifts that your family gave you. It is usually difficult to list the gifts when you are unable to forgive the hurts. How can you be nice when you are still angry at the person? You are that much closer to adulthood when you can both forgive and give thanks for your family.

But acknowledging the positive aspects is not meant to distort unpleasant realities. I'm not denying that some of us come from abusive families. Forgiveness can be a very cathartic experience, especially when you can say: "No, let the abuse stop with me. I don't want this behavior to go on to the next generation." Facing the abuse and mistakes of the past and giving thanks for whatever gifts your family contributed to your life are significant steps toward recognizing your autonomy as a separate individual, capable of taking charge of his life. Both experiences contribute to your feeling of being an adult and to your letting go of a constricting tie to the past.

Not surprisingly, as gay men are able to let go of their blame and anger about historical events, they are able to do so for more recent events as well. Forgiveness can be contagious, and many gay men find they can extend their forgiveness of the past into a new attitude toward the present. Many gay men make the connection that if they have experienced a measure of control over their lives in the past, it probably hasn't suddenly deserted them at midlife. With this awareness, they are able to include all the people who are in their present lives under the umbrella of forgiveness.

14. **What would you have to do to forgive current people in your life for the negative aspects of your life?**

Just as forgiveness of your family requires a new understanding about the past, forgiveness in the present requires responding appropriately to the negative events, not merely reacting to them. Is blame appropriate? Can you see your responsibility in the situations? Were people conscious of what they were doing when they hurt you? Have they made it worse? Have you?

Exploring such questions is not easy because blame is very comfortable. But the awareness that you have control over your life gives you the ability to be honest and to forgive. I didn't talk about forgiveness and gratitude in the material on peerships, blood and chosen families (chapter 4) because it takes time to develop this awareness. Many people are not ready for forgiveness of anybody until they feel some measure of personal power and control in their lives. Our sense of control doesn't really emerge until a thorough journey into the past brings about a recognition of our power.

15. What positive aspects of your life can you thank other people for?

The dynamic of gratitude following on the heels of forgiveness of our family applies to people in our present as well. This exercise is a variation of "count your blessings," and there are two parts: the acknowledgment that there are positives and the thanking part. The awareness of blessings and the action of counting them are equally valuable because they help you to be more realistic about your life— not pollyannaish but simply acknowledging the positives and negatives without giving undue weight to either side. Acknowledgment of other people does not take away from your own achievements, but helps to support your sense of individuality and independence.

TAKING CONTROL OF TODAY

The work you have done to recognize and respond (with either forgiveness or gratitude) to those who have contributed to your life is a major accomplishment. But it is only possible when you acknowledge your contributions to your own life. This may seem like another paradox to accept, and I suppose it is. The moments you have taken charge of your life and made life-changing decisions, especially when you came out, are things to be proud of. They reveal moments when you have been in control, but not controlling.

For many gay men, midlife is the time when they become acutely conscious of their desire for control because they feel threatened by the amount of ageism to overcome. The myths and stereotypes around aging feel like an attack on whatever sense of control we may have over our lives. Reviewing your life history at this time, you can probably divide your past into periods when you didn't feel in control and periods when you were able to guide your life.

Once you have begun to redefine your history, you can tackle your life planning with renewed vigor and focus. It is essential that goals are not seen as ends in themselves but as guideposts that keep evolving as life progresses. If goals are set from a negative evaluation of your life, you are guaranteed to fail. Even when we reach some of our goals, we may still feel disappointed because we have not changed the underlying negativity we may feel about our lives.

Successful life planning involves visualizing aspects of the life you want in the future. Once you have a clearer picture of your future (lifestyle, working conditions, friends), you can then see what steps you must take to get where you want to be. But you have to imagine positively and create the life you want. To facilitate your act of self-creation, examine the life you've had as a foundation for your new life. Another useful metaphor to apply to this life reviewing is "writing the book of one's life." It takes years of living to appreciate the richness and variety of our lives and to make the book concept applicable.

Consider your life as a book with yourself as the author and the main character. Each period of your life (like childhood or adolescence, as well as significant shifts like new jobs, relationships, moves, and so on) represents a chapter in that book, and each chapter contains its own set of characters. Like your life, your book has drama, structure, and themes. Using the metaphor of a book, you can begin to see the distinct periods of your life as parts of a greater whole, even if they have seemed unrelated in the past. The central challenge of this metaphor is keeping yourself the main character and not allowing other characters to take the lead of your story.

16. **Look back over your life and see it in terms of distinct chapters, each with a beginning, a middle, and an end.**

If done properly, this exercise can be a lot of fun and have a sense of adventure to it. Who will you, the author, cast as the Villain? The Love Interest? (Perhaps each chapter has a different Mr. Right.)

By using your imagination as well as your honesty, you can finally tell the story you've been living. This exercise can be a dramatic and effective way to embrace responsibility for your past, and after many reviews of your history, this metaphor will give you a more dynamic and committed feeling about your life. The book metaphor offers a way for you to put your past, present, and future into a positive context in which you are the central, active character—and only you know what the main character will do next.

Once a gay man grasps this concept, a new vocabulary emerges between us. During therapy, we can start talking about his life in terms of chapters. He is able to understand that what he thought were different chapters were actually the same chapter but with a different set of characters. Such insights will reveal the patterns of his past decision making, if the tapestry metaphor has not already done so. For example, in the context of relationships, it's difficult to begin a fresh one if there's lingering anger or resentment from the previous relationship. If you want to give your next relationship the best possible foundation, take the time and energy to examine how you ended the last one and look for ways to keep respect for yourself and your partner, even if the relationship has been stormy. *If you want your life to have a new chapter, you must end the old chapter in a new way so that there can be a fresh beginning of a new chapter.*

During my early life, I always assumed I needed to make a significant move for a new beginning. At seventeen, I decided to leave California and move to Chicago; at twenty-one, I left my first lover Joe to go to the University of Chicago. After my graduate work, I purposefully chose an internship in New York. Once in New York, I started to see my life as an expression of whom I was choosing to become. I began to recognize the conscious control I had exerted to create my life. I also matured enough to realize I no longer had to leave a city or a relationship to make a fresh start. My life has continued to expand past midlife as well. In my current relationship with Friedrich, I travel to Germany several times a year. My experiences abroad continue to expand my worldview, and I bring that knowledge home. In effect, I can go beyond my life in New York and no longer have to leave it.

The beauty of this book metaphor is that we know the plots are fluid and capable of changing direction on any page. Also, the story builds on each chapter that has gone before, so there's a sense that a different book would emerge with a different reordering or restructuring of the chapters. My lover Friedrich and I met on the street; what if I had walked down that street five minutes later?

Everybody has a story, and in telling our story, we record our journey through life. Using the book metaphor enables you to overlay a structure to your life, so you can begin to see cause and effect (like the interaction of characters, the role of outside forces) in your life. Building our narrative is itself an act of control.

Once a gay man becomes secure in seeing what he has been respon-

sible for in his life, and how his actions have effected goals and outcomes, he can now imagine changes—the twists and turns of the plot.
Perhaps you are at the place where you can be glad that it all happened
as it did because you like who you have become. Or perhaps you are
at the place where you realize there are new decisions to be made:
Stop pleasing other people? Change jobs? Create more leisure time?
Get a boyfriend? Nurture your relationship with your lover? Repair
your relationship to your blood family? Stop postponing your dreams
until retirement? At this point in your awareness, you are probably
conscious of steps you can take to make this vision a reality.

17. **Visualize the life you want in the future. What steps do you
    have to take to have this life?**

Visualization is a rehearsal or practice for what you will be doing.
Creating a vision of your future sets into motion a series of events
that will validate your sense of control over your life and future. You
may not actually take these exact steps, but your vision will lead you
to action of some kind. The act of planning and visualizing is yet
another step in your moving forward with your life in a positive way.
By recognizing the positive and negative chapters of your life, you
can move toward a goal that you have chosen based on a new
understanding of your history—a positive and directed preparation
for the future.

Another beauty of the book metaphor is that you can write
yourself a happy ending. You don't stop writing at midlife; the plot
just thickens, as they say (just like our waistlines). Most likely, you
stopped the "book" in the present. But taking charge of your life is
about moving into the future with the same energy and courage that
you have in the past. Maybe you're satisfied and want more of the
same. Maybe you have identified areas of change while working
through some of these exercises. Whatever your heart and mind and
body desire can be yours: Visualize it, then pursue it.

Walter's Story

Walter is a client that I had never thought I would consider as a
positive example for a book. He made such slow progress over the

few times I had seen him, which was usually when he was referred by his lover. But what I mistook for slowness were really small steps that led to major changes in his life.

When I met Walter, he had been with his lover for almost twenty years, and he was holding down a low-level job of running a mailroom at the company in which his lover had a high-level, executive position. Walter had been interested in being a featured singer/dancer all his life. He had had many volunteer roles at local theater companies, but they were usually at nonprofit companies where he did not earn money. I helped him to get his goals in order about taking music lessons and continuing with his tap lessons. He was most happy with being onstage and ultimately wanted to be a singer where he had had some success in the past. He terminated the therapy, however, when he decided to devote himself full time to getting a business off the ground with his lover.

Our therapy was unusual in that I found it very difficult to work with him since I became very bored, no matter what the topic. What he was saying wasn't boring but he had a way of being so disconnected to what he was saying that it was hard to feel emotionally connected to his reflections. I began to talk with him about this process, but it was at this time that he quit therapy.

When he resumed therapy sometime later, Walter wanted help in learning better how to adjust in his new career as a realtor. He had failed with the design business that he and his lover had tried to set up. As his lover had a full-time, very responsible job, it was difficult for him to be of much help, and Walter was too "helpless" to make decisions all on his own even though he had good taste. He was now trying to be a real estate broker, but was not making any money in it. He made lists upon lists, but never got things done—though he was busy all the time.

First, I brought up again the difficulty I had in staying connected to what he was saying. He was now ready to hear this. He remembered his home life, in which his lawyer father just lectured everyone, knew more than anyone else, and could not be proven wrong, no matter how much evidence supported the other side. As a result of his father's behavior, Walter learned very early to withdraw—one of his most memorable and miserable memories was of his father's anger and fury when his father was helping Walter with his math homework and he was not learning fast enough. He was able to relate this behavior he had learned at home to what was going on in therapy. To protect himself, he never got close to what he was saying so that he could "leave it at a moment's notice" in case he was challenged or put on the spot.

At this time in therapy, Walter wanted help in learning better how to adjust to his new career. Always keeping in mind his tendency to distance himself from what he was saying, we focused on two specific tasks: time management and his learning to be more direct with his clients. Our work was a step-by-step process of teaching him how to make manageable lists, how to prioritize his time, and how to make decisions. He focused on figuring out what could and could not be done realistically in the allotted time. The process also had a lot to do with his learning how to understand and speak to his clients. When communicating with his clients, he hadn't realized that he needed to pay special attention to the individuality and specific requests of each client.

Walter made progress with his clients after we used a very significant therapeutic technique called *a transfer of training*. This involves taking an expertise or situation where there has been a positive experience or success and transferring what he has learned from that into a new situation by recognizing any similarities between them. This meant getting Walter to see and appreciate what he could do on the stage—entertain, "work a room" with confidence, create happiness for him and his audience—and getting him to see working with a real estate client as the same thing. In short, I used his success in theater and with audiences to show him that he had been successful in another area and he could transfer that success from one field to another.

The transfer of his stage training was complete when he made the connection between the way he planned for the stage and the way he put over his performances to the way he approached his real estate work. In his singing career, he didn't simply get up onstage and sing, but he worked long hours in rehearsal on his presentation, material, delivery, patter, and so on. Similarly, he began to realize he needed to rehearse his skills as a real estate agent: finding out what the clients really wanted and helping them to see that, showing apartments effectively, seeing if it was a good match between client and apartment, being clear if the client was serious about buying or selling, and so forth.

In addition, he began to understand how lists could help him and not overwhelm him. In getting ready for a performance, he would make unconscious lists of what he had to do, and unlike the lists for work, he was usually successful in "completing" these lists. We worked on his making realistic lists of what he needed to do in his daily routine and how to prioritize what had to be done first and what could be put on the next day's list. There were daily and weekly lists. The important thing to remember was that the number of items on the list were not a substitute for actions taken—basically, the length of the list was not a positive thing in and of itself. Wanting to do many things was not the same thing as actually accomplishing a few items. It was much easier for him once he understood that lists are sometimes substitutes for taking action.

To get him to strengthen the connection between what he did onstage and what he did in selling an apartment, I used the "anchoring" technique I introduced in chapter 6. This is a kind of reconditioning that involves anchoring an experience in a moment of positive feeling with a particular physical motion, then recalling that same motion in a moment of anxiety. Because the body remembers, the anchor brings in that positive experience to balance whatever negative feelings the person is having. For Walter, he felt nervous and agitated when first meeting a client, so their communication was never very effective. I helped him to remember how he felt onstage, when he first approached the microphone, and to transfer those feelings of confidence in his talent and warmth for the audience into his first meeting with a client.

In time, he began to improve his work habits and actually take charge of what he was doing. He started selling small apartments and having better relationships with his clients. This eventually gave him the courage to take on more pricey apartments and more difficult clients. Eventually, he became quite successful and was able to bring in enough money so that he and his lover could buy the apartment next door and expand their small, present one.

Further, he has also now transferred his abilities on the job to taking care of things at home. He is making most of the decisions at home, to the relief of his lover, who is now managing two companies and does not have any time or energy left over to deal with home decisions. When they combined their apartment with the one next door, Walter handled all the details of refinancing, buying, and closing the deal, as well as the entire renovation. For the first time in their relationship, Walter is taking care of his lover and upholding his responsibilities. Their relationship, in which there had always been much love and passion, has also incorporated new aspects of sex that Walter had wanted but was hesitant to request.

Having felt secure in his relationship for many years, Walter never had an issue about aging in terms of looks or sexuality or loving—his fears around aging were more about not feeling in control of his life and taking charge. He is a good example of what can happen to a middle-aged gay man when he begins to be active in planning his life and makes concrete plans about setting priorities and following through on his decisions. The change is clearly not just his newfound material success but how he is feeling about himself as a competent man—both in his career and in his relationship, in which he is now the most loving and giving he has ever been.

NINE

Mortality and Spirituality

I was traveling out of the country when Matthew Shepard was murdered in September 1998. When I arrived home, I heard about it from my co-author, caught up on the story with newspapers and magazines, and as I learned more, I felt that the details of his death explained why his particular death had received so much attention. Anti-gay violence isn't new, and we often hear horrible stories of abuse, gay bashings, and death resulting from homophobic strangers. But Shepard's death struck a chord in many people, I think, precisely because it was so symbolic of Christianity. A figure crucified on a fence and left to die in a field recalls the image of Jesus for many. (Initially, the woman who found him thought his body was a scarecrow until she got closer.) Even his name has Biblical resonance (Matthew was one of the twelve disciples, many of whom were shepherds, and the Bible describes Jesus as a shepherd of men).

The depth of anger and sorrow within the gay community suggests, at least to me, that Shepard's death combined two emotional subjects for many gay men: mortality and spirituality. His actual murder reminded all of us of our vulnerability to anti-gay violence, and his symbolic death reminded many of us of our relationship to religion. (Even if we're not Christian, we are exposed to Christianity through the history of our country and the power of our religious media.)

For gay men at midlife, mortality and spirituality remain perhaps the most difficult concepts to face. Witnessing our own aging or the aging of those around us heightens our sense of mortality and motivates us to reexamine our own priorities, to take a hard look at what we want out of this life. Having survived an epidemic for nearly two decades, gay men are surrounded by illness and death, so we are already somewhat prepared to contemplate the larger issues of life and death. But when our bodies start to change at midlife, we can often shut down and begin to feel as if our lives are over.

Spirituality becomes a definite concern at midlife because, faced with our own sense of mortality, we begin to question what happens to us after death. What remains of us, our spirit, these created selves we have struggled so diligently to produce? As many of us at midlife review the principles by which we have lived and survived, we start asking profound questions about our existence and what tenets we want to live by for the rest of our lives. This reordering of priorities may spring from the spiritual foundation of the religion in which we were raised or a return to the religious culture in which we lived or from a serious questioning in what we have faith. What these different avenues represent is a search for meaning to our lives—why are we here? What are we supposed to be doing? These questions seriously emerge only when we begin to realize that we won't be here forever. In other words, when our mortality becomes our reality.

In many ways, the need to understand our purpose in life is always within us. But the physical changes and emotions that characterize midlife bring that need to the surface of our consciousness. We begin to step back from the day-to-day drama of our lives and question whether it's been worth it, and where are we going from here? Spirituality becomes important when we realize we won't have a body forever, and we begin to wonder if we have a soul and what will happen to it. What's next? Most of the time, I believe each soul is an essence of what has existed before, during, and after our life, and for me, spirituality is a way of honoring that soul by celebrating the life I have created. For other people, the soul can mean our human essence only, with the possibility of nothing after death. It's a matter of each individual's faith.

But when many gay men hear the word *spirituality* or *soul*, their protective mechanism kicks in and they become uncomfortable talking about anything that reeks of spirituality, religion, religiosity, dogma, and so on. This reaction is similar to what we feel during any discussion of "values," since many of us equate these concepts and have had negative experiences with some of them. Most of these words, like *church* or *dogma*, are like tripwires, immediately shutting down the conversation. But I think these words describe very different phenomena, and this confusion of terminology prevents many gay men from exploring and understanding their spirituality.

Given the sensitivity many gay men feel whenever the subject of spirituality arises, I want to clear the air a bit with some definitions. *Dogma* is the strict letter of religious law, no questions, no doubts, no flexibility, often just a rigidly literal interpretation of a religion. I use *religion* to describe any organized following of believers in a particular system of belief. Religions usually involve some form of hierarchy, with levels of authority and power among the believers. *Religiosity* is best defined as a holier-than-thou attitude. Individuals suffering from religiosity tend to be judgmental and rigid in their beliefs and very committed to determining who is and who is not following their dogma.

Finally, I define a person's *spirituality* as the principles by which he lives, independent of a specific religion. I hope the discussion of the personal value system in chapter 7 has set up a framework in which you can consider such principles, and clearly, a person's values will inform his spirituality. The difference between a value system and spirituality has more to do with a person's perspective than actual differences. Many people view spirituality as a once-a-week, special, "Sunday" behavior, whereas values are to be used every day. But that perspective links spirituality closely to religion, with its observance of rituals, practices, and ceremonies. I believe a gay man's spirituality is the expression of his values. As you'll see in what follows, spirituality can be just as manifest in a gay man's daily life as his lived values.

Gay men are not the only ones to equate religion with spirituality. The power of organized religion in this country further complicates, if not prevents, attempts by many gay men to tap into their spirituality. Since homosexuality is often at conflict with the teachings of most Western religions, many gay men do not feel comfortable in their church or synagogue or mosque, so they decide that they are not spiritual if they don't have a religion. Many gay men reject religion out of hand, but no gay man escapes the influence of religion, either in the family in which he was raised or in the community in which he lives.

Before a gay man can even approach, much less understand, his spirituality, he must tune out all the static and rhetoric and dogma of organized religion. But silencing those voices of judgment requires examining his relationship to religion, especially the religion of his childhood.

1. **What was the religion in which you were raised and how important was it in your growing up?**

Did your parents make you go to church, temple, mosque, or prayer meetings when you were little? Did they go? Did you pray before meals or at bedtime? Did you have a confirmation or a bar mitzvah? Were religious holidays observed and celebrated, not just Christmas or Passover, but other holy days like Lent or Easter? Or was religion a divisive issue in your family? Perhaps a relative's marriage "outside the faith" spawned huge discussions and bickering among the rest of the family.

As children, we do what we are told and follow our parents' instructions and don't think much about it. Before we realize our parents can be wrong, we absorb everything they say without questioning, and in those early years, we are virtual blank slates for whatever our parents pass on: religious dogma, gossip, superstition, political beliefs, classism, ageism, racism, sexism, and so on. As we grow older, these early influences can seem to disappear until one day we find ourselves repeating what our parents used to say, or the minister or elder or imam or priest or the rabbi, and we're shocked we still carry those beliefs around. In our previous work on value systems, we began to acknowledge that the values we learned from our childhoods can still influence us, and religion is a major source of those childhood influences.

Tom was born in Alabama and raised as a Southern Baptist. He always went to Sunday school and sang in the choir during his adolescence, but when he went to college and began his coming-out process, he stopped going to church and for a time, stopped believing in God. "I thought He didn't want me, so I didn't want Him," Tom remembers. He spent the next fifteen years coming out, meeting men, having relationships, establishing a career as a manager of a local video store chain, and not really thinking about God. It wasn't until he met a friend who attended Metropolitan Community Church

(MCC) that he even considered his relationship to religion. When he visited MCC, he felt like he was coming home. He remembered the words to hymns, loved the ritual of communion, and felt as if he belonged among the people he found there.

Whatever religious beliefs we absorbed as a child have probably affected our coming-out process, perhaps delaying our decision to come out, frightening us about the world we were about to enter, and so on. If our upbringing was particularly religious, many of us may feel that to come out is to reject our religion, our God, and our family, all at the same time.

But given the behavior of religious fundamentalists and the anti-gay scriptures of many religions, why would any gay man want to be involved in religion? Every major Western religion rejects homo-sexuality as a moral equivalent to heterosexuality, and to overcome this religious indoctrination is a formidable task. Indeed, how we resolve the conflict between our homosexuality and our religion is a major step in our development as adult gay men. Do we internalize the teachings of hate or do we find a different community of faith in which to express our spirituality? Or do we not bother at all? Do we ignore organized religion altogether and try to shut out those voices when they attack us? Or do we remain committed to showing our religion how it is wrong by working for reform from within the system?

Every gay man has some relation to his past religion, even if it's a total rejection and movement in the opposite direction. Religion has had some influence upon us, either negative or positive, con-sciously or unconsciously. We can feel that influence directly if we participate in a religion or indirectly by our exposure to the religious media (radio, televangelists, billboards, newspaper ads).

2. **In what ways is this religion and/or any other important in your present life?**

What about today? What have you experienced to arrive at your present level of religious belief? Do you believe in God or some Supreme Being? Do you have an idea of Heaven? Or of Hell? Do you go to any kind of services or read any sort of religious literature?

You may not be active in any religion in your present life and that's okay. You may have been strongly religious as a child, but when you came out, you shut the door to that part of your life and never looked back. That's okay, too. You might go to church or services on the major holidays in your religion, but you don't really feel connected to any community of believers or feel as if you have faith in much of anything.

But that's not to say you don't have a spirituality that your every-day life makes manifest. It's extremely difficult for many gay men to see their daily lives in spiritual terms. The confusing vocabulary, the conflict between religion and homosexuality, the treatment of gay people at the hands of the church, and the rigidity of most religions, especially fundamentalist ones, can prevent gay men from feeling like spiritual beings.

To understand his spirituality, a gay man must separate whatever spiritual teachings he has received from the religions to which he has been exposed. I am about to make some generalizations about the world's religions, but I do so in order to break through whatever resistance you may be feeling about separating your spirituality from religion, be it the religion of your birth or whatever religion you may lay claim to in your present life.

THE NATURE OF RELIGIONS

One of the philosophical purposes of every religion is to understand one's relationship in and to the present world. Some religions (Judaism, Christianity) emphasize the relationship to a Supreme Being and who communicates with that Being, while others (Buddhism, Zen, Tao) are more concerned with ethical systems: how to live in the world, how to behave, how to treat others. Religions grow and main-tain themselves through the communication and observance of certain principles and laws that usually fall into one of two categories: social laws and spiritual laws.

The *social laws* of a religion tend to reflect the needs of a certain society in a particular time, and these laws tend to differ from religion to religion, as well as region to region for the same religion (Irish Catholic versus Mexican Catholic).

In addition, there are the basic *spiritual laws* of each religion that are usually consistent with one another, across many religions. Examples of spiritual laws would include the Golden Rule, the Ten Commandments, the Four Noble Truths of Buddhism, the Four Books of Confucius. These are laws primarily concerning love, forgiveness, and human interaction, and each religion promotes these laws as "eternal truths" about how to live in this world.

The equation of spirituality with religion has its roots in the triumph of these social laws over the spiritual laws as the defining feature of each religion. The social laws were concerned with how to conduct one's daily life and historically have had to do with organizing that part of the world where they appeared. Often these rules have offered a way of unifying a geographic group of peoples— the Zoroastrians, Buddhists, Jews, Christians, Muslims, Bahai's. Most of these social laws were relevant for the time in which they were created, but unfortunately for many, these social laws have become the most important legacy of their religions.

For many people, these commandments on living *became* the religion, while the essence of the spiritual laws was forgotten or minimized. What became primary was how one conducted the rituals (food, clothing, place of prayer, number of observances per day, donations to the church), rather than the more important spiritual laws, which were about how one related to others, how one dealt with one's spiritual life, and one's relationship with forces beyond the self (Nirvana, Allah, God). Or at least, such spiritual principles were not paid as much attention to as the laws that determined, dictated, and controlled the behavior of the followers.

In addition, most major religions gained their strength by being the intermediary between a person and God. As churches grew more powerful as institutions of social unity (and governments used religion to maintain power), the leaders (priests, rabbis, and so on) convinced the followers that they were the middle person or communicant with God, Allah, or the Creator. One obvious example of this power play was the early split between the original Christians, the Gnostics, who believed (as did Jesus) in direct communication with God, without a go-between or a hierarchy among followers. Unfortunately, the Gnostics were outnumbered by the later believers who followed the Holy Roman Empire, which needed a priesthood to maintain its power. The Gnostics were largely considered the heretics, whereas they could be called the original believers. (Another interesting discovery has been their tenets on the equality of women and men and that women could be spiritual leaders. But the misogyny of early church leaders silenced such teachings and eventually, with the rise in influence of the Inquisition, witchcraft burning and the eradication of women's power in healing and medicine ensued.)

This history may seem too distant to our lives today, but a more contemporary example of a religion's spiritual laws losing out to its social laws is the Catholic church's stance on condoms in the age of AIDS. Whether it's free condoms in the public schools, or condom distribution in the prisons, the Catholic church is opposed to it on the grounds of birth control. But the issue isn't birth control, but the prevention of STDs and HIV infection. Apparently, death and disease are preferable to challenging church law (as well as more unwanted children since the Church also forbids abortion).

The conflict between homosexuality and religion springs in part from these different sets of laws. The social laws usually include restrictions against homosexuality, while the spiritual laws emphasize the importance of loving one another with kindness and respect. But since so many Western religions have elevated adherence to social laws above following the spiritual laws, the restrictions have won out over the commandments to love and honor one another. As a result, many gay men choose between two paths: joining gay versions of Judeo-Christian religions like Dignity (gay Catholics), Integrity (gay Episcopalians), Unity and Metropolitan Community Church (nondenominational Christian), or turning to Eastern religions to connect with their spirituality, rather than face more rejection and judgment from Western religions.

In many Eastern religions, there is no concept of sin, no afterlife, no final judgment, and no litmus tests of scripture or ideology: if you're this, you can't belong. As a result, Eastern religions are more about creation, rather than salvation. They are concerned with being better human beings, focusing on our way of being in the world and recognizing our connections to all others. The only "sin" in many Eastern religions is seeing yourself as unconnected to the circle of life around you. I think many gay men began to discover Eastern religions of Hinduism and Buddhism in the early years of AIDS. When there were few treatments available, many men sought alternative medicine: acupuncture, herbal remedies, yoga, macrobiotic diet, meditation, visualization. Often, there is a spiritual basis to these health practices. A gay man may have begun any of these practices to improve his overall health, yet he may have benefited spiritually as well.

Because so many gay men have left their organized religion, they feel they have left their spirituality as well. For those gay men who have maintained or reclaimed their spirituality, these exercises should reaffirm their convictions. For those men who feel they are not spiritual, these exercises will work to uncover their spirituality, which has probably become internalized without any external validation by most religious teaching.

Another assumption behind the conflict between homosexuality and religion is that you can't be both sexual and spiritual. In most Western religions, the sexual union between a man and a woman has been celebrated only on the condition of procreation. Sex that does not produce children is not allowed or must be "controlled." Otherwise, we will be dominated and consumed by sex. Religious prophets are often portrayed as asexual or celibate. The Catholic church requires a vow of celibacy from its priests, the most holy of its flock, while other Western religions like Judaism allow its rabbis some form of sexual expression. But again, sex is relegated to marriage and children.

So where does that leave gay men, whose sex is rarely, if ever, procreative? By coming out, we have chosen to express our sexuality, but many gay men, I suspect, feel that to be sexual violates the heart of spirituality. But spirituality is not a rejection of passion and sexuality—spirituality is about wholeness and passion, and how can a person be whole if he denies his sexuality?

Just as when we were coming out and gave ourselves permission to be sexual beings, we have to give ourselves permission to be spiritual beings. I heard one man describe this as instead of thinking of ourselves as human beings trying to be spiritual, we should consider ourselves to be spiritual beings trying to be human.

3. **In what ways do you consider yourself a spiritual person? How does spirituality manifest itself in your present life?**

My friend Martin was raised as an Orthodox Jew, but as an adult, he's vehemently anti-Jewish. Every Yom Kippur, he eats a big meal of spareribs, as a way of offending the religion of his birth, as well as his family. If asked, he definitely wouldn't consider himself spiritual. But his daily life as a college professor suggests to me that he does honor spiritual laws. He teaches at two colleges, and throughout his career, he has encouraged the largely minority population of students to excel. When he sees the spark in a kid, he fans the spark to catch fire by pushing her/him to go beyond the expectations of a racist world. Many of his students have gone on to become teachers, physicians, and other professionals, and they credit him with their career. For many of his students, Martin was their mentor first, then later, a loyal friend.

Clearly, certain principles of justice and equality push Martin to push his students, and despite being voted "Best Teacher of the Year" consistently, he doesn't see his work as anything out of the ordinary. It's what he must do; it's clear to him that this is the right thing to do. And that says more about his spirituality than whether or not he keeps kosher. In addition, the way he maintains his friendships, not just his teaching and mentoring, reveals him to be a loving, caring, loyal person. Martin is like many people who have been conditioned to think of themselves as not being spiritual if they do not attend church or have a regular membership at a local synagogue.

When asked if you're a spiritual person, your answer may be a gut response based on the external standards of organized religion (adherence to dogma, church attendance, prayers, tithing). That's what most of us have to go on. Surrounded at an early age by religious symbolism, ritual, and liturgy, we fall back on those same words and familiar images when we're asked about spiritual matters. But to uncover our spirituality, we may need to get away from memorizing certain kinds of prayers, or the numbers of times we pray, or the particular services and rituals, or any single demarcation that says we're "spiritual." These are the trappings of religion, not the source of spirituality.

Another reason this question of spirituality is so hard to answer is because it requires a vocabulary that is lacking in our culture and in most persons. It also taps an area of existence for which there are minimal words. Few people can agree on what a soul is, and to describe what we experience as spirituality requires imagination and metaphors. Our experience of spirituality is always removed from the language used to describe it. We talk about feelings, thoughts, images, behaviors, sexuality, and sensations, and together, they add up to what we call our spirituality. For some, spirituality is a mental and emotional state of being, meditative, quiet, reflective. For others, spirituality can be expressed only in behavioral terms, with the experience best felt during a church service or doing "good deeds" or communicating with another person or during sex or during a solitary walk in the woods or amidst a crowd on a disco floor.

If you find yourself doubting you have a spiritual side, look at the way you conduct your life. What is the relationship between how you live your daily life and the kinds of behaviors that have to do with service, appreciation, and being grateful? Be as specific as possible. You might start to list the number of times you pray or meditate each week, or you might try to remember the last time you went to church. But think about other things that you do that might reveal your life from a spiritual perspective. What about singing in a gospel choir? Or the once a week you help deliver meals to seniors or people with AIDS? Or the three-hour shift at the Gay and Lesbian Hotline you put in once a month? Or the Pride float that you helped build last June? Or the phone conversations with friends in trouble, helping them to work through emotional issues? Have you helped organize a union action or a tenant's rent strike? Are you a big brother in the community? Do you recycle or help clean up a local park twice a year?

For many of us, what we do during our daily lives could be interpreted as spiritual practices. Much of what we do as gay men reflects spiritual principles of nurturing, honesty, living each day to the fullest. We express our spirituality in our caring for loved ones, for our dying friends, and for our commitment to the community. If you want to develop your spiritual side, you don't have to go back to church, and in a very real sense, *our community has become our church— our new religion*, as it were.

THE SPIRITUALITY OF THE GAY LIFESTYLE

When we hear the words *gay lifestyle*, many images spring to mind, but "spiritual" probably isn't one of them. But the gay community has many similarities with religion, and our membership in that community, i.e., our coming out, is very much a spiritual act.

Like any religion, our community has social laws and spiritual laws (even if we don't consciously recognize them as such) that fulfill a human need for rituals. Our contributions to gay organizations (tithes), our coming-out stories (liturgy), the way we relate to one another (the commandments), could all be interpreted as facets of an organized religion (though sometimes, we're not so organized!). Even the circuit parties and discos have their place in this "church" as part of our tribal rituals. Taking care of a person with AIDS until death has become one of our rituals now, as well as the memorial service. Perhaps our biggest ceremony of communion is the Gay Pride March, which has become like our annual religious observance—a day when we all come together—Christmas, Halloween, and Thanksgiving all rolled into one. One of New York's most famous discos wasn't called The Saint for nothing!

Both Gandhi and Thomas Jefferson talked about the sacredness of public life, though they used different terms. In essence, this use of the sacred reveals the importance of community involvement and mental health. I believe our need for connectedness is actually part of our genetic makeup. We feel better when we feel connected to one another and when we are a part of the whole process of life. While some may consider altruism as a form of selfishness, I and others believe doing things for others is part of what makes us human. We volunteer and feel good about it because it is part of what sustains us—like taking a deep breath.

The gay community is not alone as it wrestles with matters of faith and spirit. This country is experiencing a growing need for spirituality on a large scale. In the nineties, the soul became a hot commodity. Books ranging from the philosophical (*Care of the Soul*) to the inspirational (*Chicken Soup for the Soul*) hit the best-seller lists, while a television show called *Touched by an Angel* was an instant hit.

Perhaps this soul searching is a reaction against the materialism of the eighties; perhaps, too, it is millennium fever, as the year 2000 approaches; perhaps, finally, it is that the baby boomers are beginning to hit fifty. Generally, this interest in the spiritual involves the conflict between the Enlightenment (science, objectivity, man over nature, alienation, life has no meaning beyond what we put to it) and Romanticism (connectedness, oneness with life, embeddedness in nature, subjectivity and inner life, there is meaning to life). What we call primitives or the primal worldview saw a participatory relationship between humans and nature and both were immanently divine.

As a society, we are now dealing with the isolating effects of technology, which is why community involvement is related to spirituality. By getting involved in our community, we repair our separateness from others and the world. But to join our community, we have to come out, perhaps the most spiritual decision a gay man will ever make.

As I've discussed, most gay men do not appreciate the total significance of their coming out. They do not recognize the courage it took and what message it communicated to the world about being true to one's essence. Coming out is a spiritual action within the context of ritual. Primitive cultures have death/rebirth rituals that prepare a person to instruct those who follow; an individual joins a culture when he or she survives the initiation rite, which acts out death and rebirth in physical and psychic terms.

For many gay men, coming out represents a significant ritual in which we prepare to leave behind all that we know and received support from. Just as the primitive shamans face death and are reborn so they can impart wisdom, so too can the gay man who has let go of what he had and moved to new position in his life. He is no longer the same person and has a vision about a new reality (camp and irony are only two manifestations of this different perspective). The positive feelings of integrity and honesty that result from coming out give us a chance to reconnect with humanity as a whole person, not a hologram and not a sexless being.

Coming out enables us to join a community of faith—faith in the goodness of ourselves and in our uniqueness as gay people. Just like any religion, you don't necessarily have to participate in every ritual in order to be a member. There are many ways for us, as gay people, to express our spirituality, and in the absence of socially sanctioned rituals (and in some cases, outright exclusion from such rituals), we are left to define and redefine spirituality for ourselves, just as other communities define their own ceremonies of meaning.

For example, during slavery, most slaves were not allowed to wed and create families, so they created a ceremony—jumping over the broom—in which a couple would literally jump over a broom placed on the floor by gathered loved ones. With that act, they were married, in the eyes of their God(s) and of their community. What the white slaveowner did or did not allow had no effect on the meaning of this ceremony to the people involved. Even after they were allowed to marry, many African-Americans continued this ritual as a way of honoring tradition. (Ron, from chapter 6, who is white, and Albert, his lover, who is African-American, included this ritual in their commitment ceremony.)

Similarly, for gay people, a mortgage might be the next best thing to a marriage license, especially in areas where "domestic partnership" remains a theory, not a reality. Much of the recent debate about marriage hasn't really touched upon the spiritual aspect of the union. It's been about civil rights, equal access under the law, and so forth. But part of the wonder of marriage is the sense of betrothal between the parties. Though rarely seen as such, marriage is a spiritual act in which two people give themselves to each other. Afterward, they *belong* to each other, not in the possessive sense of "I own you" but in the loving sense of "I have chosen you above all others to give myself to."

Since gay relationships are seen by many (both gay and nongay) as "just sex," there's little support for our relationships, no framework of commitment, and no sense of betrothal. I am sadly reminded of a story about a man who spent months nursing his lover who had AIDS. When his lover died, he wasn't allowed bereavement time since he hadn't told anyone at work about his relationship. So he went back to work the day after burying his lover.

How you think about and maintain a relationship can also be spiritual, and just because it's not acknowledged very much doesn't deny the spiritual dimension of our relationships. Again, many people, not just gay men, have a problem reconciling feelings of spirituality and sexuality, so it takes time to recognize how you can be both a sexual and a spiritual being (and some gay men even recognize sex as a spiritual act).

Just as coming out allows us to integrate our sexuality with the rest of our lives, so too does reconciling our spirituality with our daily lives (including our sexuality) allow us to become whole people. The more your life feels integrated, that is, the more consistent a person you are in all places (home, work, church, family, disco), the more fulfilled your life will become.

Whenever we deny any part of ourselves, especially our sexuality or spirituality, we sacrifice our ideals and compromise our values. It's like going back into the closet when a gay man returns home to his family or when he goes to work or when he enters the church doors.

If they don't know he's gay, he's silencing that part of himself, and psychologically, that experience represents a mini-suicide. A clear act of self-destruction. Even if he's out to them on a basic level, but they don't want to know all the details, he's still damaging his sense of self by censoring his life, compartmentalizing his emotions, and neglecting his integrity.

Given the conflict between religion and sexuality (not just homosexuality), these contradictory feelings ("I'm gay, so I can't be spiritual" or "I believe in God, but does He believe in me?") are familiar and understandable. Indeed, contradictions appear throughout our experience with religion, from the hypocrisy of televangelists and religious fundamentalists, to the mixed messages your family may have sent you. As a child, you may have witnessed differences between what your parents told you was "right" and how they lived their actual lives. Your father may have professed his love for your mother openly and often, yet it comes out later that he had cheated on her for years with a neighbor's wife. Or you were told that family is the most important instrument of God, yet your parents fought all the time and punished the children by making them go to church.

Children aren't stupid; they pick up on these contradictions. Some children rebel by totally rejecting the religion they were handed, while others struggle to reconcile the contradictions that they inherited. Gay children know these contradictions firsthand: I am a good boy but I'm also sick because of my secret. These contradictions are what makes the hologram so powerful. Like religion, the hologram is hard to reject because it reconciles (usually by denying they exist) so many conflicts: between the real and ideal self, between the lived and ideal values, between sexuality and spirituality.

The fewer contradictions a gay man experiences between his daily life and his spirituality, the more integrated and fulfilled he becomes; those feelings of strength and wholeness affirm that his life is "good." The more he feels his life is good, the less preoccupied he is with the passage of time, and the more he will accept his mortality and aging.

THE FINAL FEAR: OUR OWN MORTALITY

The majority of gay male anxiety about aging finds its source in our fear of being unattractive and in our fear of mortality. Both fears are focused on not being "enough": not having accomplished enough, not having lived enough, not being attractive enough, not having enjoyed life as much as we could have. The key to feeling "enough" is affirmation, and spirituality is a way to transcend these fears by affirming the life you have. The more your life is affirmed, the more you have a sense of being enough, and accomplishing, living, and enjoying life enough. When mortality becomes reality, spirituality becomes a daily expression of our desire to live.

One aspect of the people who age successfully is that they have faced and accepted their mortality as part of living. Not that they want to die, but they're not feeling deprived, doomed, defeated, faded, and fading, nor are they frustrated by getting older. When you approach aging from a feeling of acceptance (not being deprived, feeling good about your life, integrated), aging well becomes a matter of anticipation, of expecting the good things to come, with life getting better (not worse). The more you can see life becoming better as you age, the more you can anticipate (and bring about) the good things. When you can see that your life is better than before, it makes you less fearful of what's to come. When you approach aging from a position of fear (not being enough, being lonely, being sick), aging well means only being less afraid.

To make this shift from a perspective of fear to a heightened awareness of the good that aging can bring, a gay man has to be honest about his ideas concerning death and mortality. Exploring the fears and the fantasies, the intellectual defenses and the gut reactions, brings about an awareness that leads to an acceptance of mortality as part of life.

4.   What are your thoughts and feelings about mortality?

A subject as serious as death lends itself to intellectualizing: the distance gives us an emotional safety net. You might think, *I'm fine*. But on the inside, in your gut, you're feeling, *I'm terrified*. To sort out your thoughts and feelings about mortality will probably produce anxiety, fear, and much soul searching. The emphasis of the exercise is your *attitude* about mortality. Do you intellectualize the whole thing? Or do you feel full of mixed emotions? Explore all of your feelings of your eventual death. Sadness, anger, anticipation, relief?

You may have dealt with deaths in your chosen family or in

your blood family. Perhaps your own health status has forced you to consider your own mortality. How often do you think about death and dying? Do you block such thoughts from your consciousness only to have them resurface unexpectedly, with a memory of a dead friend or a pain in your own back? Again, our changing body at midlife gives us practically daily reminders that we are a dynamic entity, that change is the only constant, and that time is passing.

Consider the way we process the news of someone's death. When you hear of a person dying at twenty versus dying at eighty, their death feels tragic, but with the older person, you can be comforted by the thought that they had "a full life, a good life." But our reaction assumes that longevity equals fulfillment (the same way we sometimes assume that a long-term relationship must be satisfying; why else would people stay in it?). Older does not necessarily mean a full life. A young person who dies at twenty may have lived his life much more fully than someone who gave up trying to have a good life when he retired at fifty-five. Time alone does not make a life any more valuable or fulfilled. It's how that time is spent that makes a difference.

From AIDS, gay men have learned over and over again that it's the quality of life that matters most. But despite the appreciation of the day-to-day that AIDS has brought about, it's hard to let go of the idea that more is better (more time, more money, more years). When we are faced with the mortality of our community, it's understandable that we want to hang on to our peers, our loved ones, our mentors. Spirituality offers a solace because it recognizes the theory that we are more than our physical body, that time is not concrete or linear. Spirituality gives us a chance to let go of our fears about death and dying.

5. **Have your feelings and thoughts about mortality changed over the years?**

What was the first death you experienced that changed your life, that was a felt experience? A grandparent? A cousin? A friend at school or in the neighborhood? A celebrity's famous death or the assassination of a public figure? A pet?

Now what was the last death you experienced? A lover? A friend of twenty years? A boyfriend? A coworker? Your mother or father? Your sister or brother?

Consider how different that first death felt from the one you most recently experienced. Are there common feelings of sadness or anger? Do you feel numb, unable to feel anything more about death, even your own? Are you able to identify any shifts in perspective from the first time you encountered mortality, to the moment you began to consider your own mortality? What has influenced any shifts in your perspective—the number of deaths, the kinds of death, the opportunity to say goodbye if death was expected, being caught unaware by a sudden death? As we get older, our perspective on mortality will change, just as our perspective on living will change. Different priorities will emerge at each stage of our awareness, and this exercise is about recognizing the different stages of denial and acceptance that you've gone through in thinking about the mortality of those around you, as well as your own.

Before AIDS, I had observed that gay men in their forties and fifties began to deal with mortality issues in a conscious way when the body's physical changes became more evident to them. They were more able to confront this issue because, as older men, they had more experience from which to accept death and a more developed emotional support system based on their chosen family, as well as a higher level of personal maturity.

AIDS has disrupted that natural process, and HIV has forced even young gay men to deal seriously with their own mortality. A forty-five-year-old dealing with mortality is different from a twenty-year-old who feels he is just starting to have a life. These younger persons are being forced to deal with a major life issue long before they are emotionally and experientially ready for it, and the level of terror and anxiety they feel can seem out of proportion to the actual threat of infection and illness. Many young men who are told they're HIV positive react with a terror and panic that can be crippling. Most likely, their diagnosis anxiety will be the first time they've encountered their own mortality. If they had had twenty more years of experience before their diagnosis, they would have been more prepared to contemplate their mortality. For a gay man at midlife, mortality is just another one of the things on his plate already, and he will deal with it accordingly.

Gay men at midlife are caught in the middle, between the natural timing of facing their mortality and the challenge to their sense of mortality that AIDS has brought about. Like aging, AIDS has been a crisis that has made many of us conscious. For gay men in their forties and fifties, the presence of AIDS has run parallel to facing their own mortality. As a result, many gay men at midlife confuse the signs of aging with the signs of HIV illness: soreness, energy level shifts, lingering colds, muscle pains, stomach problems, tightness in the body, disruption of sleep patterns, eyesight changes, short-term memory losses, and the like. Any change in the body produces a moment of unknowing and uncertainty, into which fears of aging and HIV can crowd.

Since the advent of AIDS, I have witnessed a commonality between gay men's dealing with AIDS and the middle-aged gay men's acceptance of their own mortality: quality of life over the quantity of life. Both aging and AIDS have motivated gay men to make each day count, in all areas of their lives: how they earn a living; how they spend their leisure time; how they maintain their bodies; how they nurture, cherish, or repair their relationships; and how they begin to reclaim and express their spirituality.

6. With regard to other men your age, both gay and nongay, how do you feel your attitudes and feelings about death compare?

We are not alone in facing our own mortality. Other men your age have gone through the same series of feelings and thoughts that you are wrestling with to understand and accept, and it's important to recognize where you stand among your peers. What do your friends think about this subject? What are the feelings in your chosen family? Your blood family? Do you belong to a men's group or a support group that has approached the issues of mortality and spirituality?

There is some research that suggests that men with children have an advantage around aging. By being a parent and having intimate contact with a growing child or children, one can develop a sense of aging through watching the child's growth. As the child ages, so too does the parent. The joy of watching the child grow up displaces the parent's own fears and doubts about his aging. Few gay men have this experience directly, since child rearing is not widespread in the gay male culture and ethic. Efforts to reform adoption laws and child custody laws are changing this situation in some states, but most gay men do not have the active presence of growing children in their lives so they do not have this unique avenue into an acceptance of aging.

Most gay men, however, do have experience with the other end of the life spectrum. AIDS has brought death into our community, and from witnessing so many deaths, gay men have a window onto the life-changing effects of mortality. *An awareness of death creates an awareness of what it means to live.* This awareness is what changes so many lives. For many gay men, an intimacy with those who have died has given them even more incentive to create a life of satisfaction and fulfillment. Alone and with peers, gay men at midlife are looking for answers to deeply spiritual questions: Why am I here? How can I make my life fulfilled? Where am I going?

7.   Who are the people with whom you can talk over these issues?

The subjects of spirituality and mortality are not easy to bring up with another person, but isolation only breeds more fear, despair, and doubt. This exercise may be the first time you've considered bringing up these topics within your chosen family, or perhaps talking about these issues is what your chosen family is all about. In describing your support system earlier in the book, were there people with whom you could talk about your feelings of mortality? These sorts of feelings are difficult to express, but sharing them with another not only lends support, but direction to what you're going through. Everyone has fears, doubts, hopes, and thoughts about death and dying, and no one is alone in this process unless he chooses to be alone. To talk profoundly about life-and-death issues with others reveals and honors our human connection to one another.

8.   What are your fears about death?

Time stops, I stop. Peace. Wholeness. Calm. Sleep. Pain. Hellfire and brimstone. Nothing. I will go to Heaven, I will go to Hell, I'll go nowhere, that's it, nothing else, no pain, no joy, no sensation at all. People will forget about me. My lover will be alone. My family will suffer. My friends will be lonely. My pet will miss me.

This question may seem obvious, but it's important to be honest and concrete. During many of these exercises, I've emphasized identifying the positives in order to balance out the negatives. But it's hard for us as humans to find positives in death because we love life so much. The one positive that comes to mind is a cessation of pain if we've been sick (cancer, AIDS) or a cessation of breath if we've been unconscious (coma, paralyzed). In cases of pain or a nonresponsive state, the quality of life disappears and the distinctions between life and death fall away. If we don't feel like we're living, we have a lot of fears about death. If we feel like we're living a full life, we lose our fears about death.

Our fears of aging are intimately connected to our fears of death. The leap from "I'm getting old" to "I'm going to die" is small indeed. When we're growing up, many of us think of adulthood as a vulnerability to death. To be an adult is to knock on death's door. Children don't die, our conditioning tells us. So if one can remain a child or adolescent internally, then one does not have to face death. Trying to prolong our childhood or our adolescence is one way to deny death.

But to fully comprehend we can die is to have a different perspective on the world. It's truly a loss of innocence, in one sense, but it's a remarkable gift as well. *We need to have an awareness of death in order to appreciate what life has to offer.* A child loves to dance and thinks he can do it forever, but while an adult dances he knows he could die the next day. The difference in awareness heightens the dancing and may make it even more joyous and precious. The true gift of spirituality is joy in the moment, the now.

For many gay men, a fear of death is based on a feeling that they haven't lived. Many gay men try to prolong their adolescence by putting off settling down into careers, relationships, mortgages, savings—the "standard" measures of adulthood. But in staving off death (adulthood = death), they put off living as well. Running from death is not living; running from death is still dying.

9. What are your fears about dying?

This exercise may seem the same as the last one, but I'm making a critical distinction between death and dying. The traditional approach to understanding human mortality positions dying just before death. Dying usually means illness, getting weaker, losing energy and independence; dying represents the world closing in, circumscribed by physical and mental deterioration, leading to the moment of death, which is when the body stops.

Death is not a choice, but how we die, just as how we age, is most definitely a choice. Dying is not about physical deterioration, it has nothing to do with a diagnosis of HIV or cancer or a stroke. Dying is a form of mental deterioration, but I'm not talking about Alzheimer's. When we decide we no longer want to live, we begin dying. Dying is a conscious decision not to live, and some people spend their entire lives dying, and living just to please other people is a most insidious form of dying. Successful aging is not about dying. Successful aging is about living your own life to the fullest.

Our decision about dying can determine how quickly we arrive at the moment of death. One August, the father of a friend was diagnosed with cancer of the esophagus. He underwent surgery in September, then radiation treatment for two months. By December he was rail thin, emaciated, and depressed. He died in January, six months after his diagnosis. While he pursued his treatment, all of his thoughts were of death; he never felt much hope in what the doctors were saying. Significantly, turning sixty had been traumatic for him, and after he retired at sixty-three, he hadn't known what to do with himself. He felt most alive whenever he could pick up some seasonal work. My friend believes that his father gave up his battle with cancer so quickly because at sixty-eight, his life was not what it had been and was not worth fighting for.

In contrast, another friend of mine was recently diagnosed with pancreatic cancer. In his late forties, he had been feeling strange for about a year before the diagnosis, but the symptoms never made any sense. Finally, when his doctors figured it out, he quickly educated himself about the available treatments, consulted with several specialists on his options, and made a conscious, informed decision to undergo surgery (just one of the recommended treatments). The surgery was successful, and the cancer was caught before it had metastasized. After two months of recovery, he went back to work on a flexible schedule and continues to monitor his health closely. None of his friends were surprised at how aggressively and consciously he pursued treatment and recovery since his entire approach toward life was positive: He appreciated his blessings; devoted himself to his relationships and his activism; worked hard, traveled, and dated; and he saw the possibility of satisfaction in each new day. He doesn't deny that he will die, but he's not putting any time or energy into dying.

The reality of AIDS for many of us has been to experience the slow physical decline of our community. But there's a distinction to be made between physically dying and emotionally dying. Many gay men with HIV may be physically deteriorating but not dying emotionally or spiritually—they live until death. They embrace and participate in their lives. Some gay men with HIV are in the dying phase for a long time, while all parts deteriorate and there is no growth or aliveness before death. To see that dying is not necessarily a precursor of death requires a major perceptual shift in the way we view mortality. We cannot choose to avoid death but we can avoid dying. To achieve it is a highly mature state—to live until death. If we can do this, we have matured spiritually.

My late lover Jim was able to achieve this attitude toward death. My experience of caretaking for him enriched my understanding of him and of my own life. The first moment of truth about death came for me one day when Jim caught his reflection in a mirror, and said, "I'm just a shell of who I was." He was partially paralyzed, had facial KS lesions, and had lost a lot of weight, and when he saw his image, he began to crumble in my arms. As I helped him to bed, I knew I needed to acknowledge what he had said, but I also knew that whatever I responded with had to based on what I felt and not just meaningless words. I had to make a quantam leap to believe what I said. After a moment, I said, "Isn't that what the body is? Just a shell? What people have always loved about you is what's inside, and that hasn't changed." He stayed quiet and nodded. He also made a quantum leap internally when he was able to look beyond the physical realm to the real essence of who he was. He never brought it up again, even after his body deteriorated further. His body was no longer a point of discussion.

Throughout my Jim's illness, I made him three promises: He would die at home, I would always be there, and I would assist him if he needed the means of self-delivery. He maintained a constant awareness until the very end. The night he died, he was nearly comatose, his body was gone and wasted, and he could barely speak, but we communicated with our eyes, our facial expressions, our gestures. It was one of the most powerful and intimate moments in my entire life.

It was the night before Thanksgiving, Jim's favorite holiday. He had eaten nothing in the previous days, and the visiting nurse had gone home, after telling us (me and Jim's sister, a few others) that it would be soon. She had been saying that for a few days, and each morning she returned expecting to find him gone. But he was hanging on, barely breathing but with his eyes open and clearly conscious. On Thanksgiving eve, everybody went home around 11:30 except for our friend Joanne, who was sleeping in the living room. Just after midnight, I was in the kitchen when a bell started ringing. I had placed a handbell next to Jim, and he was shaking it for all it was worth. He was so weak he couldn't sit upright, but he sure could ring that bell. When I entered the room, he whispered, "We made it." I soothed him, and he closed his eyes to rest more. About two hours later, he opened them again and looked at me. He said, "Self-delivery," as clear as the bell he had rung earlier.

I knew the moment of death had come. When I asked him if he was sure he wanted me to help him self-deliver, he nodded. We didn't speak, but continued to communicate with our eyes, as I helped him to take his morphine. I felt like a mother giving milk to an infant; it was that nurturing, that kind of quiet intensity. It was a totally *felt* experience. There was no thinking to be done. I knew by this act that we were both going through an ultimate transformation: his was now physical, mine was spiritual. He had already made a spiritual transformation when he realized his physical body had become a shell. I was left behind, emotionally transformed, and my life would never be the same. We had discussed what he wanted, so he knew what I would be doing with his body after he died and before he was cremated. I washed his body and anointed it with oils, then dressed him in a pair of silk pajamas my sister had made for him. Then I lit candles in the bedroom, before sitting alone with him for a while. Eventually, I began to make the necessary phone calls. It was Thanksgiving morning. Since he knew the Jewish tradition of lighting candles on the anniversary of a death, Jim was grateful that candles would always be lit on Thanksgiving and his life would always be celebrated on his favorite holiday.

My experience with Jim at that moment taught me more about dying and death than any book I'd read or lecture I'd heard. I knew then that I wanted to live as he did, up until the moment of death.

I would refuse to give up whatever time I had left, and I resolved never to play games in my relationships.

10. When did you begin to see your life in terms of how much time is left?

For me, mature adulthood begins when we look at our lives in terms of how much time is left rather than how long it has been since birth. This moment of awareness is a "before and after" perceptual shift around our concept of time. For many of us, this is the line between acceptance and denial of our own mortality. The awareness that you have a certain amount of time left is probably not a positive acceptance but a simple recognition that you are not immortal. This awareness, however, is the first step toward seeing death as part of life and not to be feared. Once this shift toward an acceptance of death as natural and inevitable has begun, this knowledge permits you to focus your energy toward a more positive and creative way of dealing with mortality and aging.

11. What changes did this perception bring about?

Initially, this perception that our time is limited unleashes a torrent of fear, anxiety, and stress. All of the things we put off doing suddenly seem overwhelming and out of reach. Of course, we learn in childhood that people die and leave us, but for most of our lives, death remains theoretical, abstract, something that happens to other people, especially old people. But when we encounter death close up, usually a family member, a neighbor, or when our own health changes, death becomes something that could happen to us.

So what do we do with this knowledge? That, of course, is up to us. We could stop putting off all the things we ever wanted to do like travel or learn French or take an art class. We could pick up a hobby that we abandoned after childhood, like playing softball or writing poetry or bowling. We could postpone any major decisions because we don't really think they matter, after all. We could stop looking after our health, because what is the point, really?

The point is that you decide for yourself how you want that time to be spent. In many ways, this knowledge baptizes you an adult and your time becomes your own. This awareness of mortality motivates many people to examine their priorities and cast off whatever (habits, job, persons, behavior) has been holding them back from living their lives to the fullest. Sometimes, that person is us—we have been the one to put others first, to defer our dreams until some far-off rainy day (usually called "retirement") when we'll get what we want. Accepting your own mortality can be a heavy load of despair or it can be an explosion of life-changing energy, giving you the willingness to create the life you've always wanted.

12. At some point in your life, did you want to live only because of your fears about death?

Answering this question is almost secondary to understanding it. This is another "before and after" exercise in that there comes a day when you realize you're no longer afraid of death. For gay men, our familiarity with death brought about by AIDS combines with our natural sense of mortality that we gain at midlife to lessen our fears about death. As death becomes more familiar, the fears around the experience weaken. This is not an overnight realization, but can take many years, many deaths, and many hours of contemplating your own life to happen.

The realization brings about a major perceptual shift in how you choose to live: living in order to live richly, rather than living as a way of avoiding death. Once you have come to terms with your mortality, you realize that your life is yours to live—and it can become as rich as you can make it. I'm using "rich" in the sense of emotionally fulfilling, though your life can be materially satisfying as well. You can have joy, you can have love, you can have peace—and those things will be more precious as you live in and cherish the moment.

The alternative is to spend your life dying—watching the clock and living to please other people. This is the same decision you faced in chapter 2 when you decided to choose life, rather than death, by taking care of your health. This is the same decision you faced in chapter 6 when you decided to speak with your own voice, rather than letting other voices speak for you. Throughout this book, you've been confronted with decisions, both small and large, that will determine your experience at midlife. What's comforting, perhaps, is that any decision you make will be conscious—midlife has made you conscious of the choices you face, and no one can take that away from you.

13. When did you make a conscious decision that you wanted to live because your life was rich and fulfilling?

I realize you may not have made this decision, but I believe that you are on your way to this level of consciousness around your own aging. Merely picking up this book and working your way through these pages suggests that you want to age successfully and lead a satisfying life. *The real secret to successful aging is successful living.* The two go hand in hand, and you may have sensed the connection all along. The more life satisfaction you experience, the less fear you will have around aging.

14. If you feel you haven't made that decision, what changes would you have to make in order to make that decision?

There are two levels of change for this decision: behavioral and perceptual. At this point in reviewing your life history, you may have a very concrete sense of the changes in behavior you need to make in order to create a rich and fulfilling life. Set boundaries around your work patterns. Reestablish a relationship with your creativity or your spirituality. Repair a friendship. Establish financial goals. Reexamine the ways you treat yourself as well as other people. Changes in all of these areas can build a sense of richness (emotional, material, spiritual) to your life.

The other level of change is more difficult to assess or predict. It's your attitude toward the life you have already created. Maybe the externals of your life (career, relationships, health) appear rich and fulfilling to an outsider, but you don't feel satisfied by what you've accomplished. You always see more to do, more to achieve, more to accomplish, especially since you never feel like what you've done is "enough." Maybe it is time for you to drop everyone else's definition of "enough" and look at your life from a new perspective based on what is important to you. The work you did in chapters 7 and 8 about your values, your priorities, and taking charge of your life has prepared you to make this conscious decision to create a life that satisfies you, first and foremost. Maybe you need to change your behavior and set a new course for your life, or maybe you need to change your attitude about what you have already achieved and acknowledge its value. What's important is to acknowledge a sense of meaning and purpose in your life. Do you feel your life has meaning? Do you feel as if all this work is taking you somewhere you want to go?

15. Define your current definition of the meaning of life.

This is one of the most basic and difficult questions you'll face during your entire lifetime. It's also an easy question to avoid—"I'm too busy working and surviving to sit around and think about the meaning of life." Maybe. But what are you working and surviving for? What is all the time and energy and money and creativity you are spending building toward?

You are a work in progress. What you come up with now for this exercise today is no doubt different from what you would have come up with ten years ago, as well as different from what you will answer ten years from now. It is probably impossible to answer this question and not deal with aging. As conscious beings, we have to make some sense of our lives and their meaning, and the whole process of making sense is a component of successful aging. The question is not "What does life mean" but "What does *my* life mean?"

The meaning of your life has one source: your own sense of purpose. Many gay men have fought to end AIDS. Others have created works of art to last the ages. Having been rejected by their blood families, many gay men spend their lives trying to nurture a sense of family among their friends and within their community. Perhaps how we create meaning for our lives depends on the value we place upon our living. Faced with our own mortality, as well as that of our community, gay men know that death is close by in all that we do. Once we accept that death is a natural part of life and is not to be feared, we can begin to realize that any celebration of our lives precludes an awareness of death. If our lives have meaning, our deaths will have meaning as well. In addition, celebrating your life includes celebrating death, since it is a part of your life.

16. In what ways do you see death as a celebratory experience?

This exercise may start out as intellectual, but your feelings will get involved fairly soon. By this point in your life, you have had enough experience or heard enough about AIDS, deaths, memorials and quality-of-life discussions to begin to sense the celebratory aspects of death. Several thoughts spring to mind: death as closure, an end point to the physical life, a beginning of a spiritual existence, a celebration of transcendence by the deceased. Whether the celebration is about a life lived fully and/or about transcendence after death, both expressions represent a successful understanding of mortality that is essential to successful aging.

One of the major ways we can celebrate a person's death is with a memorial service. Once used almost exclusively for stars, public figures, diplomats, and politicians, the memorial service is fairly common these days, and its message is powerful: everyone's life is to be valued. The proliferation of the memorial service has taught many gay men a new way of dealing with death, and as a result, we have taught the nongay world how to celebrate both life and death. Instead of a staid funeral whose form is dictated by a specific religion, the memorial service allows the mourners to truly celebrate the deceased however he and his loved ones see fit. A favorite poem of the deceased, a favorite song, a favorite person delivering an eulogy are a few choices that come to mind, but what's significant is the person's life and death are honored in the way he has lived: uniquely.

17. Think about your memorial service and what you would want said by the speakers.

When my lover Jim became ill, many of his friends would call daily and want to visit, but neither he nor I had the energy to return all the calls or to spend time with visitors. In order to let people know of his status, I'd leave a long outgoing message on our phone machine, like a daily weather report of how he was feeling. At the end of the message, I'd always say that he could see people every Sunday from 2 P.M. to 6 P.M., like the regular visiting hours of a hospital. That way, the friends who wanted to see him could drop by during our open house and know that it was all right and that he was ready to visit. Jim loved these Sundays, and a few weeks before his death, he once said, "I never thought dying would be a series of parties!"

During his illness, Jim and I had chosen music for his memorial service. He had picked particular songs he wanted sung, and during one of those Sunday open houses, the women singers brought the music and performed for him. What happened was sort of a dress rehearsal for his memorial service, and Jim was able to enjoy the music he had chosen. After the performances, there wasn't a dry eye among the thirty or so friends gathered. It was a truly cathartic experience, made more so by being able to see Jim enjoy it along with his friends. Recently, one of Jim's friends told me she had been able to deal with her father's illness and death more easily because of witnessing the whole process experienced by Jim and me.

This exercise may stimulate the most emotional response of all your thoughts and feelings around mortality. The point is not to visualize your death, but the celebration of your life. To take this exercise seriously can bring you to tears. It is such an imaginative and visceral exercise because it taps into a wide range of feelings and thoughts. Sadness. Anger. Relief. Joy. Peace. Desire. Fear. To have a sad response to this exercise does not necessarily mean that all the prior successful resolutions were for naught. To create one's own memorial is one of the most difficult tasks any person can undertake. Though you may not be able to complete this task now, it will clearly be in your thoughts from this time forward. It will act as a reminder of how you want to lead your life and how you want to be remembered. While we cannot control the fact of death, we can affect how people remember us by living a life we are proud of creating.

James's Story

My client James affirmed for me how spirituality can transform our daily existence. Once James tuned into his spiritual nature, he truly blossomed. His experience is also an example of how personal one's spirituality can be, so much so that other people may not recognize it as such.

When James first came to me, he was a workaholic with constant pressures from his job and his very demanding lover who was ill with

AIDS. James was unable to speak up for himself and was a mass of nervous tension. He was also a Southerner who exuded charm and intelligence. He had a fairly typical history of someone who always tried to be "the best little boy in the world." He put his high level of energy into his career where ambition was paramount to him. In most ways, he did what was expected of him and thought of himself last, if at all—he always tried to meet others' needs before his own.

I was very surprised, given the rigidity of the way he conducted his life, that he was one of the fastest moving clients I ever worked with. From the very beginning, he heard everything I said for the first time and used it between sessions. I quickly found that I did not have to mince words or be cautious about defenses. He simply saw me as an expert in a field in which he needed some advice. He treated me as a peer. In a very short time, our relationship became one that usually happens after a much longer involvement. It was as if all he needed to hear was someone telling him what he already knew but had been afraid to voice for himself. He quickly started taking care of himself and was not on twenty-four-hour emergency call for his work and his lover. He began to set limits on both his job and his relationship while still taking care of his responsibilities. He was able to set up an emotional support system that prepared him for his lover's illness and death.

After his lover's death, James began to focus on what he wanted and what was best for his health. We talked about various programs that he could pursue—he decided to go on disability and see if he could reverse his deteriorating health. He began exploring many alternative paths and started going to spiritual retreats where he felt like he was discovering a lost part of himself. He flourished in these environments, and he was able to bring what he had learned into his daily life. This became a focus of his life. He became one of those persons who radiated a pleasure and happiness with his life so that it was a joy to be around him. In a sense, it was like being in the presence of a human bonfire that radiated warmth. Needless to say, his health kept improving and he felt equally as good. His death came as a total surprise to everyone around him because everything seemed to be going so well for him.

When James died, the autopsy revealed no cause of death. Years earlier, he had had a brain tumor that they thought was inoperable, but that had proven wrong. He was HIV positive and not in the best of health until he quit his work and started focusing on his health, which then started improving dramatically. Many people were dismayed by his death because at the time, his life was going magnificently. He had been on a very generous disability policy so that money was of no concern; he was volunteering his time using his expertise in fundraising; had just remodeled his country home and was in his first emotionally, physically, and spiritually fulfilling relationship with a true peer. He had recently finished another yoga spiritual retreat and was having the time of his life.

It was at the large memorial service (he had been director of the Big Apple Circus and before that, he had managed Carnegie Hall) at Saint John the Divine, the largest Episcopal cathedral in New York City, that new information came out about his death. A man who had been his massage therapist and now lived far away spoke at the service. He said that he and James had been having many long (two to three hours at a time) talks about spiritual issues for the past weeks and especially on the week he had died. Their usual topic was about what happens to the spirit after death. Though James's lover was the last person he spoke with, James had had a two-hour talk with this former masseur on that last night—it was all about transcendence and death. He died in his sleep that night. So to all those involved, it appeared that he knew that something was happening and that he was ready to go. Of course, there would be no evidence of cause of death because we still do not know how to look at these issues from a medical perspective.

The Last Lesson:
Letting Go

The first and last lesson of aging is letting go.

But what exactly does "letting go" mean? Much of our work around aging has to do with taking charge, deciding what we want out of life, planning how to proceed, and then taking steps (sometimes baby ones) to get it. So how does "letting go" fit in? Confusion about the concept can arise because to many of us, "letting go" may seem the same as losing control. But "to let go" is not about losing at all. It's similar to the difference between being judgmental and judging. Being judgmental is an (aggrandized) power trip, while judging requires looking to your own (inherent) power of being observant and analytical, capable of evaluating or assessing a situation. Letting go of being judgmental does not mean losing the ability to judge a situation, but it does mean no longer needing to feel superior over anyone.

Letting go is a process, an attitude, an action, and ultimately, a way of life. It's about freedom, *a release from the sense that we can or need to control everything*. Not that we don't want and have some control, but we cannot have control over all things. To let something go is to relinquish control, step back, and realize that we can control only ourselves. Just as a controlling person is usually not in control of himself, someone who rigidly holds on to something (a person, a concept, a goal, a behavior) doesn't really appreciate or understand his relationship to that something. *Letting go is the exact opposite of holding on*. Letting go is about not being attached to something in an obsessive way, or in a way that requires knowingly sacrificing one's ethics or values. That something can be just about anything: a job, a relationship, a prejudice, a habit, a family member's character traits, and most especially, expectations.

LETTING GO OF EXPECTATIONS

Much of our anxiety and stress comes from failing to realize our expectations, both for ourselves and for others. We spend great amounts of emotional energy creating a set of expectations, only to suffer continual disappointment when those expectations aren't met. Yet how often do we question the nature of those expectations? How often do we wonder if those expectations are off-base, unrealistic, or unattainable? Since most expectations are based on fantasy, wishful thinking, and past thinking, and especially some ideal or sense of "perfection," we are setting ourselves up for failure, and ultimately, for negative judgments against others and, most especially, ourselves. Expectations are rarely grounded in daily life, but they can totally ruin daily life by making us miserable with ourselves. Reality disappoints us *only* because we have too many expectations (demands, fantasies, needs, yearnings, requirements) about what life *should* bring us.

Many times, our anguish over aging comes from facing the difference between where we think we "should" have been and where we *are*, that is, the gulf between our expectations and what we have actually achieved. The metaphor of standing on a ladder is useful in illustrating how our life's priorities can change over time. Imagine your life as a ladder, with each rung representing a year in your life. From the perspective of where you're standing now, on the middle rungs, both the past and the future look different from what you expected. Where you are probably doesn't resemble your childhood fantasy of the future, but what did that child know, standing at the bottom of the ladder? Reviewing your life is not about measuring how many of your expectations you have or haven't fulfilled, it's about seeing how far you are from the rungs below and what the world looks like from this view.

Most people's expectations are stuck at the bottom of that ladder in their child's ego. Introduced by Freud, the ego is a useful concept, but as with most psychological representations, it's an evolving part of the personality. The ego is our sense of self, the "I" that operates in our world, the protagonist in the novel of our life, and the actor in our life-drama (why use one metaphor when life is so full of them?). As central as the ego is to our sense of well-being, it is a fragile thing, constantly needing attention, validation, and support.

It is out of a weak ego that perfectionist and absolute expectations spring. Whenever our ego feels weak or threatened, for whatever reason, we need to feel stronger and superior, which is where judgmentalism emerges. I think of expectations as the tool of the ego to feel superior, which usually requires judging others by obsessively rigid standards. Everyone has an ego, but not everyone operates *in* their ego. If the ego is strong, we do not feel the need to elevate ourselves by having rigid expectations that allow us to be judgmental. A person with a strong, solid ego feels his inherent power, and he appears self-focused (with his needs fulfilled and autonomous). In contrast, a person with a fragile, or threatened ego feels a desperate need to judge others by impossible expectations. His sense of power is aggrandized, and he appears self-centered (needy for attention, defensive, always thinking of "me, me, me"). Letting go of the ego allows you to release yourself from the daily craziness of trying to be everything to everybody, of being perfect, of beating yourself up when you're not perfect. When you're identified with your ego, you feel separated and alienated not only from others but also from the world around you.

To let go of expectations might be the most crucial choice of our lives. In one sense, it's a larger version of letting go of other-esteem and focusing on our self-esteem. The less we hold ourselves up to other people's expectations, the less power we give to other-esteem. But letting go of expectations means allowing choice for others as well as releasing yourself from the burden of making choices for other people. Your choices are your own, and letting go of responsibility for other people's choices signifies a major shift in attitude. The more you realize and affirm that you are responsible only for *your* choices (not your parents', not your boss's, not your lover's, not your best friend's choices), the more the world opens up and makes you feel freer to live your own life. Living your own life means letting go of other people's expectations, as well as your own expectations of your friends and lovers living only to fulfill you or please you.

Letting go of expectations doesn't mean not having standards, but it does mean being realistic about other people. The fewer expectations you have, the better you can see people for who they are, rather than your own expectations of who they "should" be. You created your support system (parents, friends, lovers, siblings, and so on—all the planets in the universe you visualized in chapter 5) by setting a standard of membership, that is, the qualities a person must have to become a member of your chosen family. But that system can change (with new planets and new orbits) as you grow and change, as well as when a person fails to meet the standards you have chosen. I'm not talking about impossible, rigid expectations of how your friends should look, act, dress, and so on, but the realistic standards of behavior and understanding that many people are capable of. Maybe you have a close peer whose friendship you enjoy 90 percent of the time (he's annoying about 10 percent of the time). Let go of that 10 percent and keep the friend who makes you feel good 90 percent of the time.

Being realistic may mean letting go of people who have qualities you may no longer want in your life. These people may not be able to be who you want them to be—just as you may not be the person others want you to be. Many of us came from families in which our parents burdened our lives with unrealistic expectations and pressures to be a certain kind of person (nongay, for a start). But coming out was a clear statement that we wanted to become our own person. Appreciating our own autonomy leads to recognizing the autonomy of others. *Letting go of other people's expectations of us empowers us to let go of our own expectations of others.* In the process of letting go of expectations, each individual becomes his own person, with his own created identity.

But the real work is learning not to hold ourselves up to our own expectations, which are too often unreal and impossible to meet. This is not to say that we can't have goals or dreams to pursue. But when those expectations require any degree of perfection, we are setting ourselves up for disappointment. Why? Because life is imperfect. Because we are imperfect. Our ability to feel compassion for others and to recognize their human imperfection is a first step in feeling compassion for ourselves and accepting our own imperfections. Like most of our abstract notions, perfection falls into the rigid, binary trap of good/bad, right/wrong, left brain/right brain, so that we equate imperfection with failure, "bad," and worthless. But imperfection is not "bad" (and is often quite satisfying and fulfilling!).

Usually, our idea of perfection is connected to what we feel we lack. These expectations of cause and effect are especially vicious around issues of aging and attractiveness. If I had a boyfriend, life would be perfect. If I were younger, guys would look at me more. If I weren't bald, I'd get cruised more. If I had a highly developed, muscular body, life would be perfect. If my job paid more, I'd be happier.

What many of us find is that those things do not perfection make. Relationships, careers, money, and a buffed body are all reasonable goals, but to *expect* any one of those things to make us perfect and therefore, blissfully happy, is to ignore what life brings us. In a sense, letting go is about accepting what life gives us, the blessings *and* the challenges. It's much too easy to focus on the half-empty glass and forget about the half-full one. As with our relationships, if only 10 percent of our life makes us unhappy, it's easy to obsess long enough over that 10 percent until it overshadows the 90 percent that satisfies us, and we end up feeling that our life seems 100 percent miserable.

Letting go clarifies the confusion. Letting go enables you to understand the limits of your reality and of your potential. Letting go empowers you to be compassionate with yourself and gives you opportunities for new decisions, priorities, and directions. Letting go means saying, "Okay, this is where I am and this is where I am headed." Letting go does not encourage or deny change, but it does imply a trust that things do happen for the best and that we are where we are supposed to be. As in the discussion of spirituality, midlife is all about faith in what you believe in—letting go is another act of faith.

By not letting go, we remain wedded to "this is not where I expected to be." Not letting go only tightens our hold on the past. By holding on to rigid expectations and past decisions, we lose the ability to be flexible and adapt to new situations, so we become even more afraid of change. Holding on means being anchored to the past and not committed to the present. William Faulkner once said, "The past isn't dead. It's not even past." What his riddle leaves unsaid is that the past lives only because we let it live. The past isn't dead until we let it go. If you're holding on to regrets and guilt over mistakes and decisions made in the past, you are losing the opportunity to have a present, a "now." Letting go makes our past choices irrelevant—and being in the present becomes the real gift of letting go.

THE PATH OF LETTING GO

Throughout this book, we have been walking the path of letting go. The first item to let go of in order to age successfully is any negative images of yourself at midlife. Only by recognizing the negatives and letting them go can we begin to let the positives in. We began our journey by letting go of other people's expectations of who we are and what is "age-appropriate" for us as middle-aged gay men.

In the early chapters, we worked on letting go of specific body stereotypes we have inherited as gay men living in a youth-obsessed sexual culture. In return, we begin to expand our definition of attraction to include a variety of body types and sexualities. Affirming our sexual lives at midlife is a crucial component of successful aging. In challenging the stereotype of the sexless midlife man, we ignited or perhaps rekindled a commitment to our health. Letting go of a passive approach to our well-being, we began to see our health is a consequence of choices we have made and continue to make.

In our discussion of role models, we let go of the invisibility that ageism creates. By looking for other gay men to guide us into midlife, we let go of nongay expectations of our development and began to recognize how valuable we are to one another. When we began to let go of traditional concepts of work, play, retirement, we begin to take responsibility for our own happiness and sense of fulfillment. Integrating pleasure and purpose into our lifestyle, we began to let go of other people's expectations of how we spend our time and money. In acknowledging our chosen family and our need to belong, we let go of relationships that did not honor our unique selves. By respecting our individual differences, we created peerships that enabled us to let go of the need to conform and began to live life on our terms. When we began to trust the sound and integrity of our own voice, we let go of the "shoulds" and came into our own as middle-aged gay men.

In examining what principles we live by, we may have let go of value systems we inherited or absorbed that do not truly reflect what we believe in, or what we choose to value. Our work on taking charge of our life shifted when we were able to let go of our anger toward other people and stopped blaming them for the bad aspects of our lives. Our deepening sense of spirituality, as well as of our mortality, has lead us to let go of preconceptions of life, dying, and death. Conscious of all that we have survived and have yet to experience, we fully embrace our midlife—to celebrate both what was and what will be.

At midlife, letting go of ageism becomes the all-inclusive task of which all the other tasks are components. *Just as having a positive gay identity required facing and lowering your internalized homophobia, having a positive identity as a middle-aged man requires confronting your own internalized ageism.* Letting go is the key to a balanced, realistic attitude about aging, and the sum of all other successful resolutions of fears and issues around aging. The more you are able to let go of your negative expectations about aging—the myths and stereotypes that our cultures feed us and that we reinforce—the better you will face your new life as a middle-aged gay man.

What new life? The one you have created, not the one you expected to have, but the one you create daily by making choices on how to live. When gay men state that they have no sense of themselves as middle-aged, they usually mean that they have a negative image of themselves at that age. This inability to visualize our middle age is due, in part, to our different development as gay men that I described earlier. At the beginning of the book, I introduced the concept of the Four Ages: our Clock Age (chronological), our Body Age (biological), our Heart Age (experiential), and our Gay Age (sexual orientation). We don't have a sense of middle age because these four competing ages leave us feeling bewildered. A gay man may be thirty-five in Clock Years, forty-five in Body Years (heavy smoker and drinker), sixty-five in Heart Years (just gone through the death of his father and his lover), and fifteen in Gay Years (sexually active and dating)—all at the same time!

With this dizzying and competing mix of needs and behaviors, as well as a late entry into their gay life, many gay men leave what feels like adolescence and enter what feels like middle age, but with no sense of adulthood. Midlife is our true gay adulthood—the time we come into our own. We develop our sense of manhood internally, without the social reinforcements available to nongay men. Letting go of nongay expectations of what our middle age should be, we are left to create it anew, on our own, just as we did when we took those first tentative steps out of the closet. When we let go of nongay expectations and develop a realistic appreciation of our gay journey, we begin a transformation into whole, unique, and fulfilled individuals.

At the beginning of this book, I asked you to work two exercises, which I repeat below. As before, I ask you what your feelings are about becoming middle-aged. Not what you think, but what you feel. And then I ask you to state the positive and negative aspects of aging. Any major life transition involves the three C's: Consciousness, Choice, and Change. By now you are conscious of the positive elements in aging, but you're probably still struggling to accept them as choices to be made. Even recognizing that you have choices in your feelings, as well as your behaviors, is a major change in perspective. Change is not only possible, but inevitable. When you work these exercises this time, be sure to notice any shift toward the positive, any minuscule shift away from your internalized ageism. Those tiny shifts (which may even appear as doubts) are the first indication you are learning to let go of what you had been holding on to.

1. **When did you start considering yourself a middle-aged gay man and how did you feel about it?**

Clearly, middle age is not a specific age, but a feeling. Like identifying as "gay," the term "middle-aged" is self-referential: only you can determine if it fits you, if it fits your life and what you're feeling. That's the basis for our dialogue about aging: What did we feel when we began to feel middle-aged? Scared? Tired? Excited? Resentful? Bitter? Relieved? Lonely? Fearful? Worried about the future? Given the ageism of our culture (both American and gay male), most of our feelings around aging are negative. In addition, our media, both gay and nongay, perpetuate these negative stereotypes of aging with their emphasis on young beauty (as opposed to showing different kinds and ages of beauty).

But as you've seen, there are also positive experiences during midlife: coming into one's own, whether professionally or personally, achieving stability, feeling your strength and power, finally realizing what makes you happy, being more comfortable with yourself, appreciating who you've uniquely become. All of these attitudes can appear at midlife, but they get drowned out by the anxiety about our changing bodies and feeling less attractive. But by taking care of our bodies, we can begin to appreciate the sexiness of a body that shows experience. Men like Rupert Everett, Barry Diller, Harvey Feirstein, George C. Wolfe and Tom Bianci can be seen as sexy and charming, but they are clearly not young. Recognition of any shifts in these attitudes, even just one, can fuel the affirmation of yourself as a middle-aged man. In reviewing your feelings about middle age, as well as the whole aging process, any shift toward the positive becomes a seed you plant. You have to water and nurture those positive feelings or they will be overrun with the weeds of negativity.

At this point, you may still just have an intellectual knowledge of the positives of midlife. Listening to and connecting with your peers or even reading this book may have given you a sense that growing older can also be a positive experience. You may know it or think it true, but you don't yet *feel* it to be true. Think back to our discussion about compliments and feedback. Intellectually, you can hear the compliments, but emotionally, you may not feel them, or worse, you deny them and brush them off. Just as it takes time and repetition and practice to learn how to accept compliments, it takes an attitude adjustment to admit feeling positive about aging.

What makes it so difficult? Our expectations of what it means to age, of what it means to be older and gay. Only by letting go of those expectations do we begin to recognize the complexity of aging, the need to balance the positives and the negatives, without either one becoming more important than the other. Letting go allows you to reinforce the positives, and the more experience you have affirming those positives, the more you will realize that the presence of negatives—a changing body, less energy, whatever troubles you—does not minimize or eliminate the positives. Both can exist simultaneously when you age successfully. Not aging successfully accentuates one over the other, so that you become Perky Paul (always seeing the positives) or Bitter Bob (always complaining about something).

2. What are the positive and negative issues about your aging?

Has your answer to this exercise changed since the beginning of the book? Do you feel freer to express your mind? Do you have a clearer idea of a career change you've been wanting and waiting to make? Do you see any work to be done in your relationships? Have you been able to identify patterns of behavior you want to change or affirm?

Do you feel overwhelmed by the aging process? Do you feel negative about the whole thing? Do you want to run away and hide? Do you feel uncomfortable telling people how old you are? Do you not relate well to peers or have difficulty seeing men your age as positive role models? Have you always had these feelings?

These exercises are not easy, and it still may be difficult to find the good in aging. But even one little glimmer of a change in attitude—about any of these tasks, whether it be work, relationships, health, control, self-esteem—can brighten the horizon. A chink in one brick can start breaking down the wall of ageism. The seeds of self-esteem we are planting will soon put down roots to undermine that wall even more.

COMING OUT (AGAIN)

Remember when you were in the closet and you listed all the reasons not to come out? Most of us believed all the lies and homophobia in our culture, and most likely, in our own families, and yet we still came out. In asserting your right to love another man, you proved all those myths wrong and you did it. Now is the time to do it again: shatter the myths of aging by coming out as a middle-aged gay man. As another coming out, midlife can involve rejection of a group of peers or a frame of reference that no longer values you. Now, instead of letting go of people because of their homophobia, you have the choice to let go of people because of their ageism, which comes out as a resistance to honor the life you are creating. It's time to enter a new community of peers who appreciate you for who you are, which is more than a number on a birth certificate.

When we first cracked open that closet door, we looked out on the positives of being gay and blocked out the negatives the nongay world had conditioned us to believe. At midlife, we face that same forest of positives and negatives, but we lose the path when we allow negativity to overrun the positive aspects of our current life. Given our cultural realities, there will always be negative attitudes about aging, both internal and external. We can hope for balancing them out, not their total eradication.

Draw upon the courage you used to come out to face down the myths and stereotypes of midlife. Remember: Courage is action in the presence of fears. It's hard to challenge the status quo of ageism, but you've done it before with homophobia and you can do it again. You know you can. Fight ageism with the same vigor and tenacity that you used against homophobia—catch yourself and others when you find ageism in our thinking, in our speech, in our media. By perpetuating ageism, we are only making our aging all the more difficult. As gay men, we know that life is difficult enough without making it harder on ourselves.

We reinforce these ageist attitudes whenever we name our age as a reason for not doing something or as a cause of our unhappiness or as something to be ashamed of. Sometimes we are conscious about this reflex of always comparing ourselves to younger men, but mostly, we follow the cultural patterns and repeat the ageism without examining it. One of my goals in this book has been to make gay men more conscious of how much damage they do to themselves when they give in to the ageism, when they shrug and say "that's the way it is, now that I'm old." Or "I'm not sexy, I'm not this, I'm not that, I can't do that anymore."

By rejecting ageism wherever you see it, especially in gay male culture, you continue the process of self-invention that began when you were a child and first realized you were different. Even before you attached "gay" to your desires or to yourself, there was a feeling of difference, and that feeling freed you to invent your self. By joining the first generation of openly gay older men, you pass on a legacy of pride and self-love that young gay men need. We have lost a generation of role models because of AIDS, and we stand to lose another because of ageism. Don't let ageism make you invisible. Some of us drop out of the gay community when we get older, but our participation in our culture is vital. Maybe the younger generation embraces ageism so easily because of the way they see older gay men embrace it. We are at the brink of the new millennium, and it's time for gay men to show the world, and especially themselves, a new breed of gay man: older, sexually active, positively visible in all arenas, productive, adventurous, energetic, and committed to every generation—*including their own*—in our community. Such Golden Men will be worth far more than their weight in real gold.

In his latest book, *Dry Bones Breathe*, Eric Rofes has observed about the "generation of gay men who . . . are now in their forties, fifties, and sixties": "Rather than addressing their own misgivings about aging, ageism, and the gay sexual cultures they inhabited in the 1970s and 1980s, some men may be transferring a powder keg of fears, disappointments, guilt, and rage onto young gay men and their emerging post-AIDS cultures." Whether we choose to be or not, we will become role models for younger gay men, and if we do not engage ageism, personally and collectively, each generation that follows will merely reinforce the negativity and perpetuate the stigma around aging.

I'm talking about cultural change, what Gloria Steinem has referred to as a "revolution from within." Change starts with each individual, but can expand to become a collective experience. By telling our stories of survival and aging, we begin to shatter myths and disrupt the expectations of our community. But we can only do that if we're visible, present in the community, not removing ourselves by retreating to couplehood or a closeted life in the suburbs. We owe it to ourselves and the younger generations, our spiritual children and the inheritors of our liberation.

3. **In what ways can you see yourself as a positive role model of a middle-aged gay man?**

A role model? Me? You probably didn't start this book thinking you were a role model. Maybe you went looking for one and realized, eventually, that you could've looked in the mirror. By stripping away the ageism of our culture, we begin to appreciate our journey more, what we have done and gone through to get where we're at. In that journey, we have developed skills and traits that served us well, and those are what constitute a positive role model. Not necessarily that we make money or are famous or have a good relationship or do good deeds in the community, but that we have integrity, we feel good about ourselves, we have a decent sense of our strengths and weaknesses, and we don't beat ourselves when we make mistakes, but we learn and adapt to new behavior. Recognizing our unique experiences, we can claim authority for our created life, and we begin to *own* our life—in the way an artist forever owns his work, though he may sell it to another.

4. **Describe yourself in positive terms without making reference to any other age group.**

One indication of successful aging is when you can make positive statements about yourself without making any reference to a younger age group or how much "youth" you have retained. For example, a measure of successful aging is the ability to describe yourself as enthusiastic, sexually attractive, vibrant, mentally and physically active, spontaneous, risk taking, inquisitive, and nurturing. You do not say you are "young at heart" or "young for my age" or "a young forty-seven." You can recognize the ageism of such statements and move beyond them.

Ageism moves in the other direction as well, with comments made to younger men like "You are wise for your years" or "You're so mature for a twenty-five-year-old." Wisdom and maturity are available at any age, and our Clock Age has little to do with it. The combination of our various ages enables us to get away from a strictly linear, chronological assessment of our life. Fighting ageism is about getting into the present for all of us, and never using age—a number or a decade—to define who we are and who we are capable of becoming.

In my work on life planning (detailed in chapter 8), I ask a gay man to think of his life as a book, with periods of his life as succinct chapters that build to create a whole narrative. Extending the metaphor a bit, each of his younger selves has been a character in that novel, and each chapter reflects the end of that character's part of the story. But the story doesn't end there, it continues with a new character, a new self for each period of the man's life. In this context, successful aging incorporates some of the qualities of grief. But instead of grieving for a particular person, we are grieving for younger versions of ourselves. By being able to accept the "death" of his younger self and yet maintain a continuing essence of himself, a gay man is better able to continue this process at each stage of his later life.

5. In looking over your life history, can you see the different lives you have led and said goodbye to?

We often don't realize how much we've changed over the course of a life, and reviewing our life through the metaphor of a book, we can look at the different lives we have led and see the different paths we have taken in our journey. Think back to a significant moment in your early life when you may have felt sad, alienated, or alone. Knowing what you now know, what would you say to that younger self? How would you present your life to that child?

Try to embrace your younger self in all its richness, then let him go. Use this leave-taking as a foundation for a new life. Incorporating the experiences of our younger selves expands our Heart Age, which contains the lessons we have learned and not-yet-learned. Letting go of a younger self means recognizing its value, then moving on to the next stage. This attitude will enable you to view aging as a lifetime process in which there will be more stages and challenges, as well as riches and gifts. Just as we learn to see death as part of life, we begin to see our younger selves as part of our middle-aged self.

As many of us have experienced in this time of AIDS, the ability to incorporate and let go of our younger selves is akin to uncondi-tionally loving someone who is dying, cherishing his unique history, and being able to say goodbye. Despite the pain or feelings of loss at the moment of his death, our life is richer, even after his death, for having known and loved him. For many gay men, this experience is the dividing line between youth and adulthood, and it has the depth, power, and complexity to serve as our community's most life-changing ritual. Coming out may be the initiation rite of our gay adolescence, but knowing and possibly caretaking a person until his death is a measure of our true adulthood.

What's perhaps surprising is the renewal of life that comes after these experiences of caretaking and survival. Confronted with many deaths, we learn to value our lives even more, and quality of life motivates many of us to reorder our priorities and begin a life that fulfills us. Many of us who have survived an intimacy with the dying are finding ourselves less anxious and concerned with our own aging.

This shift around their own aging is not about denying death or their own mortality, but having survived so many deaths, many gay men know what it is to cherish life, despite its changes, despite its potential for pain and grief. So many gay men whose lovers have died are not afraid to love again, and I know many HIV-negative men who enjoy dating HIV-positive men because of their positive attitude toward living. When HIV testing first began, many gay men observed how the whole language around the test was ironic and contradictory: To be "negative" was healthy; to be "positive" was unhealthy. But for some gay men, the test wasn't ironic: turning positive was a positive, life-changing experience that made them conscious of many things—their desire to live, their real priorities, their spirituality. Just as aging can make us conscious of our own mortality, our intimacy with those who are HIV positive can make us conscious of the way we live our lives. Are we genuinely living or are we preparing for death?

The measure of our capacity to live a life of our own choosing depends upon how much we live in the moment. Closely related to letting go, living in the moment is also an attitude, an action, and an approach to life. Living in the moment is about not letting the past or the future determine your present. Living in the moment is about taking charge of your present, making it your own, not somebody else's. In order to live in the moment, you must constantly let go of past frustrations and events, including death, illness, business failures, relationships, whatever you have survived and experienced. Recalling the moments we have spent with those who have died, many of us have learned to let go because we had to—the person we loved died and we learned to live beyond his death. Some of us remain stuck in a cycle of grief, unable to move beyond the person's death, while others transfer what they have learned from the person (and from the experience of caretaking) to a life in which they can choose to let go or not.

Ultimately, living in the moment is about letting go of the future as well as the past. Living in the moment is about enjoying what life brings you each day, each hour. But what's to enjoy about losing a job or a friend dying or a lover who leaves? The joy will come from knowing that you have choices, that you have decisions to be made in responding to what life brings you, that you are aware of how precious life can be.

6. In what ways do you live in the moment compared to the way you used to live?

Review your life history for episodes in which you lived in the moment. If this is a new concept, it may be hard to identify such periods in your life, but your recent history might be more revealing. In what ways do you live life differently from the ways you did in your twenties? Do you treat yourself better? Do you worry about what people think? Are you spontaneous? Do you hold on to grudges and resentments, or do you let them go quickly?

The more you can recognize when you are living in the moment, the more comfortable you will be in aging. Why? Because living in the moment means letting go of stereotypes and myths around aging. Because living in the moment means realizing each moment has value. Because living in the moment in your twenties is rarely possible given the level of parental and social and cultural influences. Because living in the moment frees us to have a future, and not just a repeat of the past. Because living in the moment at midlife recognizes the full breadth and depth of life each moment can bring: joy and heartache and death and goodness and growth.

All these benefits of living in the moment are available. But only when we learn to let go of whatever is keeping us from living our life fully. By now, you can probably identify things you have let go of that freed you to live your life. Pleasing other people. An ex-boyfriend. Your parents' unhappiness. Are there any areas where you are resisting letting go? What's the one thing you would let go if only you could? By pinpointing whatever blockage we may be feeling in the present, you are identifying opportunities for growth, change, and more satisfaction with your life.

7. What in your present life do you see yourself having to "let go" of?

A fight with your parents that has totally shut down your communication with them. A diagnosis of AIDS. A job promotion or scholarship that went to a rival. An arrest. Not being available for a friend when he was dying because you just couldn't go through it again.

We can live our lives haunted by the ghosts of past decisions and behaviors or we can change our lives by choosing to make each day better than yesterday. Earlier in this chapter, I described how holding on to expectations only brings disappointment and despair. Expectations are like the deferred dream of retirement: it's the one thing you think you need that will make everything else be all right. But there is no magic pill, there is no silver bullet to aging. And holding on to that kind of salvation (a magic pill, a silver bullet) only defers action and delays change—but it doesn't stop change. This is not to say there's no such thing as hope, but hope is a living thing, a dream or goal that motivates, not medicates. Hope is proactive, not passive. Hope is faith in the possibility of change and working toward it.

8.   Describe how you see change as an integral part of your life.

Change is just part of life, and so much of our frustration and pain occurs because we hold on to our expectations and resist change. During the course of this book, you have reviewed your life and the changes you have gone through in great detail ("enough already with the exercises!"). With that knowledge, you have gained insight into the patterns of your past decision making, and you can now develop a blueprint for living your life based on all you have learned. We survive change each day; the key is to harness the changes that will come, rather than remaining passive and feeling like a victim. For many gay men, the first decade of being out can seem totally directionless, but the awareness that comes at midlife (through the hard work of self-reflection, compassion, and understanding) brings it all into focus. Blueprints, however, are not set in stone, but are fluid documents, open to change and revision. By accepting change as an integral part of life, we can begin to look *forward* to change: What will life bring us next?

9.   In what ways can you see yourself celebrating your life?

Count your blessings. Do something just for yourself. Celebrating your life can be planned or spontaneous, a dramatic display or a small gesture. Throw yourself a big party for no reason at all. Create a scrapbook of memories, some happy, some sad, but each one a significant moment in your life.

One can celebrate oneself only from a positive and self-affirming stance—which was not our birthright as gay children. It can, however, be the gift we give ourselves and the legacy we pass on. Our middle years will become golden only if we treat ourselves as if we were carved from real gold: precious, sexy, infinitely malleable, and priceless.

I'm a Virgo (as is my co-author, and actually, we have the same birthday), and I like lists. My gift to you has been pages and pages of observations on gay male life, but if you can take away one item from the list below and really, really take it to heart, my work—and especially, all of your work—will come to fruition.

DO'S AND DON'TS FOR GOLDEN MEN

Don't confuse youth with power.

Do recognize the power of gay midlife.

Don't use age as an excuse for rejection.

Do value your own wholeness.

Don't negate any positive statements made about you by others.

Do learn to smile and accept compliments.

Don't confuse muscles with health.

Do exercise—your mind and your body—regularly.

Don't use age to justify abuse of your body.

Do take care of your body—for your pleasure (and others'!).

Don't confuse perfectionism with self-nurturing.

Do nurture and exercise self-control.

Don't allow ageism to make you invisible.

Get involved in the community. If there isn't one where you live, build one.

Don't let the voices of the past silence you today.

Do learn to trust your own voice.

Don't pursue other-esteem.

Do esteem yourself.

AFTERWORD

HAL

As you can now understand, this book is an exploration process that, in a sense, is never ending. In conclusion, three points still remain: my acknowledgments of Charles Flowers's work, what working with him has meant to me personally, and how the writing of this book has changed me. These three are very interconnected and a bit of my history is important for understanding the impact that writing this book has had on me.

I began organizing my ideas about aging during the last year of my late lover's life. The process of caretaking and his death were transforming experiences for me. Though sad and painful, those experiences became a very rich part of my life. Literally, on Jim's deathbed, I vowed to myself that I would not let his death be in vain: I would try never again to play those games that prevented me from being happy in a relationship, and that I would incorporate his zest for life and his ability to have fun into my own life. I was not sure that I would be able to accomplish these things without him. Needless to say, they were difficult tasks for me since I also had to contend with my own grief, health issues, and my own destructive patterns. The personal direction I wanted to move in was now clearer for me. At the same time, I was more confident that my years of both personal and professional experience had now given me insights into the aging process for gay men that could bring about a better and richer life. It was important to share that knowledge. I wanted what had been my own private ownership of ideas and experience now to become the common property of gay men—my major intention of this book.

And this is where Charles came in. Within a short time into my first meeting with Charles, it was clear that he understood why this book was so important for our community. He had read my proposal, introduction, and one chapter as well as the professional paper on which all this was based. Besides his conceptual understanding of what I was saying, he felt the urgency of the message that I wanted to communicate to my gay brothers. His obvious intelligence, wisdom, and warmth immediately impressed me as well as his confidence in his ability to work with these ideas. I knew that this collaboration would only work for us if it were an equal partnership whereby we both brought all we had to offer to the project. This was also a scary and exciting challenge in that he was exactly half my age. This was going to be a living test of what I believed about peership—that similar worldviews and experiences defined peership more than chronological age. Of course I had years of more experiences but he clearly had a depth and awareness that I only wished I could have had at his age. It was also obvious to both of us, as well as to others in the publishing business, that I needed to collaborate with someone who could put my ideas into a more accessible form for the reader. Thanks to Charles's sophistication and writing skills, this has been accomplished. Never did I think that writing a book would be fun! The back-and-forth process of developing each chapter from basic concepts to exercises to full-blown chapters with stories was always easy—each of us could channel our energies into what each of us could do best. The weekly and sometimes daily exchange of what we had each worked on was always done comfortably with complete openness. Not only was he able to articulate the concepts and ideas, but he was also able to embellish many of them so that the final product was truly a collaboration. When all the chapters were finished and I sat down to read the final manuscript from beginning to end (as opposed to the chapter-by-chapter reading as we had been working), I was overwhelmed. I was close to tears at seeing how much the book was saying exactly what I had in my head but could never have put into words as clearly. I just want to say, "Thank you, Charles. You got it exactly and even more."

The working across generations and the blending of our voices has produced a text that contains many other voices as well. As my friend Sam would say, "We are the custodians of the past and the future." One of the silent voices is that of Friedrich, who has been a further validation of this book. We met about the same time that Charles and I did, so that my past and present personal life became a confirmation and reflection of what was in the text. In addition, having or having had love in one's life, whether from friends or a lover (like Friedrich) or co-author or other sources only reinforces my belief in the sense of a positive present and future for us all.

I have also been significantly affected by a recent experience that reenergized my commitment to working within our community. I have increasingly felt that what I had to offer was being "someone from the past." Last fall, I was asked by the National Gay and Lesbian Task Force to be one of the plenary speakers at the closing ceremony of the annual conference, "Creating Change." I had prepared what I wanted to say but left it unfinished as I knew that I always had some consciousness-changing experience whenever I attended workshops. Well, I attended one on "Intergenerational Dialogue," where a self-identified youth of eighteen years was speaking about what angered her. She said, "I resent being called the future—I am not the future, I am the present." I was struck by that comment and later that night, while rewriting my speech to incorporate what she had said in my reference to the importance of youth in our movement, I had a sudden and profound awareness. *If she is not the future but the present, then I am not the past but the present too!* When I saw her the next day and began to thank her for what she said, I only got as far as, "When you said, you are not the future but the present," she interrupted me and said, "And you are not the past but the present too!" In that moment, I knew that she and I were peers and I could continue my activist work with all the energy that I had in the past. Each of us could bring our total selves in working together. I talked about this encounter with her in my speech and the audience applauded that recognition—we all are of the present as long as we want to keep working together. This experience totally energized me. It reinforced all that I believed in—it was a recharging of my batteries! Without being able to articulate it clearly, I knew that something significant had happened, which told me that I was now occupying a place in the world different from what I had thought.

That feeling of change brought me back to my experience with the book. I truly believe in the process of transformation, so that the challenge has been to create a book that would become a tool for change within the reader so that he would see himself in a new place in a different world. That sense of transformation happened for me as I wrote this book. Though I did not intend it nor suspect it would happen, my life has significantly changed by working on this book—in a sense, I ended up working the book just as I have been asking you, the reader, to work it.

Since part of the collaboration meant reviewing my history and explaining my rationale for many of the ideas, I had to do a review of my life and explain how each task in the book was reflected in my own life experience. I gained a new appreciation of the richness of my life and saw how and what I had created. I did not realize that doing the book would do this for me—I was just focused on getting the message out to the community. After the writing was over, I thought my profound sense of completion had to do with finishing the book, but I was wrong. It was about my own completion of an all-important process. Without fully understanding it at the time, I had somehow completed this latest phase of my life. I had finished the book but I had not completed it—until I recognized how I had been transformed by it. My feeling of completion was further proof of what I have said for years—*we always teach that which we have to learn.* I never suspected that there would be a significant chapter in my life entitled "Writing and Working the Book." Now, it is not just another chapter that awaits me but a new place in the world from which to write the next chapter of my life.

It is a strange feeling to realize that I am at the end of middle age but I do not know what to call what is coming next. As I have been saying throughout the book, we continue to create ourselves and now I am in this process again. I do not know what awaits me—I just know that I have completed an important process and a new one is beginning. It is a peaceful yet exciting feeling. So I have to thank you, the reader, for helping me to get to this place. Without you, I would not have written this book and possibly not gotten here so soon. It truly has been a rewarding process and worth the time and effort. I know it is going to be interesting and fun. And so the adventure continues . . .

CHARLES

"What do you know about being middle-aged?" I heard that question many times while writing this book with Hal. During our collaboration, I have been in my early thirties, and I would joke that since Hal was in his early sixties, we averaged out at about forty-five: a prime midlife age.

But the question has haunted me, and I have felt the nagging self-doubt any writer faces: Who am I to talk about this subject? Well, I am a gay man living in a culture that worships youth, and just as many gay men, I have internalized ageism, believed the stereotypes, and feared my own future. While working with Hal to get his ideas down on paper, I have faced my own sense of my aging, explored my doubts and fears, and identified places where I still need work.

When I read Hal's article on which this book is based, I knew he had a strong message to send to other gay men, but I worried if we would be able to pull it off. I had edited a book on gay teenagers, so I knew how the other end of the spectrum felt about growing up and older, and I had begun to sense how ageism kept the generations apart in the gay community—not just sexually, but socially as well. On a more personal level, I didn't know if I could relate to a man thirty years older than me. Much to my relief, we found that despite being men of different generations, we have much in common: the shared experience of coming out of the closet, a mutual passion for dancing and travel and romance, a similar understanding of family, a progressive social and political worldview—plus, we have the exact same birthday (September 4), so in a way, we're twins across three decades, "separated at birth."

Before meeting Hal, I hadn't given too much thought to aging, one way or the other. I remembered how miserable my dad was when he turned sixty, and I didn't understand his anxiety. He was healthy, active, married to a wonderful woman, and financially secure. When my parents retired (my father at sixty-three, my mother at fifty-five), I witnessed how differently you can handle that transition.

My father had never had many hobbies, other than hunting and fishing, which you can't do all year, so he drifted through his retirement, bored and unfulfilled. At one point, he got a part-time job and he was excited to be working again, to have somewhere to go, something to do. Meanwhile, my mother volunteered at the local hospital, got more involved with her Sunday school, and took up ceramics. She'd often say, "I don't know how I had time to work, I'm so busy these days."

With my parents' different models of aging, I didn't really know what to think about my own aging. I worried about never meeting Mr. Right or having someone to grow old and fussy with. I also came of age during AIDS, so the fear of "no future" was real. Maybe I would live past thirty, maybe I would die quickly (though probably not painlessly). I don't think we can overestimate how much damage such AIDS-related thinking can do to a young gay man's vision of the future, much less to the day-to-day choices he makes, whether consciously or unconsciously, about his own well-being.

Perhaps the first of Hal's concepts that I would eagerly embrace was the idea of our different ages (Clock, Body, Heart, Gay). By identifying the different components of "how old I feel," it explained to me the conflicting emotions I have often felt: I'm a kid, I'm old, I don't know how I got here, I'm running out of time, I still have a future, and so forth. The idea of a Heart Age quickly put into context an experience that has "aged" me more than anything else: the death of my parents. My father died when I was twenty-five, and my mother died twenty months later, when I was only twenty-seven. As a result, I went through a double dose of major grief in my twenties that many people don't experience until their fifties or later. So my Heart Age is significantly higher than most men my age, another element that has prepared me for understanding and appreciating Hal's observations on midlife.

Perhaps the two chapters I have benefited from the most while writing this book have been Work/Play (chapter 4) and Relationships with Family and Friends (chapter 5). After working seven years at two major publishing houses, I left full-time employment at the age of thirty to pursue a freelance career as an editor and writer. My major goal is to pursue my writing, whether fiction, poetry, or nonfiction, and with this book, I have obviously made progress toward making that dream real. But in pursuing a writing career, I have devoted my life primarily to work. It's very hard for me to have fun—there's always more work to be done, and given the erratic cash flow of a freelance career, I never know when or how I can afford to play. Integrating more play into my life remains a daily challenge for me, but I know from working with Hal and listening to his stories of other gay men who've struggled with this, that change is possible.

I have already experienced dramatic change in another part of my life. While working on the manuscript, my relationship with my sister, my closest blood family, underwent a transformation as I began, for the first time in eight years of being out to her, to integrate her with my "real" life in New York. My sister is thirteen years older than I am, so we have a generational divide, as well as gay and nongay differences. We've always been close, especially after my mother's death, and unlike many horror stories you hear about settling estates, we never fought about selling my mother's house and dividing up the belongings. It is a relationship I have always cherished, but I realized how much I don't share with her: my romantic life, my political views, my religious beliefs, and so on. In the past year, many of these walls have begun to break down, and we have been very open and honest about our feelings for and understanding of each other. At the core is a love that has sustained the relationship even when we've disagreed or misunderstood each other. While working with Hal, I realized that I needed to take the time to teach my sister about my life. She wouldn't learn who I am from a magazine or book or a random image of gay people in the media. She had to hear it in my own voice. In a way, I have begun to let go of the hologram of "little brother" and face my sister as an adult. And she, in turn, has begun to consider me an adult, not just her brother, not just a gay stranger. I have Hal to thank for showing me the way to this understanding.

Ultimately, I have been changed by the ideas in this book, and perhaps the most important lesson is that I will continue to change. The areas in my life that need work now probably won't be the same areas ten years hence (I hope not!), since new challenges and people and events will continue to enter my life. I look to Hal's embrace of his life as a heroic model for the future: His passion for living makes the future more real, more possible, more fulfilling than any images I can see in our gay media. It is my hope that whoever reads this book will come away from it changed: proud of what they've already accomplished in their lives and inspired to enjoy midlife.

INTRODUCTION

page 2   "some very good books . . .": John W. Rowe, M.D. and
          Robert L. Kahn, M.D., *Successful Aging* (New York: Pan-
          theon, 1998);
          Daniel Levinson, with Charlotte N. Darrow, Edward B.
          Klein, Maria H. Levinson, and Braxton McKee, *The Seasons
          of a Man's Life* (New York: Ballantine, 1978).
page 5   "Studies conducted . . .": C. Almig, *The Invisible Minority:
          Aging and Lesbianism* (New York: Utica College of Syracuse
          University, 1982).
          Keith C. Bennett, BA, and Norman L. Thompson,
          Ph.D., "Accelerated Aging and Male Homosexuality:
          Australian Evidence in a Continuing Debate," in *Gay
          Midlife and Maturity*, edited by John A. Lee, Ph.D. (Har-
          rington Park Press, 1991): 65–75.
          Richard M. Berger, Ph.D., *Gay and Gray: The Older Homosex-
          ual Man* (Harrington Park Press, 1982; 2nd edition, 1996).
          K. Dawson, "Serving the Older Gay Community," SEI-
          CUS Report (1982): 5–6.
          J.S. Francher and J. Henkin, "The Menopausal Queen:
          Adjustment to Aging and the Male Homosexual." *American
          Journal of Orthopsychiatry* 43 (1973): 670–74.

Richard A. Friend, "Older Lesbian and Gay People: A Theory of Successful Aging," in *Gay Midlife and Maturity*, edited by John A. Lee, Ph.D. (Harrington Park Press, 1991): 99–118.

J.J. Kelly, "The Aging Homosexual: Myth and Reality." *Gerontologist* 17 (1977): 328–32.

Doug Kimmel, "Psychotherapy and the Older Gay Man." *Psychotherapy: Theory, Research, and Practice* 4 (Winter, 1977): 386–93.

Doug Kimmel, "Adult Development and Aging: A Gay Perspective." *Journal of Social Issues* 34 (1978): 113–30.

Harold Kooden, Ph.D., "Successful Aging in the Middle-Aged Gay Man: A Contribution to Developmental Theory." *Journal of Lesbian & Gay Social Services* 6 (3) (1997) 21–43.

John A. Lee, Ph.D., "What Can Homosexual Aging Studies Contribute to Theories of Aging?" *Journal of Homosexuality* 13 (1987): 43–71.

Fred A. Minnigerode, Ph.D., and Marcy Adelman, Ph.D., "Elderly Homosexual Men and Women: Report on a Pilot Study." *The Family Coordinator* 27 (1978): 451–66.

S. M. Raphael and M. K. Robinson, "The Older Lesbian." *Alternative Lifestyles* 3 (1980): 207–29.

M. S. Weinberg, "The Male Homosexual: Age-related Variations in Social and Psychological Characteristics." *Social Problems* 17 (1970): 527–37.

M. S. Weinberg and C. J. Williams, *Male Homosexuals: Their Problems and Adaptations* (Oxford University Press, 1974).

page 5   "less rigid gender roles": K. Dawson, "Serving the Older Gay Community." SEICUS Report (1982): 5–6.

J. S. Francher and J. Henkin, "The Menopausal Queen: Adjustment to Aging and the Male Homosexual." *American Journal of Orthopsychiatry* 43 (1973): 670–74.

Richard A. Friend, "GAYging: Adjustment and the Older Gay Male." *Alternative Lifestyles* 3 (1980): 231–48.

Richard A. Friend, "A Theory of Accelerated Aging Among Lesbians and Gay Men." Paper presented to the combined annual meeting of American Association of Sex Educators, Counselors, and Therapists and the Society for the Scientific Study of Sex, Boston, MA (June, 1984).

Levinson, pages 197–98.